The Odds

The Odds

One Season, Three Gamblers, and
the Death of Their Las Vegas

CHAD MILLMAN

DA CAPO PRESS
A Member of the Perseus Books Group

Book design by Barbara Werden.
Composed in Stempel Garamond at Texas Type & Book Works.

Cataloging-in-Publication data for this book is available from the Library
of Congress.

First Da Capo Press edition 2002
Reprinted by arrangement with PublicAffairs
ISBN 0–306–81156–1

Published by Da Capo Press
A Member of the Perseus Books Group
http://www.dacapopress.com

Da Capo Press books are available at special discounts for bulk purchases
in the U.S. by corporations, institutions, and other organizations. For
more information, please contact the Special Markets Department at the
Perseus Books Group, 11 Cambridge Center, Cambridge, MA 02142, or
call (800) 255-1514 or (617) 252-5298, or e-mail
special.markets@perseusbooks.com.

For Barry, Temmy, Linsey, and Stacy.
They've earned it.

Contents

\

Acknowledgments

The words of encouragement, nuggets of information, and sage advice I received while writing this book sustained me through the entire project. For these random acts of kindness, most likely forgotten by those who passed them along, I am grateful.

Specifically to Gary Hoenig, executive editor at ESPN The Magazine, for reminding me that, as a reporter, the eyes often work better than the ears. Also to ESPN The Magazine deputy editor Gary Belsky, who planted the seed that ultimately became the book you're now holding. To Mark Helm, whose mind is a treasure chest of Las Vegas facts and law, for his willingness to spread the wealth. To Trent Garcia, an intrepid researcher whose work filled in holes I didn't know existed. And to the Sports Illustrated library staff, who let me pillage the stacks and get in their way at the most inconvenient time.

To Geoff Shandler, my friend before he was my editor, whose deft touch with the copy and enthusiasm for the idea made this book better every time he read it. And finally to those I profiled. Thanks for sharing.

Introduction

During the first round of the National Collegiate Athletic Association (NCAA) basketball tournament in March of 2000, I won $300 on an inconsequential game between two teams no one cared much about, except for me. The game went down to the final play, with the team I bet on winning after a sophomore hit a miracle shot at the buzzer. I jumped, I exhaled, I screamed, and I nearly threw up. I was exhausted, shaking, and felt warm all over. I had just won $300 I had no business winning. Not too shabby, I said to myself. I could easily do this for a living.

I looked to my right. The man sitting there was a professional, and I wanted props from him for my betting skills. *Three hundred dollars, on one bet. Come on, man!*

He ignored me. He ignored the other people in the room. His shoulders were tensed and stiff like Frankenstein's monster. His hands trembled. He screamed obscenities and numbers into a telephone. His posture betrayed the fact that he had won $20,000 on the same last-second shot that won me a measly $300. He was too busy putting that $20,000 back into play to acknowledge anyone other than the bookmaker on the other end of the phone. Numb to winning or losing, only the betting gave him a tingle. After hanging up the phone he looked relieved, like a heroin addict who had just pulled the needle from his arm. This was the moment when he felt warm all over.

Who was I kidding? I couldn't do this for a living.

Following sports had been my hobby as a boy, but only when it became my vocation (as a reporter at *Sports Illustrated* and then an editor at *ESPN The Magazine*) as an adult did I realize the sway betting had on fans' interest in the games. People didn't ask me who won, but by how much. Friends picked my brain about NFL teams to glean the slightest advantage against their bookies. My dear mother woke me with calls in the middle of the night demanding I help her fill out her NCAA brackets. She wasn't alone. Over the last twenty years, in line with the explosion of sports on television, sports betting has become America's obsession to the figure of about $80 billion a year. To my friends and family, I was a tout sheet.

Las Vegas is the only place in the country where sports betting is legal. And the hard-core bettors I met while researching this book, "wiseguys" as they're known in town, are a mixed breed of sports fans, outlaws, and artists. They rooted for teams that covered the spread, not players who scored the most points. They bet $10,000 when they had only $10,000 in the bank. They tortured themselves over abstract details.

My friends and relatives were rank amateurs. But the professionals were different. They were the characters I wanted to meet when I started working on this book.

For nearly fifty years, Las Vegas has been the capital of sports betting. Every point-spread, every favorite, every piece of language we use to describe winners and losers has grown from the desert town. Considering the billions bet on sports each year, the impact Las Vegas sports books have on the line is the economic equivalent to the Federal

Reserve's impact on interest rates. But, today, sports books—local establishments that accept sports wagers—are getting attacked from every angle. Offshore books based in far-off Caribbean islands are using the Internet to attract more and more bettors. Meanwhile, Vegas has become family-friendly and is run by cost-conscious corporations. Wiseguys are being squeezed out.

The turmoil surrounding the sports books' demise is eerily similar to the circumstances that made Vegas a sports-betting paradise to begin with. When Nevada legalized gambling in 1931 the state, and particularly Vegas, evolved from a dusty stopover for weary travelers into a desert paradise for the unwanted. It's where the gangster Bugsy Siegel built his first hotel for the sole purpose of going legit, where a recluse like Howard Hughes was considered royalty, and a former mob lawyer like Oscar Goodman became the beloved mayor. And of course, the city pulled in the good, the bad, and the ugly from the gaming community, from the workers to the players.

In Nevada and elsewhere, sports betting had generally been considered a victimless crime, getting no more attention than a wink from local police. That all changed in the early 1950s. During those years, Tennessee Democratic Senator Estes Keafauver's investigation into mob activity determined that the Mafia's main source of income was from sports betting operations. It also concluded that, because of sports betting, the mob's influence extended to players, police, and elected officials. Immediately, there was an increased crackdown across the country on bookmakers. The bookies who used to coexist so peacefully with cops were now on the run, changing apartments every two weeks to evade stings and making their clients use passwords. But Vegas presented an alternative. It was a chance to play in the show. There would be no police harassment, no need for subterfuge. Quickly a virtual farm system of bookies made their way west.

Only one problem existed: Nobody wanted to play their game.

Sports betting has always been the misunderstood stepchild of the gaming family. And after the Kefauver hearings, even if betting was legal in Vegas, the government wanted to make it as unappealing a proposition as possible. It levied a 10-percent tax on all sports-betting establishments for every bet they took in. In layman's terms, for every $10 wagered, $1 went to Uncle Sam, whether the house won the bet or not. Even without the tax, the vagabond bookies faced a serious deterrent. While parlor games made for easy winnings, betting on sports was more unpredictable. The bottom line for casino execs (mob-influenced and otherwise) was that anyone could make sure the house won at blackjack or poker. But, unless they fixed every game, how could they ensure coming out a winner on sports bets? The fact was, they couldn't.

Shunned by the casinos, career bookmakers looking to make a go of it in Vegas did what they did best: They took a calculated risk. If sports betting was legal and if it was popular—their client lists from back home proved that—they would open up their own shops with their own money. They'd run them like they ran their corners in their hometowns, only now they wouldn't have to change their phone numbers every few weeks to keep the cops off their tails.

Despite the facade of legitimacy, the atmosphere inside Las Vegas's early stand-alone sports books was as reckless as any back-alley joint. Unlike the casinos, which catered to the wealthy weekenders, the sports books attracted local degenerates, transplants from New York, Chicago, or Philly who, like the bookmakers, got tired of outrunning the law and wanted to bet their balls off without going to jail for it. For the first time as career bettors, they had a place to go and work everyday.

They were guys everyone knew by nicknames like Dick the Pick or Montana Mel or Crazy Kenny. Hole-in-the-wall sports books named after familiar sporting venues, like the Santa Anita, Churchill Downs, or the Rose Bowl, were pretty much the only home any of these bettors knew. The old joke around town was that Montana Mel could tell you every college football team's nickname, but couldn't tell you his address. Meanwhile, Crazy Kenny showed up at various books every Saturday and Sunday morning with a new bottle of vodka, because he had finished one off watching games the day before. Getting drunker and angrier as the day went on and the games were lost, he'd insult every race, color, and creed. Watching a game at the Del Mar sports book one afternoon, he pulled out a pistol and shot the television when the team he bet against scored a touchdown. On another particularly unhappy occasion, he rammed his face into the wall, caving in the thin Sheetrock and getting his head stuck.

"One day we had a guy running in from our alley entrance and there was a guy running behind him swinging a pick axe, and people are screaming," remembers Vic Salerno, CEO of the Leroy's Sports Book chain. "We finally get them stopped and we say, 'What's the problem?' The guy that was doing the chasing, the one with the pick axe, says, 'This guy is really pissing me off. I owe him money and he keeps bothering me about it.'" (Of course, the book wasn't always wrought with danger. One slow afternoon at Leroy's Sports Book, Barry the Donut man bet Hungry Hal he could eat more donuts. The over/under for both of them was thirty-eight, which they covered by one when Hal polished off twenty donuts while the Donut could only muster nineteen.)

The betting in such joints revolved around the point spread, which had been invented in the 1940s by a University of Chicago grad named Charles McNeil. Traditionally, odds favoring one team over the other had been used to choose favorites. But McNeil's point spread ascribed a number value to each team, making the favorite the team with the higher value. The line—or point spread—is the number of points bookmakers predict one team should be favored over the other. For the bettor, it is the barometer by which they make their decisions on whom to bet and for how much. The line in the Super Bowl between the St. Louis Rams and the Tennessee Titans was St. Louis minus seven, meaning the Rams were favored by seven points. If someone bet the Rams side (known as "laying the points") that meant the Rams would have had to win by more than seven points to cover the spread and for the bettor to win the bet. If someone bet the Titans side ("taking the points") the Titans would have to win outright or lose by less than seven to beat the spread and for the bettor to win the bet. It's a common misconception that when bookmakers make one team a favorite over another they think that team is actually better. Not true. The line is there to draw people in, to entice people who think they know sports to make a wager. Bookmakers don't have an opinion on which team is better or worse. They have an opinion about which point spread will make people want to bet and what, in turn, will make them a lot of money.

Before the mom-and-pop books opened in the 1950s, the point spread for the same game would vary wildly from city to city. Somedays the line emanated out of a bookmaker in Lexington, Ky.; other days it was someone in Chicago or Minneapolis or even Montreal. There was no linemaker who established a baseline that all others followed. But gradually the Vegas bookmakers—and their lines—earned credibility through publicity, something they had once strenuously avoided. And as their status grew within the betting community, so did their legend. Seeing up close their quirks, traits, and physical features made the books destinations for out of town sports bettors. People wanted to watch the diminutive Harry Gordon at Churchill Downs count out cash that piled so high on the front counter he couldn't see over it. Or they'd visit the Santa Anita for the privilege of being yelled at by bookmaker Sammy Cohen, the way tourists flock to the Soup Kitchen in New York City to get berated by the real-life Soup Nazi from *Seinfeld*. And everyone knew that if you wanted to make a bet no one else would take, you should see Gene Maday at Little Caesars. Suddenly the attention bookmakers had shied away from while running illegal operations had turned them into celebrities. Their opinions of which team should be favored *mattered*.

And none mattered more than Bob Martin's. Martin began booking sports when he was a teenager in Brooklyn. He'd lure other high schoolers into what he called the "six-hit bets" in which bettors could pick any three players in the major leagues to get six hits between them in their next game. When he served in World War II, he booked the baseball games he and his fellow soldiers listened to on the radio. He left France $30,000 richer, and had found a career as well.

In the early 1960s Martin was living in Las Vegas and working as a professional bettor. Harry Gordon grew tired of Martin beating him and offered him a job managing Churchill Downs. Sick of risking his neck, Martin accepted and, almost instantly, Gordon and the rest of Las Vegas recognized that the lines Martin put up garnered nearly perfect two-way action. Rarely did Martin have to move the original line he posted to entice bettors into taking one side over the other. If a bookmaker's ultimate goal is booking equal two-way action and making money off the vigorish—a 10-percent commission bookmakers charge. Martin was a master. "Shortly after he started booking, you would see guys from the other books staking out Churchill everyday with their clipboards and lists of games," says Vegas sports-betting historian Peter Ruchman. "When Martin put the line up they'd run to the pay phones and call their bosses, letting them know what to post."

Martin's line became known as the Las Vegas Line throughout the country. It was the standard by which every Vegas sports book and every corner bookie set his spreads. And Martin took his responsibility seriously, assiduously researching every team. He'd have assistants meet early-morning arrivals at the Vegas airport to scour the out of town sports sections passengers left behind. He'd work every morning from seven A.M. until eleven A.M., formulating spreads for every game on a yellow legal pad.

Frequently, gamblers who were tired of getting slammed at the blackjack table left the larger properties to bet and watch a game in the sports book. To combat this, in the mid-seventies, hotels lobbied to have the betting tax lowered from 10 percent to 2 percent, which allowed them to justify putting sports books in the hotels and which, in turn, kept bettors from walking out the door. When the Union

Plaza became the first hotel to open a sports book on its property, Martin was the bookmaker it hired. His celebrity status breached the tight-knit betting community into the public at large. He hosted a weekly radio show that could be heard from Vegas to Los Angeles every Monday morning during football season. He invited well-known wiseguys as guests to talk about the games, and then, before every guest left, Martin gave them a crack at his unposted line, which was like giving them a license to steal. "He earned a huge amount of respect because he was willing to take so much money on a line no one had tested yet," says Salerno. "The rest of us all waited until after his show to put up our numbers."

Soon after the Union Plaza, the Stardust opened its sports book in 1976, followed by nearly every major hotel on the Strip. No longer just the domain of Crazy Kenny or Dick the Pick, sports books catered to the hotel customer more than the wiseguy. "What casinos did was bring sports betting to the masses in a way the mom-and-pop books along the Strip couldn't do," says Arnie Lang, the former host of the Stardust Line radio show, which dissects weekly matchups. "It glamorized and sanitized it at the same time."

By the early 1980s, the Justice Department was in the midst of wrestling control of Las Vegas from the mafia and large-scale corporations such as MGM and ITT were supplanting mob families as the town's dominant players. The sports books in these high-profile locations suddenly had high expectations as well. Just making a buck wasn't enough anymore. Hotel executives had bottom lines to meet and shareholders to answer to, and the limitless wagers bookmakers allowed at the small shops and in the last days of mob rule were counterproductive. They were too high risk, even for the business of gambling. "In the 1970s the mafia guys understood that in the gambling business you would take a licking every once in a while," says Chuck DiRocco, editor of the newspaper *Gaming Today*. "All that changed with the MBAs. I think the biggest problem they have is that they are very bright in the pure business world, but gambling is not selling neck ties; the commodity you sell is gambling."

The era of the independents changed for good in 1983, when Bob Martin was arrested for illegally transmitting wagering information across state lines. He spent thirteen months in federal prison and, during his forced retirement, the bookmakers and the bettors fell in line with corporate structure. The Stardust picked up where Martin left off as the home of the Las Vegas Line. But instead of relying solely on their wits, the Stardust's bookmakers were more practical. There were more games than ever to book and bettors had access to more information. The bookmakers realized they were at a severe disadvantage when it came to making the point spreads and they needed help. In the void that Martin's absence created, Las Vegas Sports Consultants was born. The brainchild of a failed bettor named Michael "Roxy" Roxborough, LVSC (or "Roxy's place" as it is still known) acted as an independent odds-making consultant. A staff of full-time oddsmakers studied every game and, for a monthly fee, supplied every bookmaker in Vegas with a number to start with. Some books posted the number as is; others tweaked it.

While times forced characters like Crazy Kenny or Dick the Pick to go the way of eight-tracks, the new breed of bettors was no less eccentric—only now they were techno-savvy entrepreneurs who took advantage of everything the decade of cable and computers had to offer. One such syndicate—a group of bettors who pooled their resources—was aptly named The Computer Group. Plugging every game of the week into a computer formula, and betting limits at every casino as well as with illegal bookmakers all over the country, The Computer Group wagered nearly $140,000,000 on football between 1980 and 1985. They cleared $13.9 million. Billy Walters, one of the principals in the group, came to Las Vegas a dirt-poor gambler from Kentucky, and, after The Computer Group's run had ended he was a millionaire several times over.

In the fall of 1999, when I made my first trip out to Las Vegas, Billy Walters was still one of the biggest sports bettors in the business. But he was also a prominent real estate developer and philanthropist, a minicorporation, surrounded by layers of lackeys and lawyers. Ultimately, he was insulated from the problems the rest of his betting bretheren faced.

Most bettors and bookmakers I met that fall, and during the subsequent winter and spring I was there, felt that Vegas's reign as the sports-betting capital was nearing an end. There were laws being proposed to ban betting on college sports. And the FBI was raiding the secret bank accounts of several high-profile wiseguys. But the real threat to the way things were was coming from the Internet. "You'd be crazy not to see this as an unstoppable force," Salerno told me one day shortly before the NCAA Tournament. "Over the next five years, who knows if they'll even need us in Vegas anymore."

Like the mom-and-pop shops in the 1950s, offshore books take any bet for any limit. Now, bookmakers and wiseguys alike are fleeing the desert for the unregulated islands. They are betting vagabonds looking to hit it big.

I'm glad I caught them before it was too late.

Chapter 1

"Death Is Not the End"

A lot of gamblers say the action replaces sex, but I really think they mean it replaces relationships and a fear of socializing. We're all outcasts and gambling occupies our time and we get paid for it.

For me for sure it was a way to make money and be by myself. Now, it's become an obsession. I don't think it's an addiction. I don't think. But then again, I have no life.

—ALAN BOSTON, SEPTEMBER 1999, IN OLD ORCHARD BEACH, MAINE

Alan Boston walked into the Corvette dealership fourteen years ago wearing a ripped University of Pennsylvania T-shirt, shorts and a pair of boating shoes, looking like some twenty-seven-year-old punk coming to jerk the salesman's chain. He hadn't slept in two days. A binge of betting, boozing, and partying left him more wired than Con Ed. Alan knew the guys hawking cars would brush him off. He knew the dealers would see another young kid eager to take the 'Vette for a spin, and then leave them with the keys in one hand and a promise to come back soon in the other. That's what Alan was counting on, actually. He reveled in finding a mark and making his head spin.

Alan understood human nature. He bet his life on it everyday. And, as sure as he knew the Red Sox would cover against the Yankees later that night, he knew the car jockeys would ignore the opportunity that was right in front of them, bulging from Alan's pocket. That's where Alan had stuffed his life's work, what he had to show from instincts, luck, research, brass balls, and guts that translated into big wins at the track or on the game or at the card table. That's where he stuffed enough cash to buy a Corvette with all the options and maybe even leave the poor schmuck who sold it to him a tip, if anyone took him seriously. After all, what good is the money without the respect?

One by one, just as Alan expected, the dowdy group of salesmen ignored the strung out kid with the unruly mop of red hair. Finally the manager, as if by default, asked Alan if he needed any help. *Damn right I could use some help,* Alan thought. *I've got more than $27,000 in my pocket but I pulled up to your lot in a 1972 Impala I bought for $150. Get me a 'Vette.* Alan picked out a car—a metallic rose t-top—filled out the paperwork, and laid the money in a neat pile on the table. He drove off the lot with the music loud and enough cash left over to get down some decent action that night.

He didn't bother leaving a tip.

Fourteen years later, rose would become yellow, yellow would become purple, and purple would become gold. Batman has the Batmobile and Alan has Corvettes, even when he has nothing else. They're not just transportation, but 200-horsepower boosts to the ego. When you spend six months of the year in Las Vegas as Alan does, betting as much money in a day on sports—college basketball, specifically—as some people make in a year, gold Corvettes are a stylish statement. Another wiseguy, as professional sports bettors are known, sees the car parked in the lot of a casino and says to himself, "Alan is here. I wonder what he's getting down on."

But Alan spends the other six months of the year in a cozy seaside town in Maine, where he's known as a small-time harness horse-racing owner with a two-bedroom condo on the beach. For Alan, Maine is the perfect antidote to Las Vegas. It is an ocean whose breeze recharges him after the desert has sapped his strength. It is wide-open beachfront property after he's been trapped in the congested basin. It is the place he chooses to live, not the place he has to live. But mostly, a raw nerve like Alan living in tranquil Maine is a contradiction, like fire burning in water. For a guy who revels in the shock factor, that alone makes it worth living there. "No one expects a guy like me to say they are from Maine," Alan says. "New York or Boston maybe. But not Maine."

Up there, a gold Corvette raises suspicion. Drive it at breakneck speed with Chuck E. Weis or Tom Waits blasting over the loud-speaker, the top down, the seatbelt unbuckled, and two cell phones attached to your ears like gaudy, oversized earrings, and you might as well have a bull's-eye on the hood. Amid the practical trucks built to survive bitter Maine winters, Alan's Corvette looks like a spaceship that has landed in the middle of Amish country. "Driving this car around here," he says, "people always think I am a drug dealer." And then he guns the engine.

It is late September, and Alan is speeding down Route 11 like a golden bullet, headed for the last day of the Rochester State Fair in New Hampshire, where he has a horse named Wingate Hanover racing in the finals of the thirteenth race. At the start of the fair two weeks earlier, Wingate Hanover was closer to the glue factory than the winner's circle when Alan picked him up at an auction for $2,000. Wingate Hanover paid Alan's largesse back with an upset win in the first week's race that paid $750 to the owner. A win in the finals might help Alan break even, although the price of the horse actually meant nothing to him. Alan holds most animals in higher regard than people. One year, he spent $40,000 of the $60,000 he had in the bank on a yearling his trainers told him would never win a race and, if he didn't buy it, was destined for an early death. He bought it anyway, then he refused to let the trainers work the horse into shape. He promised them that if they hit the horse, Alan would hit them back twice as hard. If they tried "preparing" the horse—drugging him up—he'd fire them on the spot. Their hands tied, the trainers could only treat the animal like a pet rather than an investment. For months, the horse took leisurely afternoon trots on the track, ate fresh bails of hay, slept in a clean stall, and lived better than one of the Budweiser Clydesdales. When Alan finally saw the horse in a race, it finished sixth in a seven-horse field. The next day the owner with the deep pockets and the horse with no speed shared a sweet potato pie to celebrate their second-to-last-place finish.

Cruising along towards the fair, one hand on the steering wheel and one on the sports pager with scrolling scores that he checks more often than a paramedic looking for a patient's pulse, Alan deftly slips in a CD by the band Nick Cave and the Bad Seeds called "Murder Ballads." It's a charming collection of songs in which all the lyrics center on death and dying, including such paeans to death as "Songs of Joy," "Lovely Creature," and "Death Is Not the End."

"Lighten up," Alan says when he sees his passenger cringing. "It got an A in *Entertainment Weekly.*"

With the sun out, the top down, Nick Cave whispering sweet nothings out of the Corvette's supersonic sound system, and the horse he rescued from the scrap heap racing on the last day of the fair, life seems pretty sweet. What more does he need?

"Winnings," he deadpans.

It's been six months since the end of the college basketball season. A season in which Alan established himself as *the* preeminent college basketball handicapper in Nevada's small community of professional sports bettors. We're not talking about Jimmy the Greek types or the crooks who tout their 900 services for $50 a pop. Those guys are no more respected in Vegas than political pundits are by Washington politicians. Handicapping, like playing the stock market, rewards good instincts, long hours of research, and an acute awareness of how fickle human beings and human nature can be. Most of all, however, it requires guts of iron and the resilience of a Super Ball. It's not easy losing $10,000 because an eighteen-year-old freshman choked on two free throws late in the game. Bettors live their lives on the edge of financial and emotional ruin. One night they win ten grand and on others they lose twenty. It's not sports that pulls them in, but the rush of winning a bet, of getting something for almost nothing. For Alan the goal is simple: Make enough one year to be able to come back and do it again the next.

Just the rumors about what Alan has won—"I hear people say I won more than $1 million betting on college basketball, which is ridiculous," he says—are enough to garner respect of the entire community. But, it wasn't just what he earned; any guy off the street with money to burn could parlay a few lucky picks and a small pile of dough into a Fort Knox–sized bankroll. In the handicapping underworld the strength of your system and ability to move the spreads with your bets separates the posers from the players, the squares from the wiseguys. Some players don't even need to put their own cash on the line. Instead they make six-figure salaries acting as consultants, supplying wannabes who are long on money and short on skills with the probable winners to every night's games.

For a true wiseguy, however, consulting is what you do when you've lost your nerve, your bankroll, or both, like a cop who takes a desk job because he's too scared to walk the streets. Consultants are paper-pushing desk jockeys analyzing teams' past performances, doing all the work it takes to make a smart bet without experiencing any of the thrills.

Alan found the consulting track particularly unfulfilling when it came to college baskets and always worked on his own, building up a small bankroll and then blowing it on bad bets, bad drugs, or bad buys. He was the equivalent of the rookie pitcher with the million-dollar arm and the five-cent head, too talented to ever go broke but too brash to get too far ahead. Then, in 1997, two guys who had been tracking Alan's work decided to back him. The deal was this: Alan, the expert, would do most of the work, they would front all of the money, and they would split all winnings three ways. The partnership was the perfect remedy to reign in Alan. With two other people involved, he couldn't go overboard on his gut-check bets. And, with a deeper pool of money than he'd ever had, he could also bet bigger, and win bigger, than he ever had. As long as his system didn't fail.

After pulling into the Rochester Fair's front gate, Alan's Corvette kicks up dust on the gravel lot as he makes a sharp turn into a parking space next to a pickup. He stops by the race office, where he drops off two bumbleberry pies he bought for the office workers. Every year, the fair organizers ask Alan to reprise his role as "Rochester Red," a handicapper who writes up the daily tip sheets the fair sells for a dollar at every race. He won't take any money for the gig, won't even accept a free tip sheet, and he exasperates the fair workers who, after saying thanks for the pie, remind him that he still hasn't picked up any of the checks he's won in the past two weeks from Wingate Hanover. "If you buy the damn horse, at least take the money," says an office worker. He ignores her. He saved a horse. Get over it. Does he really need to cheapen the deed by making money off of it?

Behind the office, in the corner of a horseshoe-shaped ring of stalls, Wingate Hanover stands on spindly legs mindlessly munching on some hay. She's a nine-year old mare with a graying mane, skin the color of wet cement with black spots, a thin beard of white whiskers, and yellowing teeth. She looks like the equine version of Miss Havisham from Dickens's *Great Expectations*.

"She had a good night and has been alert all morning," says Alan's trainer. "She'll run a good race for you."

"It don't matter," says Alan, patting her long gray snout. "She's a good girl."

That someone may feel the rush of winning, or even come close, is what drives that person to take their first steps toward a betting window. It's why some of Alan's friends had been at the track since sunrise that morning and, when the fair ends, why they were heading to another harness-racing track in Brunswick that night. It is why the Rochester Fair would make $86,000 on this sunny Saturday in early fall on racing alone, even though there were never more than 1,000 people in the stands for any of the fourteen races.

Before a race the cavernous walkway beneath the grandstands, where the betting windows are, fills up like a train station during rush hour. Bettors walk up to the windows absentmindedly staring at Rochester Red's tip sheet and clutching their money in an outstretched hand. Fat men who were stuffing their faces with fried dough from the carnival next door thoughtlessly lay down $20s like they're pitching pennies. Grandmas with blue-tinted hair wearing T-shirts that read "Property of the Foxy Lady" smack a couple hundred bucks on the counter hoping to score a winner. Maybe this time their horse will come home. Even more than the rush of winning, hope is the most compelling component of a bet.

As the horses line up for the thirteenth race, Alan pulls a $100 bill from his thick, rubber-banded roll of cash. Before he can turn around, people are already asking him, "What did you bet? Who did you take? Who's the favorite? What do you like?"

"Idiots," Alan mutters. "It's illegal for me to bet against my own horse. Not like I couldn't get away with it. But, it's not right."

Settling into the aluminum chairs in the grandstands, Alan pulls out a vegan pumpkin-crunch cookie to munch on. There's always something to keep him occupied, someplace else to direct his energy toward besides the race or the bet. Seven years ago he would have pulled out a vial of cocaine to snort during the race. Three years ago it would have been fries and a milkshake that soothed his nerves. Each fixation is indicative of his all-or-nothing lifestyle; there have never been any compromises in Alan's life. During his drinking days, he didn't just have a few drinks, he'd get wasted. He couldn't accept going bald, so he shaved his head. He didn't just snort cocaine, he inhaled it like it was oxygen. When he decided to get healthy he didn't just work out, he developed the physique of a bodybuilder. Compared to Alan, extremists lack focus.

Alan once had curly red hair, glasses, and a tire around his waist. But when he started working out—to build his self-esteem as much as his physique—the baby fat around his face melted away and his skin became taut around his skull. He transformed himself from a grown version of a Raggedy Andy doll into a walking, talking, breathing version of Mr. Clean. He also turned himself into a winner.

"Before that I was always making good numbers but bad decisions. I got more confidence once I started liking myself more," Alan says. "But it's still all mental. The working out only helps so much."

Wingate Hanover draws an inside position for the race. From the start, Alan knows she doesn't have a chance. She is boxed in between the railing and another driver who won't relinquish his position. As the horses on the outside maneuver freely, Wingate Hanover maintains her speed and pacing, hoping to pounce on any opening. But it never happens. She finishes third, winning $600 for her owner. Combine that with the $750 she won for Alan the week before and she'll only cost Alan $650, not a high price to pay for saving a horse's life.

"For the horse," Alan says, a smirk forming at the corners of his mouth, "death is not the end."

Going broke, however, would be the end for Alan. Because that would mean he couldn't bet, which could be the worst fate imaginable.

Not that he economizes. He is a profligate spender. It is the gambler's code of silly pride and outright boasting that says he must pick up the tab whenever he is out with friends. At a table full of gamblers, the most successful bettor does the honor. These days, that's Alan.

Making investments on horses that end up losing you $650 is not the best way to make your money last either, and Alan's nest egg from college basketball is dwindling fast. In fact he's very nearly running on fumes. In addition to the payments he has on the $356,000 house in Las Vegas, there is also the two-bedroom beachfront condo he's renting in Maine. He estimates that he gave back 25 percent of his winnings to bad bets placed on the NBA and NHL play-offs as well as poker. He pissed the rest away on horses, food, and travel. A two-day trip to New York City in midsummer included two nights at the Four Seasons, car service to and from Yonkers to see his horses race, and the requisite two cell phones, one with the Maine area code and one with the Nevada, wherever he went. But it could be worse. "If I had $1 million dollars sitting in the bank earning interest," he says, "I would be miserable."

However, considering the six months he's had since college basketball ended, having one mil in the bank might come in handy. The last month has been particularly unkind. In early September, he endured a wicked NFL losing streak. Other sports were no kinder. Late in September, Alan turned on the Ryder Cup golf tournament between the United States and Europe to see that American Payne Stewart, in match play with Colin Montgomery, conceded a forty-foot putt, the hole and the match to Montgomery because the U.S. team had already clinched the victory over Europe. Alan had bet $1,500 that Stewart would beat Montgomery. He lost. "I'm at a real low point in my gambling career," Alan says. "Just when I thought I had lost every way there was to lose, I outdo myself."

Because his shrink told him there must be something in his subconscious disturbing him, Alan blamed the cold streak on sleepless nights and a lack of concentration after watching a Discovery Channel special about the slaughtering of elephants by poachers harvesting their tusks. He laughs as he says this, throwing his clicker on the table that is littered with fax paper, a laptop, dirty dishes, and old racing forms. But it's gallows humor. Come November, when he gets to his fancy house in Las Vegas with the kidney-shaped pool, he'll pull his gold Corvette into the three-car garage, riding on nothing but vapors. And vapors only last so long. He needs some wins.

Chapter 2

"It's Us Against the Wiseguys"

The psychology of a bettor is someone who is constantly second-guessing. You wouldn't believe how many people out there wanna bet one way but they come into the sports book, talk to bookmakers like me or just another bettor in line, and change their minds.

Part of that is because there is so much money floating around right now that isn't smart money. Just a lot of squares walking around with a lot of money in their pockets who are sports fans and think they should be able to bet sports. Just because they have a lot of money doesn't mean they know what's up.

But, we'll happily take their money. They are not the ones who we go up against. It's us against the wiseguys, like Alan Boston.

—JOE LUPO, RACE & SPORTS BOOK MANAGER,
STARDUST HOTEL & CASINO, LAS VEGAS,
NEVADA, OCTOBER 1999

There are more than fifty wedding chapels in Las Vegas. None of them hear as many prayers as sports books. Sports bettors beg God more in one hour than Muslims pray to Allah in a day. Phrases like "Dear Lord, let him make this kick," or "Please God, gimme this one game and I'll never ask again," or "Jesus Fucking Christ, can I get a break here?" are the Hail Marys of those who put their faith in the bounce of a ball and the will of an athlete. Sunday afternoons in a sports book resemble a revival meeting at Our Lady of Perpetual Sorrow.

It's appropriate then that the Stardust Race & Sports Book is laid out like the interior of a church. A wide swath of purple and green flowered carpet, the center aisle, separates the book's two sets of pews: the race side, where bettors playing the ponies sit, and the sports side, where people betting on athletic events hunker down.

Bettors sit quietly in their seats, studying racing forms and tip sheets and rotation guides—which are master lists of every game in every sport being played that the sports books will post a line on. These are the bettor's bibles, holding the keys to happiness. If gamblers can only interpret them the right way, they will be born again. They will have seen the way to betting enlightenment, a righteous moment when the collection plate is theirs for the taking. No questions asked.

Suckers. That's what the high priest of the sports book, Joe Lupo, is thinking. Good customers surely, but suckers. Day in and day out they throw good money after bad. Lupo stands behind the betting counter, protected by a line of employees called ticket writers—the people who listen to a customer's bet, punch it into a machine, and hand them a ticket—watching his congregation's every move. When they can't find the answer in the racing form or tip sheet, the customers will come to Joe, begging him, "What do you like today, Joe?"

"I've got $5,000 in the bank," says Kevin Phillips, a 28-year-old security guard at the Flamingo hotel. "I'm only betting to make more money. Believe me, if I had more cash, I wouldn't do this." Customers stop in on the way to their mechanics jobs in blue work shirts with their names sewn on the front. They pull crumpled dollar bills from their pockets, trying to string together $20 to drop on a game. They come in straight from night shifts in the Stardust's gambling pits, with clip-on bow ties dangling from their tuxedo shirt collars, to lay down crisp $100 bills from their just-cashed paychecks on UCLA or Florida

State or the Minnesota Vikings. The money the casino paid them goes right back into the Stardust's coffers.

Another group of bettors, called runners, spend their entire waking lives camped out in the sports book. They are lackeys who carry thousands of dollars of someone else's money, making bets for players too big-time to leave their homes. They spend twelve hours a day watching games, watching point spreads, and watching their waistlines expand. Two years ago, the Nevada Gaming Control Board, in an attempt to stem the flow of money from illegal bookmakers outside the state who laid off some of their bets in the sports books, made using runners illegal. Now, no one is allowed to make a sports bet in Nevada on behalf of anyone but themselves unless they are earning a percentage of the bet. But, in Las Vegas, some laws get as much attention as a Tony Danza movie. The runners that don't make a percentage get a few hundred bucks a day, if their wiseguy is benevolent.

And Joe Lupo is the runner's best friend. So many runners spend so much of their time in the sports book that they're disconnected from the rest of the world. The war in Bosnia? Unless there's a favorite, they didn't follow it. Monica Lewinsky? Isn't she 40–1 to win the U.S. Open? Lupo gives them free drink-and-buffet tickets. He tells them the weather conditions where games are being played and who is umpiring. And he lets them go about their business.

The Stardust is off the main drag of the Strip, a fifteen minute walk from upscale properties like Caesars Palace and the Bellagio. Sit in the sports book at one of these two opulent hotels and, compared to the Stardust, it's the difference between being in a stadium luxury box with cushioned seats and the bleachers with backless metal benches. And, in contrast to the roller coasters and faux skyscrapers in front of the New York, New York–themed hotel and the pirate ship in front of Treasure Island, the purple and orange Stardust sign with hundreds of bulbs bathing the night in fluorescent colors seems decidedly understated. New properties like the Venetian feature marble foyers, trendy nightclubs, hot bars, and four-star restaurants catering to high-rolling big spenders flush with Wall Street cash and good looks to spare. The Stardust, however, looks like it hasn't undergone an overhaul since the Rat Pack reigned. And while the Mandalay Bay has the House of Blues and Wolfgang Puck eatery, the Stardust features steak-and-egg breakfast buffets and lounge acts older than Don Rickels's shtick. At one time, when it first opened, the Stardust was the biggest hotel in the city. Now it's a relic.

"The other books," says Phillips, searching for the diplomatic phrase, "well, if you want a nice place to sit and a free martini, go to the Bellagio. But if you wanna gamble, you come here."

The Stardust's main attraction—other than being the hotel immortalized in Martin Scorsese's movie *Casino*—is the sports book. "Lupo is captain of the most prestigious sports book because most of the betting numbers that come out of Vegas are tied to the Stardust," says Peter Ruchman, a longtime bettor and sports betting historian. "The Stardust has been the legendary home of the opening line. It really is the place that people look to get their opening numbers."

And, indeed, there are moments in everyday when Joe Lupo wields more power than anyone else in the sports betting industry. Everyday, it is the Stardust that posts the first line for every game in every sport. He can set in motion a chain reaction that spreads from Las Vegas to New York to Costa Rica and Australia. Millions of dollars will trade hands based on what he says, what he thinks, and how he reacts to the information before him.

Lupo relies on a half-dozen consultants to ply him with their opinions of what the spread should be on the various football, basketball, baseball, and hockey games. But most of all he relies on his assistant manager, Bob Scucci. Scucci, a former all-state baseball player in Nevada and a teammate of Mark McGwire's at USC, has the short, stout body of an ex-athlete. He is a former bettor turned bookmaker after going broke. A hard-core numbers guy at a hardcore sports book, Scucci once eschewed the top job at the Hard Rock Hotel's book despite a bigger paycheck because there wasn't enough action.

He also has a storyteller's eyes and ears for details and an uncanny knack for predicting the future. "Basically," says Lupo, "Scooch knows shit before we do. It's kind of freaky." But handy when your livelihood is based on prognostication.

Between the two of them, Lupo and Scucci will make point spreads for dozens of games as well as create totals, which are the combined number of points that bettors wager the two teams will go over or under. The spread's goal is to put all the teams on even footing. Bookmakers take points from the favorite and give points to the underdog. That's why a team favored by five points is always listed as "minus-five" while a five-point underdog is "plus-five."

Meanwhile, as Lupo and Scucci work the numbers, wiseguys are privately creating their own personal point spreads for the same games. They'll use these as guidelines for what games they feel are most worth betting on. If the Stardust posts that the Lakers are favored over the Blazers by five points—Lakers minus-five—but a handicapper thinks the Lakers are only three points better than the Blazers, he'll take points—meaning bet the Blazers—in the line being offered by the Stardust. If another handicapper thinks the Lakers are seven points better than the Blazers, he'll lay the points—meaning he'll bet the Lakers.

Nobody in Vegas or anywhere else posts their line until Scucci and Lupo post theirs. It's an honor and a tradition they have carried on for years at the Stardust. But it also puts them in the role of bettor, as they lay their reputations and their jobs on the line every morning. In a very real sense, Lupo is as much a gambler as Alan Boston. Being the first line up wreaks havoc with the bottom line. There's a reason, after all, they call handicappers wiseguys. The slightest discrepancy in their line versus the Stardust line will make them bet heavy. Then it's Lupo and Succi's job to adjust the Stardust line up or down based on which team the money is coming in on. The book makes money off of the "juice," the 10-percent commission they collect on every bet. If two bettors bet opposite sides of the same game for $100, each bettor puts up $110. The book now has $220 total bet on the game. The winner gets back $210, his $100 bet plus the $10 commission he paid. The loser gets nothing. Meanwhile, the book clears $10 between the two transactions. If everyone is betting on one team it puts Lupo at risk for a huge payoff if that side covers.

Only after the Stardust has posted its line and the wiseguys have pounded it for a bit do books around the world start posting their numbers. Almost unilaterally, the spreads at other books fall in line with the adjusted numbers at the Stardust. That line then gets posted at every street corner and corner office as the Vegas Line, the spread everyone uses to decide who should win and by how much. The trickle down impact is enormous, reaching tens of millions of dollars everyday. By posting the opening line, the Stardust purposely puts itself on the front line of the betting war between wiseguys and book-makers on a daily basis.

While there is glory in being the kamikaze of the betting world, Lupo is also taking a tremendous risk. No hotel in the city depends more on its sports book. Not just because, in the same way that Siegfried & Roy defined the Mirage, the sports book is what the Star-dust's reputation is built on, but because of the financial gains. At most casinos, the windfall from sports betting accounts for about 2 percent of the bottom line. But at the Stardust, where a four-story marquee on the Strip touts their football handicapping contests, the sports book can sometimes generate 5 percent of the casino's revenue, making it a more significant cog in the Stardust's revenue machine.

All of this is obvious at 7 A.M. on a Saturday morning in early October, five weeks into football season. Inside the book, it's already standing room only, with all eyes fixed on the three-story board lit in green, orange, and yellow bulbs burning brighter than a Times Square bill-board, listing every game available for betting. There are NHL games, Canadian Football League games, first-half wagering on college and

NFL football, second-half wagering on college and NFL football, straight point spread bets on college and NFL football, college and NFL football totals, and baseball play-off games. To the left of each team is a code number like 584 or 672. To the right of the team that's favored is the point spread. When someone comes to the counter to make a bet on the Michigan vs. Ohio State game, they don't say "Give me Michigan minus-seven over Ohio State for $22." Instead they would say, "Gimme 584 for $22."

This—two hours before gametime—is the most crucial part of the day for the bookmakers. Lines of people stretch from all thirteen betting counters to the back of the book, with hundreds of thousands of dollars coming in on nearly 100 different games. Most sports books have a limit of $10,000 a game on football and $3,000 on basketball. But it's at the discretion of the bookmaker to move that up or down. Lupo and his staff have to balance being aggressive and letting bettors bet with being responsible and sticking to the house limits. Rarely is a wiseguy, or a wiseguy's runner, extended the courtesy of an above-the-limit bet. He knows too much and chances are good that if he's betting $5,000 on a game, he's heard—and Lupo hasn't—about a quarterback's injury or a change in coaching strategy or a fight some point guard has had with his girlfriend. Squares, John Q. Public, can bet as much as they want whenever they want. "Those guys are just gambling," says Lupo. "We don't respect their plays. We'll take their money anytime."

Every bookmaker and wiseguy has a computer with software that links them to point-spreads at any book in the world. Like day traders watching for the right price, bettors keep their eyes glued to the screens, waiting to see a number on a game they view as a good value. Bookmakers watch the same screen to see what the other books are doing. As soon as one book moves a number on a game from 6 to 6.5 or 10 to 9.5, usually because of a big bet made by a wiseguy, the screen flickers with action as every other bookmaker moves their number in the same direction. If they don't, the wiseguys will catch them napping and make them pay. During the week it's easy to watch the screen, manage the numbers, and stay on top of the game. But at 7 A.M. on a Saturday during college football season, it's like trying to keep a daisy planted in a tornado.

Behind the counter at the Stardust, it looks like NASA's mission control. At one end of a long counter, two computers hooked up to the ticket-writing machines log every bet that comes in and gets paid out, keeping a running tab on how much money the book has on each side of every game. Another program on these computers lets Lupo or Scucci or another one of their lieutenants move the line up or down. At the other end of the counter is the desktop computer with the software linking the Stardust to all the other sports books. When the Stardust is busy, this computer is always manned. Next to the computer are the phone banks, where customers calling from within Nevada can place bets as long as they have sufficient funds in an account with the sports book. Above the counter and computers are seven, ten-inch television screens, which at various times everyday are messengers of hope, joy, or suffering to Lupo and his staff.

When the system is running smoothly on a Saturday morning, there is a seamlessness to the staff's movements that belies the frenzied scene behind the desk. Lupo's men scream out numbers—amounts bet, spreads moving, game codes—in cadences reminiscent of a quarterback yelling signals. To the bystander the numbers mean nothing. To the guys behind the counter, they're the play.

"QX4A 472 three dimes," yells ticket writer Jim Russell from the bank of phones. A stick-thin, smooth-talking washed-up pro pool player who is only twenty-one, Russell hustles tips from big winners in the sportsbook during the day and blows them at the craps tables at night. He just told Scucci, standing by the computers monitoring the bets, that the player with the account number of QX4A wants to bet $3,000 on team 472.

QX4A is someone whose bets Scucci respects. Team 472 was the Rams minus-2.5 over the 49ers. Scucci gets on the sports book's public address system and says, "Game 472, St. Louis, minus-3." A wiseguy just moved the line.

The faster the bets come, the more Scucci or Lupo are on the PA announcing the line movements, and at the computer tapping in their changes. "304, plus-4, 323 minus-10, 351 minus-12, 405 plus-7, 5148 total 52." At times, they are simultaneously approving bets, moving numbers, keeping tabs on other sports books, watching games, granting drink requests for the bloated runners, and making announcements in a voice pattern that could rival any auctioneer. For every one of their actions, there is an equal but opposite reaction across the counter. A small ripple becomes a tidal wave as a square runs up to bet his favorite team. A wiseguy calls in because he saw a line move to a spread that he liked. A runner makes a play for his boss. Another bookmaker at a different book moves his line to match the Stardust's. Nothing is done that won't impact the bottom line of someone in that casino, whether it be Lupo, the player, or the bartender. And at the sports book, the tsunami won't stop until NFL games end on Sunday afternoon.

Joe Lupo sits down behind the desk in his office, sipping on bottled water. It's 4 P.M. and the late Sunday games are wrapping up. For the first time in thirty-six hours, Lupo is able to take a breath and assess the damage or count his winnings. For a guy who grew up in Stow, Ohio, and had a picture of bookmaker Jimmy "The Greek" Snyder on his bulletin board when he was ten years old, this is his afterglow. He spins a beloved souvenir Cleveland Browns football (commemorating their first season back in the NFL) and cranes his neck forward to stretch out the kinks.

Scucci walks in carrying a clipboard and printout of seventy-four of next week's college games and fourteen NFL games. The Stardust will post its numbers by 5:30, just ninety minutes from now. A few other books will follow and put up point spreads a couple of hours later. But most books won't have anything to bet on until 9 A.M Monday morning.

During the previous two days, before every game both college and pro, Scucci and Lupo played the betting man's version of a word association game: Quick—Florida State is playing Florida next week, what's the first spread you think of? They'd compare answers, winnow down the information the consultants have sent in, and compare some more. They become part psychologist, part mathematician, and part sports fan as they try to predict who the sharp players will favor, where the public will bet (almost always the favorite), and where the line will ultimately end up. The goal is to have your opening number stay as true to your closing number as possible. If you open a game at seven points and move it down to four points over the course of a week, you have liability at four, five, six, and seven. When you run a sports book, the one thing you can't afford is exposure.

Then, of course, there are actual game factors to consider: the talent of the two teams, the coaches, their strategies, where the game is being played, the weather, the time of day, who the teams played the week before, who they are playing the week after. Yet, none of this guarantees that some eighteen-year-old freshman kicker won't choke when you need a field goal to cover the spread.

RULE NUMBER ONE
The only sure thing is that there is no sure thing.

Lupo and Scucci have the New York Mets vs. Arizona Diamondbacks play-off game muted on the television as they work on the lines. From the book you can hear faint chants of "Let's Go Mets," as the score is tied 3–3 in the ninth inning. Lupo, clearly jaded, looks at a guest and says, "So you know, they are not really Mets fans."

Suddenly, the chanting stops and the book falls silent. The lack of screaming is as foreign in the book as it is in a nursery. Instinctively, Lupo checks the TV mounted on the wall. It's nothing but salt-and-pepper static. The satellite carrying the game has wandered into a sunspot. All over town, anxious bettors and bookmakers are hopefully staring at static, trying to revive the signal with their will, as desperate as doctors facing a patient who is flatlining.

Jim Korona, a twenty-four-year-old supervisor and Lupo's golden child, is manning the counter. A handsome kid with a chiseled face, slicked-back black hair and cool demeanor, Korona came from the posh New Jersey suburbs to the University of Nevada–Las Vegas. After graduation he settled in New York City and worked as a stockbroker. "It sounds weird," he says. "But there wasn't enough action out there. I needed more…"

Before he can finish his thought, anxious bettors are screaming at him.

"Jimmy, fix the damn TV!"

"It's not me," he yells back. "It's the sunspots."

"Jimmy, what's going on?"

"Jimmy, give us an update!"

"Jimmy, give me some volume at least!"

Korona just stands in front of the transmitter, adjusting the volume, which is all static and shaking his head in disbelief. "God, I love this clientele. In five minutes they will all be asking me for comps since they missed part of the game."

"Jimmy, give me a radio, give me an update. Give me something!"

Lupo, who had been standing out of sight to check on the commotion, watches proudly as Korona fights back the crowd. "He's a real go-getter that guy."

As he turns around Scucci hands him the final point-spreads. It's 5:40, time to put their reputations on the line. Again.

Chapter 3

"Get Out of My House"

He grew up in a beautiful home and we bought him a beautiful car and we gave him the best of everything. My job was to put my two kids through four years of college, and we would have done that with Rodney if he hadn't dropped out after two years. Then he just gambled.

He's twenty-two and I think he needs to focus on a career. Gambling is not going to get him anywhere. But that is all he did here so I finally said, "You have three alternatives. You can stay here and get a job, you can go back to school or you can leave. But if you are so good at gambling, go to Las Vegas and gamble." Even when his money runs out I told him he can't come back home unless he works.

So now he says he feels guilty when all he does is sleep in, gamble, and watch sports on TV. Well he should feel guilty. Then he should double that and he'll understand how I felt telling my son to get out of my house.

—VICKIE BOSNICH, MUNSTER, IND., FALL 1999

Why shouldn't he go, Rodney Bosnich asked himself. Why shouldn't he practice the only thing he really learned in college? Why should he risk betting with these two-bit bookies in a small-time town like Munster, Ind., when he could do it for real, for big money, against the best bookmakers and the smartest wiseguys in the palatial sports books of

Las Vegas? Screw getting a job, screw his mom, screw going back to school. He's got the cash. Those stupid frat guys who bet with him in college never had a chance with Rodney as their bookie. He may have been majoring in business while at Indiana University, but all he studied were the point spreads. And frat guys were easy marks. They were IU fans, stupid homers; Rodney would change the point spread in his favor every time one of them called to make a bet. "You want Indiana over Purdue? Well the spread is Indiana minus-7," Rodney would say. "Okay, I'll take $200 on that." Dozens of times a day he would enact a similar transaction, even though the spread across the board in Las Vegas was never more than Indiana by four.

Yeah, he could do it, he convinced himself. He had a $20,000 bankroll, courtesy of the stupid frat guys and a few good bets himself, a good grasp of how the system works, and a full tank of gas in his 1999 Grand Am. He could leave $10,000 in Munster for a fallback and take $10,000 to play with. He'd think to himself how nice it would be to make a legal bet, get a real ticket from the sports book, and then cash it in without any hassle. It would beat that time at Thanksgiving in 1998, when he won $5,000 on the Vikings over the Cowboys and the bookie had to hide the loot in a bathroom at the Harrah's Riverboat Casino in East Chicago, Ind. Rodney, a Harrah's security guard, couldn't even pick it up until after the boat was closed to the public at 6 A.M. and his shift was over. For eight hours, he felt nauseous waiting for the sunrise, worried some customer would snare his stash. No, he wouldn't have moments like that out in Vegas.

Heck, his girlfriend, Missy, could transfer from Purdue to UNLV. He could make a life of it real easy. Easier than at home, that's for damn sure.

It all made so much sense. Without hesitation, Rodney rolled on toward Vegas from Indiana in May of 1999, with Sin City's neon marquees his beacons, as they had been for so many other sporting souls before him.

"Driving in from over the Hoover Dam you feel the lights of Las Vegas," remembers Rodney, "and it's like a drug."

The lights—just the vision of the lights—pulled him in with the force of a black hole sucking down a galaxy. Rodney drove in with his sister's boyfriend, Jeff, and for the last twenty-four hours they went nonstop. The thirst for gambling parched their throats. Rodney didn't steer the car so much as let momentum and his instincts drive him there. All roads led to Las Vegas Boulevard, the Strip, as naturally as the Colorado River winds through the Grand Canyon and flows into the Gulf of Mexico. The final few miles are still a blur.

Rodney and Jeff arrived at 4 A.M., which in Vegas is no different than noon. They pulled the car into the valet at the gleaming new Venetian Hotel, a $1.5-billion complex where an Italian-style bridge leads into the casino entrance, men in black berets give gondola rides, and cocktail waitresses wear "authentic" uniforms skimpy enough to make Madonna blush. Rodney and Jeff sat down at the blackjack tables, where the felt was smooth and green and the cards dealt were shiny and clean. The waitresses flirted with them and brought them free drinks. The dealers showed them regal kings and queens paired with beautiful aces, magical figures with more cache and purchase power than a gold card. "Twenty-one," the dealer shouted. "Blackjack," the dealer screamed. "Dealer busts," the dealer fretted as Rodney and Jeff cheered. They won big and tipped the scantily clad waitresses with the free drinks and felt like big players in a city where big players are more revered than priests in Rome.

Long after the sun came up, they hobbled out of the Venetian and headed for the race and sports book at the Stardust Casino. "That was like nirvana," Rodney says. It was early in the NBA playoffs. The 31–19 Atlanta Hawks were playing the 29–21 Detroit Pistons. On any night this would be a tough game to pick between two division rivals who, during a lockout-shortened NBA season, had played each other three times during the regular season and had already played four times more in the play-offs. The play-off series was tied 2–2, with each team blowing out the other on their home courts.

Choosing sides in an even matchup like this was why Rodney

came to Las Vegas. This was his first chance to prove he belonged with the big boys. That it came during a basketball game was even better. After all, he was an all-conference basketball player in high school. He still held the school record for most three-pointers in a career. He planned on becoming the Dean Smith of high school basketball, as soon as he was done betting. He was from Indiana for God's sake, he knew basketball better than the Bible. If you cloned the greatest basketball team of all time and had those two teams play each other, Rodney felt he could figure out who would have the edge and why. No matter what the circumstances surrounding the Hawks-Pistons playoff game—be it pride, desperation, money, or bragging rights—he felt it was a no-brainer. He liked the favorite, which was the Hawks minus-4. Rodney sidled up to the counter like an old gunslinger and threw $220.

Rodney placed his bet like a Vegas vet, announcing the number of the game he wanted and for how much, including the vigorish. The ticket writer punched the numbers into the computer and a slip of paper popped out of a slot at the top of the machine like a lottery ticket. Rodney had been making bets under the table for so long, and taking bets from college kids with one eye on the door for the cops for so long, that the basic steps required to make a legal sports bet in Vegas made him giddy. He took the ticket from the slot, examined it carefully, and folded it into his wallet. This is nice, he thought. Later that night he would win his bet. But for now, he settled into one of the chairs at the Stardust and slept, waiting for the game, and his life, to start.

Chapter 4

A Nation of Sports Bettors

Whoever being engaged in the business of betting or wagering knowingly uses a wire communication facility for the transmission of interstate or foreign commerce of bets or wagers or information assisting in the placing of bets or wagers on any sporting event or contest, or for the transmission of a wire communication which entitles the recipient to receive money or credit as a result of bets or wagers, or for information assisting in the placing of bets or wagers, shall be fined under this title or imprisoned not more than two years, or both.

—U.S. CODE: TITLE 18, SECTION 1084, TRANSMISSION OF WAGERING INFORMATION AND PENALTIES, AKA THE 1961 WIRE ACT

umans are all intrigued by risk. Adam and Eve took the biggest one when they bet God wouldn't punish them for biting the apple. Boy were they wrong. The sixteenth-century Italian physician Gerolamo Cardano even prescribed gambling for melancholy, noting that, "play may be beneficial in times of grief and...the law permits it to the sick and those in prison and those condemned to death."

But, as Americans, we are inherently predisposed to bet on ourselves, more so than any other culture. It's the fabric of our existence. It started with our forefathers and -mothers getting on boats to come to a new colony, a new city, a new farm, and make new lives for themselves that they couldn't anywhere else. It's a computer geek dropping out of Harvard to become the richest man in the world. It's a white trash motorcycle rider called, of all things, Evel, becoming an American icon for jumping over flaming cars. In American culture, people who take risks and win are deified. We'll take a risk on an idea that only we believe has merit even when everyone else says it's stupid. "People don't want to admit it, but a great part of gambling is consistent with the American way," says James Frey, the dean of UNLV's liberal arts college who studied people and gambling as a sociologist. "We admire people who take risks, and we have even treated the very colorful historical gamblers such as Doc Holliday in a positive way."

Bonnie DeSimone of the *Chicago Tribune* wrote in 1999:

> Odds are you don't go a day without using a figure of speech rooted in gambling. You roll the dice. You root for dark horses. You pay attention to the high-stakes issues. You scoff at penny-ante schemes. You maintain a poker face and call your buddy's bluff. You put down your money and take your chances and hope that no one has your number. Betting is in our blood. It helped the homesteaders win the West acre by acre. It is the motif of every immigrant who lands here sight unseen. It is, in many ways, our most universal form of recreation, conducted in places still quaintly called parlors. It appeals to the naughty part of us that wants to walk on the shady side, to get something for almost nothing.

Of course, normal risk-taking is a fact of life. It's what we do when we leave ten minutes later than we should. It's crossing the street when the light flashes "don't walk" or going forty-five mph in a forty-mph zone. We are all predisposed to accepting some sort of risks if for no other reason than to move forward in life. And the greater the risk—being offered a job we're not qualified for, getting married, having kids—the less often we're confronted with taking it.

But it's different when we gamble with money. Former Treasury Secretary Robert Rubin's mantra as a Wall Street trader was "bet until your balls hurt." He was talking about more than the old notion that the greater the risk, the greater the reward. Rubin was also talking about the adrenaline surge leading up to the outcome. After all, part of betting's allure is how good it makes us feel. The boiling in our stomachs is exciting. (It's just a coincidence that the nerve signaling our brains that our stomachs are digesting is called the Vagus nerve.) The heat in our cheeks feels like the first time we fell in love. (Or even better, the first time we had sex. For some poor souls, gambling replaces sex altogether.) It's not just the rewards of winning, but the physical rush of anticipating the win. It's the delusions of grandeur we harbor that the win will change our lives. Winners are special. Winners hang out with Regis, get free trips to Disneyland, and have press conferences where the media ask them lots of questions about...them. We are a competitive culture, and it's the losers who get left behind, laughed at, and forgotten. And winning once is never enough. Usually winning once makes us feel like we are starting a hot streak. No one ever considers that what just happened *was* the hot streak.

Never have we been more aware of all this than over the last five years, when we have all become gamblers playing the fickle stock market. For every broker preaching patience and practice, there have been novice players taking a shot on the next new big thing. Nobody wants to be the guy who couldn't crack the code, be it point spreads, blackjack, stock picking, or choosing lottery numbers. Taunting the odds is a little sexy, a little dangerous, and straddles the line between unimagined success and nauseating failure. It's our chance to feel the rush of life as a rock star compressed into the few seconds it takes us to turn wins into losses and cash into debt.

Of course risking and winning is as much about luck as it is about skill. And who doesn't want to be lucky? Who doesn't want to be seen as charmed or special? Being branded lucky—or unlucky—says as much about us as our jobs, religions, or politics. The lucky ones are the chosen few.

The difference between the weekend gambler and the pro is the weekender's ability to separate fact from fiction, reality from dreamland. The casual gamblers don't depend on betting as a revenue source; they see it as entertainment. They don't accept being lucky as a preordained right or their winnings as anything more than chance. Most people know when to walk away satisfied they beat the house. And what they remember is the anxiety of the risk. They don't crave it. They gamble just enough to get a cheap thrill. When they get too close to the ledge, their desire for self-preservation pulls them back in.

But professional gamblers aren't like that and that makes us envious. They've shed the inhibitions the rest of us hold sacred. They live by rules that say security is for sissies, having a boss means being someone's boy, and money in the bank is money wasted. We see them as Indiana Jones, Fast Eddie Felson, and Dirty Harry rolled into one. They are masculinity personified, mythical characters that are so sure of themselves they'd rather be broke and alone than walk away without proving how smart they are. And while we respect hard work, we revere guts. Guys with guts take risks, they gamble, test the odds, and push the limits. Laying it all on the line is also a slap in society's face. They're saying they don't need money and all the trappings that come with it. They can throw it all away. They are rebels. To make a bet, a big bet, shows they believe in their own intuition above all and don't need anyone's approval.

Risking it all means losing it all, and losing it all includes not just tangibles like money but intangibles like sanity, stature, respect. Worse yet, it means starting over. Most of us feel like we have worked too hard to go back to the beginning. But for the addicted and the unaffected, that's the appeal. To paraphrase F. Scott Fitzgerald, gamblers are not like you and me.

But at what point does normal, healthy risk-taking become dangerously self-destructive? What makes some people recognize that the upside of winning a bet doesn't outweigh the risk? Until recently, psychologists and society at large assumed problem gamblers were sociopaths. In the eighteenth century, the word "gamble" was slang for a "term of reproach" and "gambler" originally meant "a fraudulent gamester." Only in the past twenty years, since the American Psychological Association began recognizing gambling as a disease, has it gotten the same attention as an addiction that drugs and alcohol do. The APA describes gambling as an impulse-control disorder, but according to Harvard Medical School's Director for the Division of Addiction, Howard Shaffer, there is new evidence that shows gambling and other physical activities can stem from altered brain chemistry and cause dependence.

The wiseguys, as opposed to slot players, are what Las Vegas psychologist and addiction specialist Dr. Robert Hunter calls "action gamblers." Unlike slot players, considered "escape gamblers" who want to get lost staring into the windows of the machines, action gamblers crave intellectual competition. They are, almost without exception, young, educated, and competitive. The initial attraction for them is the rush of the risk, like a runner's high. But they come back to prove they are brasher and brighter than the average person. Challenging the unknown, doing hand-to-hand combat with karma, is one of the driving forces taunting the compulsive or pathological gambler. While the casual bettor weighs common sense and financial realities with every bet, the wiseguy pushes those aside. His brain chemistry is geared to seek out the pleasure he felt the first time adrenaline rushed through his body. These are the same factors that lead people to drug or alcohol addiction. The bettor's battle isn't with what makes sense; his battle is with anyone who gets in the way of making his bet a euphoric experience. It's the public, the bookmakers, other wiseguys, the government that is out to get him, or the technology that moves too slow, or the overpaid athlete who doesn't care anymore or the freshman who cares too much. It's enough to cause vertigo—which, perversely, is exactly the way they like it. "Without exception," Hunter says, "sports bettors are action-seeking gamblers."

To wiseguys, gambling is not about the money. It is about the art, the experience, the desire to always be in pursuit and on the edge. Alan Boston talks about the day he woke up as a ten year old and realized he wasn't immortal. "Do you know what it's like to be that age and understand what it means to die while all your friends are eatin' freakin' popsicles?" Boston asks. "It's exhausting." He has spent the last thirty-one years making Hades revise his tune. If you can beat the odds on University of North Carolina vs. Duke or New Mexico vs. Utah, you raise the ante. Maybe you can beat the odds on anything. Maybe you can live forever.

Indeed, the act of gambling feels like dying and being reborn. And that's not an entirely novel concept. Egyptian tombs dating back to 3500 B.C. have been found that depict noblemen in the afterlife playing a crude game of dice. Animal anklebones, assumed to be dice, are often found in prehistoric tombs and burial caves around the world, believed to have been put there so the dead could re-create life. Icelandic, Hindu, and even Native American myths claim that the gods routinely destroy and recreate the world on a dice board. For mere mortals like the men who come to Vegas, every game is a new opportunity to prove you're smart, intuitive, analytical, a winner. Ultimately, it's a chance to prove your omniscience and, to a certain extent, your godliness.

The fact is, gamblers are not always the stoic men of conviction we've romanticized them to be. A professional gambler is characteristically an anxiety-riddled neurotic who doesn't relax until he's lost it all. Social bettors enjoy gambling as much for the atmosphere as for the game. They watch the Super Bowl together. They join pools. They trek to the sports books for the Final Four in packs. Any flight heading into Las Vegas is a virtual party plane, with dice rolling in the aisles, cards stacked on the tray tables and a communal sense of good fortune filling the cabin. But the wiseguys are loners. "Gamblers are by nature antisocial, and we'd rather not talk to anybody about what we do," says wiseguy Dave Malinsky. "In fact, it's kind of stupid for us to try and do what we do. So we don't want to tell anyone who may think we are stupid."

According to Michael Brubaker, a national certified gambling counselor based in Arizona, "compulsive gamblers have the highest suicide rate of any addiction." Is it any coincidence that the suicide rate in Nevada, the only state in the Union where all forms of gambling are legal, is the highest in the United States? But before laws were even on the books, lawmakers had been willing to accept the potential dangers surrounding the bet, as long as the benefits outweighed the costs. The Great Virginia Lottery in 1612 provided half the budget for the settlers of Jamestown. Lotteries funded George Washington's army as well as roads and mortgages.

Nevertheless, in the 1870s, when a massive bribery scandal involving state and local officials was uncovered in the Louisiana Lottery, lotteries were banished by the federal government. For nearly a hundred years after that, all forms of gambling were the domain of the Wild West, the underworld, and the misbegotten.

When New Hampshire became the first state to reinstitute the lottery in 1964, it deemed that the proceeds go toward education initiatives. It was a brilliant political move. Suddenly, every other state legislature felt like it could reap the rewards of gambling without suffering political repercussions, if the programs funded were virtuous. We may be legalizing a dangerous habit, they said, but it's a chance worth taking if it raises enough money for schools, hospitals, or the elderly. The good would outweigh the bad. Today gambling in some form, be it pari-mutuel, lottery, riverboat, or Indian casino, is legal in 48 states. Nine of the eleven states with casinos earned them via the ballot box, as did twenty-seven of the thirty-eight states with lotteries.

"Now, gambling," says Fred Preston, a UNLV sociology professor, "is no different than going to a golf course."

In fact, gambling is different than golf: Gambling is much bigger business. According to I. Nelson Rose, an expert in gambling law and a professor at Whittier Law School in California, the "total action in casinos and on slot machines, wagers on sports, bets made in licensed card rooms and expenditures before prize payments in charity gaming and Indian bingo, the total amount bet legally in the United States is estimated to be well over half a trillion dollars, $638.6 billion, to be more precise. Looking just at revenue, Americans spent more on gambling, $50.9 billion, than they did on all live events, concerts, plays, all movie theaters, all spectator sports, and all forms of recorded music—combined. In 1994, Americans spent more on gambling than they did on toys for their children." With this onslaught of lotteries, powerballs, and riverboat and Indian casinos, gambling is not only acceptable now, it's commonplace. From televised megabucks drawings, to parlor games at the church, to senior citizen day trips to casinos, betting is like the old mob figure who has gone legit. And Las Vegas has transformed from Sin City to Disney in the Desert, with the fastest population explosion in the country—one that rivals the expansions of San Francisco during the gold rush and New York City during the heyday of immigration through Ellis Island.

In 1999, the National Gambling Impact Study Commission, a group formed by President Clinton in 1996 and charged with studying the positive and negative effects of gambling on U.S. citizens, released its report. In it, the commissioners stated that 86 percent of Americans had gambled at least once in their lives. Seventy percent had done so in the year prior to being surveyed by the commission. The commission also noted that, in 1998, Americans lost more than $50 billion gambling, a figure that has increased every year for more than two decades, sometimes at double-digit rates.

In 1974, the Nevada Gaming Control Board lowered the state tax on sports bets to be paid by sports books from 10 percent to 2 percent. Instantly, running a sports book could be a profitable, large-scale business that had the added bonus of keeping guests on the property. In 1975, hotels along the Strip began building sports books on their property to accommodate their biggest players. In the early 1980s, when the tax was lowered again, this time to .25 percent, casinos didn't just build standard sports books, they built 10,000-square-foot super books. Suddenly sports books weren't just stopgaps to keep bettors from leaving the property, but destination spots. The profile of sports books regulars subsequently changed from downbeat locals to upscale guests, and the profits from sports betting grew like Jack's beanstalk. In 1975, there was $13 million legally wagered at the Nevada sports books. Twenty-five years later, the amount had risen to $2.6 billion in 147 sports books.

As big as the legal take is, it is dwarfed by what goes on under the table. Estimates of illegal gambling wagers—the handshake bets, office pools, and sophisticated college operations—range from $80 billion to $300 billion. The Internet also gives gambling an audience it could never reach before. Americans gambled $651 million on-line in 1998 and that figure is expected to quadruple over the next seven years. Analysts expect that 40 percent of this money will come from sports bets.

The 1961 Wire Act made transmitting sports information over the telephone between states illegal. In 1985 the Bank Secrecy Act targeted gamblers, mainly sports bettors, who were dropping more than $10,000 at a time in a sports book by requiring them to fill out forms notifying the Interal Revenue Service they were making the bet. The 1992 Professional and Amateur Sports Protection Act made it illegal for any state that didn't already offer sports betting to do so. At the time that the bill was passed, then Democratic Senator Bill Bradley from New Jersey, who had proposed the bill, said, "I am not prepared to risk the values that sports instill in youth just to add a few more dollars to the state coffers. State-sanctioned sports betting conveys the message that sports are more about money than personal achievement and sportsmanship. In these days of scandal and disillusionment, it is important that our youngsters not receive this message...sports betting threatens the integrity of and public confidence in professional and amateur team sports, converting sports from wholesome athletic entertainment into a vehicle for gambling...sports gambling raises people's suspicions about point-shaving and game fixing. All of this puts undue pressure on players, coaches and officials."

Seven years later, the report released by the National Gambling Impact Study Commission concurred with Bradley. The committee's recommendation "that the betting on collegiate and amateur athletic events that is currently legal be banned altogether," was one of the report's shortest suggestions, but it used the strongest language. It was the only recommendation not couched with safe words like "should" or "urges."

To those on the committee, sports betting, unlike parlor games or slot machines or lotteries, carried a stigma that it couldn't escape. The face of poker was an old cowboy with six-shooters at his waist and a gentlemanly drawl that oozed charm. The face of slot machines was a grandma holding a cup of quarters in one hand and the pull in the other. The face of lotteries looked like you, your neighbor, your kid's teacher, or anyone else who thought they're number may come in. But, the face of sports betting was sinister and evil, topped off by a fedora, chewing on a cigar, sucking down whiskey, and looking to stick its chin in the middle of trouble. It was bookies, bad bets, big debts, and broken legs.

In 1950, Senator Estes Kefauver of Tennessee held hearings to investigate the influence of organized crime. For the first time, gangsters were paraded in public, and they were striking, intimidating figures on the new medium called television. Even when their faces weren't shown, their scratchy, thickly accented voices and their mannerisms were memorable. New York's crime boss Frank Costello refused to appear before the committee unless he was guaranteed his face wouldn't be shown on television. During the entire testimony, the camera stayed focused on his hands, which fiddled with his watch and his cuff links so incessantly his performance at the testimony became known as "the hand ballet."

At times, 100 percent of the television viewers on the 108 local stations throughout the country were watching the Kefauver hearings. What they learned was simple: Bet on sports and you will be tied to gangsters. Cops in New Orleans, viewers learned, supplemented their $186 a week income by being on the take from mob gambling syndicates, syndicates that profited mainly from bookmaking. Some of those who testified admitted to having $150,000 in the bank. Chicago police captain Dan Gilbert admitted to not invading any bookie joint for over a decade while confessing he had accumulated his wealth by betting on sports, elections, and the stock market. When Kefauver released his report after a seventeen-month investigation, one of his main points stated: "Big-time bookmaking operations, largely monopolized by big mobsters, cannot be carried on without the rapid transmission of racing information and information about other sporting events." This, of course, laid the foundation for the 1961 Wire Act.

Around the same time the Kefauver hearings were ending, in February of 1951, investigators from the Manhattan District Attorney's office met the train of the City College of New York basketball team in Penn Station as the squad returned from a road trip to Philadelphia. The CCNY team was beloved in Manhattan because they were an undermanned, under-talented team with a legendary coach, Nat Holman, who in the previous season had pulled off the most unlikely of feats: winning both the NIT and NCAA championships. At a time when college basketball was strictly a back-page item whose games were barely covered by television, CCNY dominated the newspapers and newscasts as the feel-good story of 1950. They were poor city boys who had done good.

But when the train pulled into Penn Station, the collective good will the city held for their team was on the verge of turning sour. The district attorney arrested, and eventually wrangled confessions from, seven CCNY players for point shaving. Paid as much as $1,000 a game for their sins by a local bettor, the players not only admitted their crimes, but confessed that shaving points at City College had been a long-standing tradition. Sadly, they weren't alone. They were caught in the web of a nationwide investigation that snared 32 players from seven of the top basketball schools at the time: CCNY, Long Island University, New York University, Manhattan College, Kentucky, Bradley, and Toledo.

It wasn't the first time the nation had been rocked by a point-shaving scandal orchestrated by unscrupulous sports bettors. But it was the first time during the post–World War II era, the modern era, when news and pictures could be disseminated to the world in a matter of minutes. The images of the fresh-faced boys of CCNY walking into the local police precincts were a blow to fans' faith in amateur athletics. And the scandal guaranteed that opposition to sports gambling would remain strong for years to come.

Despite the importance we place on being lucky, we still don't honor lottery winners with trophies and commercial endorsements and breathless cheers. They're just lucky. But athletes are different. They are special, skilled beyond normal limits. Strip away the salary disputes and strikes and sports, at their core, are still fun. They're what we would all do if we could jump higher, lift more, or shoot better. Even when Sportscenter goes ten minutes without reporting a single score because so much of the news is about athletes being arrested, we are always shocked when it happens again. We want to believe.

The threat of athletes betting on sports, and what it can do to the integrity of the game, is more daunting than any murder and mayhem they may cause off of the field. "(Betting) is the hydrogen bomb of the leagues," Milt Ahlerich, senior director of NFL security has said. "I can't tell you how much damage it would do. We operate under the assumption that it would be enormously dangerous to the integrity of competition."

Former Knicks coach and current broadcaster Hubie Brown once joked about his last-place Knicks team, "We play hard, and we cover. We lead the league in covering the point spread." The NBA, however, takes the threat of gambling so seriously it wouldn't allow Toronto to field an expansion team until Ontario, where Toronto is located, made betting on NBA games illegal. In 1991, Charles Barkley of the Philadelphia 76ers and the New York Knicks' Mark Jackson made friendly $500 bets with each other if one of them hit the game-winning shot against the other. In one game Jackson hit what appeared to be a game-winning shot with less than ten seconds left, only to be outdone by Barkley, who scored at the buzzer. Jackson and Barkley joked on the record with reporters about the bets after the game, but NBA commissioner David Stern wasn't laughing. He fined them both $5,000.

The examples of corruption are many. There are the 1919 Chicago White Sox, infamously known as the Black Sox, who threw the World Series to make some money and to spite their chintzy owner, Charles Comiskey. In 1963, Pete Rozelle suspended two of the NFL's most popular players, Green Bay running back Paul Hornung and Detroit defensive lineman Alex Karras, for one year for betting on their own games. Pete Rose, baseball's all-time hits leader, is not in the Hall of Fame because he bet on baseball games as a manager.

In the 1990s alone there have been five major point-shaving scandals involving college athletes. In 1992, nineteen University of Maine football and baseball players were suspended for participating in a $10,000-a-week gambling operation. At Bryant College, also in 1992, four basketball players who were $54,000 in debt to gamblers were suspended. In 1996, thirteen Boston College football players were suspended after they bet on college and pro games. Two allegedly bet against their own team. A year later, in 1997, two former Arizona State basketball players admitted shaving points during the 1993–94 season. One of the players, Isaac Burton, pled guilty to conspiracy to commit sports bribery, and in June 1999 was sentenced to two months in jail, six months of home detention, and three years' probation. He was also fined $8,000. The other player, Stevin Smith, pled guilty to point shaving, and in November 1999 was sentenced to a year in prison and three years' probation. He was also fined $8,000. (The ASU scam was uncovered when two ASU students allegedly bet $250,000 on a game versus Washington State, an amount that led suspicious Vegas bookmakers to pull the game off the board, sparking the investigation that eventually led to the point-shaving convictions.) Finally, in 1998, two Northwestern basketball players, Dion Lee and Dewey Williams, were indicted on point-shaving charges for conspiring with former Notre Dame football player Kevin Pendergast to fix Northwestern games during the 1994–95 season. Eventually Lee pleaded guilty to sports bribery and was sentenced to one month in prison and two years of probation. Pendergast, who orchestrated the scandal, was sentenced to two months in prison. Dewey Williams got a month.

A 1999 University of Michigan survey of 758 college football players and female basketball players showed that 3.4 percent said they had bet on games in which they played, given inside information to bookies, or taken money to change a game's outcome. Another University of Michigan study, done in conjunction with the NCAA and released during the 2000 NCAA basketball tournament, polled Division I football and basketball officials. Of the 640 people who responded to the questionnaire, 84.4 percent admitted they had gambled since becoming an official. Forty percent had gambled on sports and 22.9 percent had even bet on the NCAA basketball tournament. A little more than 2 percent had used a bookie while two officials said they had been approached by someone about fixing a game. Two others said their awareness of the point spread resulted in "their officiating with a level of bias" and twelve officials said they knew of colleagues who had not called a game fairly because of gambling.

Nevertheless, while sports betting is still a crime in forty-nine states, law-enforcement officials prosecute it as often as they go after someone for driving sixty in a fifty-five-mph zone. In 1960, nearly 123,000 people were arrested for illegal gambling activities, or 3 percent of all arrests made nationwide. In 1999, just 15,000 were arrested, less than one-tenth of one percent of all arrests. By comparison, drug arrests in 1960 numbered 27,000; today the figure is over one million annually, or more than 8 percent of total arrests. A 1983 study by the New York–based research firm Christiansen/Cummings Associates put the total amount of illegal sports betting at $8 billion. In 1995, they revisited the study and raised their estimate to $84 billion. By contrast, at the time the government figured that the U.S. illegal drug trade totaled $49 billion.

While local and state law-enforcement officials have come to see time-consuming investigations of illegal sports-bookmaking activity as a waste of time, the federal government has been schizophrenic in its approach: Some laws have made matters more difficult for sports gamblers, while some have made matters easier. In 1986, six years before Bill Bradley authored his antigambling legislation, the U.S. Supreme Court gave betting some legitimacy in the case of the IRS vs. Robert Groetzinger. A former traveling salesman, Groetzinger became a full-time gambler, wagering on greyhound races. In 1978, he bet $72,032 at the races, coming away with losses of $2,032. Groetzinger, who worked up to seventy hours a week studying the dogs, claimed on his taxes that he was a professional bettor and deducted the more than two grand he lost. The IRS however, believing that Groetzinger's gambling activities did not amount to a legitimate business, refused to allow him to deduct the money as a business loss on his income taxes. Groetzinger's lawyer, an old gambling buddy named Carroll Baymiller, argued all the way to the Supreme Court that his client not winning at gambling was no different than an unpublished author claiming his expenses or a cattle rancher who didn't sell any steer claiming his losses.

Justice Harry Blackmun and five of his colleagues agreed, ruling 6–3 in Groetzinger's favor. Blackmun wrote for the Court that to be engaged in a trade or business, a taxpayer need only be involved in that activity continually and regularly for the purpose of producing profit or income. (When he finally heard the decision, after nine years of battling the IRS over what had become a measly $2,142 tax bill, Groetzinger said, "Do you think they'll still go after the money? I'm not taking any bets against it.")

The Court's decision helped blur even more the already vague line between what was an acceptable legal bet and what was an illegal wager. The Groetzinger case also pointed out the cognitive dissonance Americans have when it comes to sports betting. On one hand, there is social stigma and a belief that gambling leads to trouble. But when it comes to individual bettors, it's hard for us to distinguish between what's harmless and what's not. Rarely are gamblers on trial seen as criminal by a jury of their peers. "The jail time is minimal; fines can be paid; felonies can be knocked down to misdemeanors," says Edward Galanek, a detective who works with the Brooklyn District Attorney investigating gambling operations.

"It's extremely hard to prosecute because sports betting has a blanket of legitimacy," adds Sergeant Mike Bunker of the Las Vegas Police Department. "It is difficult to educate people on why betting illegally is wrong because they don't see betting as being wrong." The fact is, people hate point shavers and bookies, but almost everyone can sympathize (if not agree with) the desire to take a chance and make a few bucks.

RULE NUMBER TWO
Winning is a work ethic.

More than any law, new casino, lower tax, or some kind of sociological acceptance of gambling, the one entity with the single greatest influence on sports betting has been television. In the 1950s, the nascent television networks may have demonized sports betting by showing young athletes who shaved points and testifying gangsters. But, by the 1980s television, specifically cable television, helped turn the tide in favor of sports betting.

By bringing sports into people's homes on a regular basis, television networks built a captive audience with enormous potential for gambling. Jimmy "the Greek" (who was once convicted for transporting gambling information across state lines) handicapped games every Sunday on CBS's *NFL Today* during the 1980s. Newspapers published the point spreads. In the early and mid–80s, ESPN broadcast *Sportsline*, a half-hour show broadcast from Caesars Palace in Las Vegas that provided lines and pregame information on upcoming NFL play-off games. Play-by-play men and analysts made it a practice to talk about point spreads.

"With the boom of cable TV in the 1980s, it changed everything," says handicapper Ken White, a second-generation sports bettor in Las Vegas. "Now everybody bets sports because there are more games to watch on TV and when there are more games to watch more people need a reason to be interested. Betting fills that hole.

"Of course, this makes it a lot more competitive too. In the 70s, even if there were a lot of people betting, they were hush hush about it. Even though it was legal you were considered a degenerate if you were betting sports. People would snicker and say, 'there goes the sports bettor,' when you walked into the book, which was always tucked away in some tiny corner of the casino. Not anymore, now no one is afraid to talk about it."

This puts the leagues in a catch-22. "The NFL is a business, and they know their revenues are determined by viewership and viewership generates ratings and ratings sell advertising and potential advertising dollars are what drive up the cost of programming," says Bill Bible, the former chairman of the Nevada Gaming Control Board and a member of the National Gambling Impact Study Commission. "A lot of people are going to watch these games because they are participating through wagering." In fact, it's the NFL and the NCAA tournament, the two sporting events that generate the most action in Las Vegas sports books, that also garner the highest rights fees from the networks.

The increased exposure has not only changed how sports betting is perceived by the public, but who in fact is making the bets. Two generations ago, most gamblers bet on the ponies. But about 85 percent of the bets made today in the sports book are on team sports. And there is not a finite number of dollars being funneled into this industry; for example, there hasn't been a decline in pro football betting because betting on college games increased.

"Conventional wisdom now is that sports bettors are younger and better educated," says Arnie Lang, former host of the Stardust Line, a radio show broadcast from the Stardust and dedicated to betting. "They are attracted to the value of betting on sports because it's beatable to them. They know the game, and sports betting is a bargain in that respect."

Only in Vegas could someone consider a losing proposition a bargain. But the truth is, despite all the game broadcasts, chat rooms, magazines, and sports radio, the vast majority of people who bet on sports lose. They put their money down, and they never see it again. That's what the sports books are counting on. The bookmakers' greatest fear is the bettor who wins. The one who has figured it out. The one who puts his money down and consistently gets a whole lot back. Such gamblers are rare characters, but when they get on a roll is when things get interesting.

Chapter 5

Let the Games Begin

It's November 13, late in the college football season and the Stardust sports book resembles an airport at Christmas, right down to the bathroom sinks where there's a line three deep to wash your hands. A cell phone's ring intrudes on the rhythm of toilets flushing and water running.

"What do we got on West Virginia-Boston College?" a voice from behind a bathroom stall asks.

All anyone can see is a pair of sneakers and all they hear is a voice, but instantly the others in the bathroom check their lineups, silently thinking, "Let's hear what he has to say."

"Nothing," the voice screams. "I got that game cold." A pause. Some shifting in the stall. A pencil falls to the floor. "We better get some action on it fast."

Another pause.

"I don't know what time it starts." The voice is desperate and strained.

He waits. The people in the bathroom wait.

"I can't right now," the voice says, hesitating a bit.

Another pause.

"I can't get to my pager now, okay," he whines.

His feet tap, his belt buckle bounces on the Stardust's faux Italian tile.

"I JUST CAN'T."

A deep breath, papers shuffle.

"God Dammit, you moron. WE ARE MISSING THE GAME!"

Two weeks. That's how long Rodney lasted at the construction job his parents set up for him when he got to Vegas. "I just couldn't deal with the long hours, the heat, the labor," he says.

Before the job, the first few days in Vegas felt like spring break. Smoke dope and party late, gamble all day, eat, smoke some more dope. They were rolling good times. After a week his sister's boyfriend left. Rodney would set arbitrary deadlines to get a job—once the summer is over, once college football starts, as soon as college basketball begins—and they'd pass unceremoniously. Missy was taking classes at UNLV and working at Abercrombie & Fitch nearly thirty hours a week, while Rodney rented movies, played video games, rolled joints, and, of course, gambled. They would sit in the dining alcove of their small prefab one bedroom twenty minutes from the Strip and she would hand him the want ads. At first, she was subtle, leaving the whole section, unopened, on the table before she hustled off to work. Each week she became more direct, eventually folding them open to the jobs she thought he'd be interested in, and finally circling the places she assumed he'd be happy at. The want ads became a part of the apartment's decor, like the Serbian flag—acknowledging Rodney's heritage—that hung over the couch and the portrait of Jesus Christ displayed next to the television.

By November the euphoria of those first few days has dulled like shine on a year-old car. The thrills in his day—placing a bet, the hope and optimism it brings, and the game itself—are sandwiched between watching *Days of Our Lives*, trips to the mall and buying Missy dinner. He has squeezed in a little job hunting: Rodney has applied to nearly every sports book on the Strip to be a ticket writer. His Stardust interview was in late October.

"We really needed to get some people in here," says Scucci, who did the interview. "Joe was on vacation and he was pressuring me to get someone in. In fact, before he left, he mandated I get a ticket writer in here by the time got back.

"I had seen this kid in the book a lot, so when he applied I called him in for an interview."

Rodney prepped hard for the interview, which meant drinking a whole bottle of a masking agent that conceals marijuana use on any drug test. Otherwise he felt prepared. He had been coming to the Stardust for a couple of months, watching Lupo and Scucci put up the lines, deal with customers, and get respect. He knew bookmaking, he loved sports and, to him, Lupo and Scucci were bigger stars than the loudmouthed players he saw making bets. A little more than two years in college hadn't helped him find his life's work. But now he had seen the light: He would be a bookmaker.

"So, why do you want to work in a book?" Scucci asked.

"I spend most of my time here, and I can make numbers," Rodney answered.

"Do you like sports?"

"Yeah."

"Do you work well with people?"

"I can."

"Why did you leave your job as a security guard?"

"They were fucking with me."

"Normally," Scucci remembers, "I would have blown it off right there. But Joe was adamant I get someone in here. I'm shaking my head in disbelief at how bad this interview is, but I give him the benefit of the doubt."

"You said you're in here a lot. Do you gamble?" Scucci asked.

"Fuck yeah, I got $600 of your money in my pocket right now."

At this point Scucci had had enough, but he decided to send Rodney for a drug test regardless, just in case he didn't see anyone even remotely more qualified. As Rodney left the office, he turned around and said, "Oh yeah, I need off from Christmas through New Years."

"That was the last straw," says Scucci. "I mean come on, that is one of our busiest times of the year. I called the drug tester and told her to send him back without the test. Then I told him we weren't interested.

I still see him coming in here all the time. He bets a lot of parlays. He might get hot with those for a year or so, get up maybe $30,000 or $40,000, but parlays don't turn into a career. He better be careful."

Scucci's prescience is, as usual, uncanny. Rodney thinks of the wiseguys with three-ring binders who have committed twenty-four hours a day to making sense of irrational behavior and he laughs. Since his arrival in May he is up $9,000. After a baseball season spent betting on the Cubs out of blind loyalty and losing about $2,000, Rodney has been making most of his money since college football started in September. And his wins have come in big chunks, not from small, consistent wagers. Twice in October, he's successfully made $100, five-team parlay bets that pay $1,200. That means all five teams Rodney picks have to cover for him to win his bet. It also means if he wins he's just earned six months' rent. "I like just going in cold," he says. "I mean, I'll read some stuff on the Internet and I watch a disgusting amount of games. But I see people with these books charting every play and taking notes and I don't know how they do it," Rodney says. "I don't buy into that. I just check games on the Internet and make a bet." And every week he wins is one less legitimate job interview he'll go on.

By November, Rodney's developed a rhythm to his habits, a confidence in his voice, and strategies for his betting, all shining like klieg lights on a fledgling gambling career. "You just know in your head what's gonna happen. You start to catch on a little bit," he says. "I mean when you first see that board all lit up, you wanna bet on everything. Then you learn to pick and choose fewer games and just bet a lot on those."

Yet, his brash confidence, born of some big wins and the street savvy that earned him his bankroll to begin with, contradicts his ignorance about the professional betting scene. Here's a kid who ran a bookmaking operation on a college campus and was smart enough to manipulate the lines based on the fanaticism of his clients, yet he's stunned to learn you can bet over the phone in Nevada. The fact that wiseguys use runners to stake out different books and lay money down when the spread changes astonishes him. He's got four bricks of $5,000 each hidden around his apartment in places like the freezer and a shoe box, yet he needs to ask the Stardust ticket writers for change to call Missy from the payphone. Instead of shopping for the best lines on the Strip like most wiseguys, he bets at the Stardust everyday. Is it the service? The concession stand's food? The soft lines? Nope. It's the only place that won't check his ID anymore.

"I went to Bally's a couple of times and the same guy kept asking me for a driver's license every time I bet. This was two or three times in the same day," says Rodney. "I got sick of it. I'm not some fucking kid."

It's easy being a sports fan in St. Louis, New York, San Francisco, or every other city where sports betting is illegal. You root for the home team. Period. But being a sports fan in Las Vegas is complicated. In 1991, after the number one–ranked UNLV Runnin' Rebels basketball team was upset by Duke in the NCAA semifinals, men at Caesars Palace sports book in Vegas started dancing on the tables and ripping off their shirts in celebration. Why such joy when the home team, UNLV, just lost? Because it's illegal in Nevada to bet on games involving UNLV. If the Runnin' Rebels had beaten Duke then the NCAA basketball finals, on par with the Super Bowl as the most wagered on event in the country, would have been taken off the board. Without the possibility of action, interest in the game, for those in Vegas and for the public at large, would have been seriously diminished.

RULE NUMBER THREE
Vegas doesn't root for Vegas.

For the first couple months of the fall sports schedule, Rodney had been managing his bankroll wisely. On college football Saturday's he'd make the usual five-team $100 parlay as well as two or three $200 straight bets. In total, he'd lay between $500 and $1,000 on the line every Saturday. A big Saturday win and he'd treat himself to a twelve-pack of Corona. On days when he lost, "I'm too upset to drink."

With football his action was confined to the weekend. Basketball, however, is daily and as a native son of Indiana, Rodney was born with a basketball beating in his chest. A little taller than six-feet, with thick features padding his 180-pound frame from head to toe, closely cropped hair, and permanent remnants of stubble on his cherubic face, Rodney, at twenty-three years old, is not far from his playing shape at eighteen. In memory, those days are even closer. He could have been a banger underneath the boards—he was big enough even against those corn-fed Indiana teenagers—but he liked to stand on the perimeter and shoot. And shoot. And shoot. It's not his style to do the dirty work. He wants to score and score big. Rodney could have played college ball, if he wanted to go to a Division III school. At times, when he drifts off into talking about being a part of the best season his high school team ever had, he seems to personify a Bruce Springsteen song about lost youth and past glories. Of course, becoming another small-town stereotype is what drove him out of Munster to begin with. He wants more than drinking in the same bar, smoking dope with the same friends, and talking about the same damn shot in high school that, if he made it, could have made him a star. At least, he thinks he wants more.

Betting on basketball, the chance to win big at something he knows so well, was Rodney's perfect excuse to leave his parents' house and come out to Vegas. He looks at the teams playing, and, because he's followed them for so long, he can picture in his mind's eye an instant scouting report: which players do what well, a team's style of play, who will guard who, and so forth. Making wagers on basketball is like betting on an old friend. Once the season finally starts, and he sees the games and the spreads light up the board like a Christmas tree, he has to control the urge not to blow his whole bankroll.

Rodney starts collecting on November 16. There's no significance attached to the date itself, other than the fact it's the day Rodney started parlaying his football streak with an even hotter basketball streak. The sports book became his personal cash machine, spitting money at him like he had the magic code. His feel for the numbers—which were a good value, which were off target—was as instinctive as a great hitter's feel for pitches. On the field, when they are in "a zone," players call it "seeing dead red." For Rodney, being in the zone meant seeing dead presidents.

He's sitting at the MGM sports book, wearing Birkenstocks, an Arizona State baseball cap, and twirling his keys around his finger. The MGM, for all its fanfare as the biggest hotel in the world, has traditionally had one of the weakest sports books on the Strip. The reason has always been as much a function of design as it is a lack of interest by management. Unlike most books, which have the board hanging over the betting windows so customers can see the games as they wager, the MGM's board hangs in the bar area, where all the televisions are, while the betting windows are in a connected, but separate room, where they show the horse races. Rodney sits and watches half-drunk or absentminded bettors wear a path in the carpet after checking the board, walking to the window to make a bet, forgetting the bet, and walking back to the board to check which game they wanted.

RULE NUMBER FOUR
If you forget your bet on the way to the window,
forget your bet.

There are two types of bookmakers: 1. those who throw caution to the wind, take any big bet regardless of the gambler, and treat the corporate book like their own corner shop. (The legends like Sammy Cohen who ran the Santa Anita and Gene Maday who operated Little Caesars could afford to take or refuse whatever bet they wanted because they ran independent books.); 2. then there are the guys like

Joe Lupo, who could care less if they're liked and are more interested solely in beating the wiseguys and making as much money as possible—whether it's for the corporation or not is irrelevant.

But MGM's Richie Baccellieri is a throwback. His renegade attitude is more wiseguy than bookmaker. Born in the Bronx (his parents moved to Vegas when he was a teenager) Baccellieri still has traces of a New York accent and attitude. He made a name at Caesars as the one bookmaker who would post numbers—and take large bets—on small, Division I college games that no other bookmaker dared take a chance on. He'd arrive at work early, research the Samfords and the Colgates and dare people to take their best shot. For the wiseguys, the games were as good as freebies. No matter how much time Baccellieri spent reading that morning, he didn't have the same depth of knowledge as the wiseguy who spent all day pouring over stats and figures and player profiles. Those lines brought in a lot of business for Caesars.

When, in 1999, the MGM decided it was time to remedy their sports book ills, Baccellieri was the guy it called. During his first football season, Baccellieri challenged the Stardust supremacy as the first book up with a line by posting his odds earlier. After two weeks, he was back to waiting, but the betting community took notice, with dozens of Web sites that cover the industry and the local newspapers commenting about his brashness. He endeared himself to smart players by opening a high-limit window that allowed bettors to wager more than the standard MGM limits. Once college basketball started, he put the small college games on the board, just like he did at Caesars. And that drew in players like Alan Boston and Rodney, exactly the type of player MGM higher-ups expected Baccellieri to attract to bring the book credibility.

Last night, Rodney's hunches about Arizona, Notre Dame, the Toronto Raptors, Portland Trailblazers, and Indiana Pacers paid $500. It was a turning point. He had the confidence to bet five different games at $100 a piece, rather than putting $100 down on a five-team parlay. Parlays are for suckers who don't know what they're betting on; they are the Internet IPOs of the sports book. Betting individual games, on the other hand, is like putting your money on an undervalued stock. It takes research, skill, and, most of all, confidence.

Winning individual bets also means Rodney can take a little bit of his winnings and put it back into a five-team parlay without being ashamed. He's proven he can win the straight bets; now he's just putting this money on the parlay to give himself a rooting interest, a little bit of a sweat. So the next night he laid $100 on a four-teamer that picked the Knicks plus-7 against Utah, Kentucky minus-12 against Princeton, the Sonics minus-10 against Golden State, and the Bulls plus-15 against Phoenix. As the Knicks tip off, he settles into a black-cushioned chair and puts his sandaled, blocky feet on another one. "Basketball is still the only sport I can watch without having to make a bet," says Rodney. "Although I'd rather not have to."

Immediately, the Knicks are down by eight points as Utah starts the game shooting five of five from the field. Rodney's bet, the measly $100, is hardly enough incentive to work himself into a frenzy. In fact, the more he wins, the more difficult it is for him to get worked up about anything. Coaches always chide their big-name, big-money players for losing their motivation once they've signed a lucrative deal. Rodney, the wannabe coach, can't see that's he's falling into the same trap. He considered volunteering at a junior high school as a basketball coach, but decided against it. Instead of applying for jobs, he wants go to school to learn how to be a blackjack dealer, but he'll wait until after New Year's to worry about it. It's hard to get motivated to look for a job paying minimum wage when you are covering your monthly nut with one day's worth of good bets.

In many ways, Rodney is living the life of the NBA player he so wanted to be. After the games, he stays up until 5 A.M. getting high, playing with his cats and watching movies like *Full Metal Jacket, The Godfather,* or *Goodfellas* over and over. Then to bring down his buzz he plays the video football game Madden 2000 before going to sleep. "Without that video game, I don't know what I would do," he wistfully says. "Since I don't work, I haven't met anybody here except the roofers who worked on our building. And I don't want to hang with them." Tonight, his biggest responsibility is making sure he gets home to see *Beverly Hills 90210*.

Even as the Knicks end the first quarter down 36–23, six points out of the money, Rodney's thinking not about his losses but about retirement.

"How much money do you think it would take to retire?" he asks. "I heard of one gambler who was thirty-eight years old when he hung it up. I doubt the guy had a family—how could any woman handle someone in this lifestyle? Maybe it would take $1 million to retire if you have a house and no kids. If I had kids, I'd want boys. No girls. I want boys more than anything so I can get 'em good at something like basketball or baseball. Girls no way. You can't be a man with a girl if you're out there teaching them softball or girls basketball instead of teaching a boy. No way."

By the fourth quarter, Rodney has shed the cool demeanor and big talk about retirement. Suddenly he's an unemployed twenty-three-year-old kid who's about to lose $100 on a "freaking basketball game." He is visibly anxious, twirling his keys around his finger, playing with the wrapper on his water bottle and quietly chanting the phrase "Dee-Fense, Dee-Fense," to himself. He's got his feet off the chair and firmly planted on the floor. He leans his elbows on his knees, his chin on his upturned palms, and hunches himself forward, concentrating all his efforts on willing a Knicks comeback. With 1:40 to play, the Jazz are up by ten points. While the Knicks have no chance to win the game, it's still a tightly-contested three-point game for Rodney. This is the ending most bettors experience: the game itself is out of reach, but the chance to cover is still a reality. It's not who wins, but by how much.

At 7:30, Rodney needs some divine intervention. The Knicks are down by ten points with less than a minute to go. Kentucky, who he picked to win by twelve points over Princeton in the second game of his four-team parlay, is up by eleven with minutes to go. *Beverly Hills 90210* is on in half an hour, and he lives twenty minutes away. Something has got to give.

With seventeen seconds left, the Knicks have the ball for what could be the last possession of the game. They are down 98–89, two points from a push (meaning the game lands on the spread and bettors neither win nor lose) and three points from covering. The Knicks' wispy center Marcus Camby catches a pass underneath the basket and goes up for a dunk. As he is about to release the shot he gets hammered by someone on the Utah Jazz. The referee blows his whistle. The ball is in the air. If it goes in, the Knicks are down by seven points, with Camby on the line shooting a free throw to cut it to six. That's money, baby.

The ball rattles in, rattles out, rattles in again, and finally rims out. Not all is lost. Camby is on the line for two. If he makes them both and the game ends as a push, Rodney can still make some cash on his parlay. But, Camby bricks the first shot. The second one he makes is moot. The Jazz run out the clock, winning by eight, covering the spread by one point.

Rodney, the man for whom teaching his daughter to play softball would threaten his masculinity, looks at his watch. It's 7:40. "Well," he says. "At least I've still got *90210*."

While parlays can pay back big returns with relatively low risk for the bettor, they are a high risk, high reward proposition for the sports books. In 1999, parlay cards, which work the same as a parlay bet only the spreads are fixed, accounted for 24 percent of the money won in Las Vegas sports books. That number is three times higher than any other revenue source. During the football season, when 41 percent of all sports wagers in Nevada are made, a number that has surpassed more than $900 million each of the last three years, the Stardust displays preprinted parlay cards on Tuesdays, a full 24 hours before other books print theirs. The numbers on the card are based on the spread Lupo and Scucci and Korona established that Monday, six days before the games. During that week, a quarterback may get hurt, a coach may get fired, or a wide receiver may get arrested. Suddenly, the team that was favored by four when the card was printed is now a two-point underdog on the board. "Because the line on the card can't change," says Scucci, "it's easy for the wiseguys to pick one up on Friday, pick out a few weak lines, and bury us."

There are betting syndicates that rely solely on their plays off of parlay cards. And college-aged kids in shorts and T-shirts carrying empty backpacks will come in, poach a stack of cards, and fill out as many as they can in different combinations. It's like buying $100 worth of $1 lottery tickets for a $20-million payout.

Mostly though, it's the tourists, the squares, and the novices who play the parlay cards. Because every game is bet in tandem with at least one other game, the liability is magnified. None of the bets made exist in a vacuum. And, while the bookmakers can control how much money comes in on one side of a game by adjusting the spread, they have no control over who parlays which games together. Bettors can fill out preset parlay cards or make parlay bets involving anywhere from two to six teams of their choosing. Then the bookmakers can only watch as they see their liability pile up on a pair of games that, if the book won them separately, would be big wins, but because of parlays could be huge losses.

For every football weekend, there are certain games that get paired up more often than others, usually a high-profile Sunday game and the Monday night game in prime time. Parlays are the greatest barometer of what teams are most popular and what games everyone will be watching. It is not the wiseguy breaking down an offensive line's blocking assignments who usually bets the parlays, it is Joe Fan who knows who the starting quarterback is but couldn't tell you anything else about who is playing.

Only occasionally will someone hit it big and pick all fifteen winners on a preset parlay, like the forty-five-year-old Asian woman from Los Angeles who put $5 on a card in early October and was rewarded with more than $100,000 in cash in a silver briefcase straight out of a James Bond movie. The local paper came by to take her picture and it made Lupo sick to smile and pretend to be happy as he gave away six figures of his sports books' money to some amateur who wouldn't know a forward pass from a romantic one.

It's unusual when Lupo can spend a Monday doing paperwork and recounting the glories of a weekend's spoils without worrying about his liability on a Monday night game. But on this crisp day in mid-November he's gotten an unexpected reprieve. Yesterday, the sports book had a magnificent run. Lupo and Scucci and Korona all moved numbers with aplomb, anticipating where the bettors were going and beating them to the punch. They won nearly every game, turning what could have been a normal $100,000 football weekend into a $285,000 windfall. And better yet, all the parlays had been knocked out. Tonight the three of them—Lupo, Scucci, and Korona—could go out for sushi—a payday tradition—drink a few beers and enjoy the game as fans, because whatever happened it wasn't going to impact their Sunday windfall. They too had gambled. And they had won big.

Lupo rips open a gold-foil package of vitamins, takes a big gulp of water and sighs. Leaning back in his chair, spinning his ubiquitous Browns commemorative football, Lupo double-clicks the mouse on his computer. Marlon Brando, as the Godfather, whispers in a raspy and forceful voice, "I'm gonna make him an offer he can't refuse." Lupo laughs out loud, feeling as though he just did the same to every wiseguy in Vegas, and then took them to the bank.

But the weekend's euphoria masks a bigger problem, not just for the Stardust, but for the entire betting community in Las Vegas. The Wednesday before, a crazed and jealous boyfriend opened fire at the Golden Gate Casino, killing a dealer who happened to be his former girlfriend. For the first time, casinos across the strip were considering plans to station armed guards inside their doors. But what really spooked Vegas was how the incident mirrored what was happening to the gaming industry as a whole and the sports-betting industry in particular; the industry was under siege.

Lupo knows firsthand what sort of pressure is building. The new mayor, former mob lawyer Oscar Goodman, is pushing to get an NBA team in Las Vegas. But the NBA is adamant that Las Vegas can't have a team unless they drop betting on pro basketball. Goodman has floated the idea to the public and gotten enough of a response in favor of dropping NBA betting to open talks with some NBA owners looking to relocate. "I've got enough going on thinking about, Glenn Robinson gonna play tonight and should I move this Alabama game from 6.5 to 7?" says Lupo. "Now I have to care about whether or not we are going to get rid of NBA betting completely."

It's not just pro basketball he should be concerned about. The same day as the shooting at the Golden Gate, Lupo attended a meeting at the Bellagio Hotel that included several hotel owners, CEOs, him, three other bookmakers, and Frank Fahrenkopf, the president and CEO of the lobbying group the American Gaming Association. Fahrenkopf had once served the longest tenure ever as chairman of the Republican National Committee under Ronald Reagan. Now he represents the multibillion-dollar gaming industry on Capitol Hill. Although he has spent a lifetime listening to rhetoric, innuendo, and empty threats coming from breathy politicians, he had been hearing rumblings about a bill, an anti-sports-betting bill, whose potential for becoming law worried even him. Sports books may account for only two percent of a casino's revenue, but because they provide a fun place to watch a game, they keep customers on the property, which increases their importance ten-fold.

At 4 P.M., in a corporate meeting room with a long oak conference table, plush leather chairs and platters of richly colored fruit, Fahrenkopf laid out the scenario. In October, Cedric Dempsey, President of the NCAA, met with Fahrenkopf in his office in Washington, D.C. The NCAA and the American Gaming Association are as natural enemies as cats and dogs. When one of them wants to get together, it's not to sign a peace treaty, but to fire a warning shot. That's exactly what Dempsey did.

"We have met with members of the Senate, and we've decided we are going to push for an amendment on the Bradley bill and lobby for a ban on all legal wagering on amateur athletics," Dempsey told Fahrenkopf.

Fahrenkopf was surprised, mainly because when the NCAA testified before the National Gambling Impact Study Commission, not once did they push for such a recommendation. Dempsey continued.

"We are concerned about widespread betting on college campuses and we want to do away with sports books in Nevada. Every newspaper in the country runs the line and we feel if gambling was illegal in Nevada, and therefore illegal everywhere, they would stop."

Following the meeting, Fahrenkopf drafted a letter to Dempsey, citing the Tenth Amendment, which guarantees an individual state's right to determine public policy toward gaming within its borders. But, as he polled his contacts in Congress, Fahrenkopf recognized Dempsey wasn't looking for a debate. At the Bellagio meeting, Fahrenkopf reported his findings to the assembled gaming executives and confirmed that the notion of banning betting on amateur sporting events was gaining support in Congress. And, with an election year coming up, attacking sports betting would be an easy, nonpartisan, and popular stance for politicians on the campaign trail.

"It was strange for them to call me into this meeting, which makes me think it was much more serious than I anticipated. Way in the back of people's minds here in Vegas they thought this issue would go away. But it's tough to prove a negative and that when kids are gambling on college campuses it isn't coming to Vegas," Lupo says. Being there, surrounded by the industry's leaders, meant a lot to Lupo. "But I didn't come away thinking this is a good time to be a bookmaker. Not a real positive outlook right now."

Lupo has other problems, too. His personal life is a mess. He's been married twelve years, has two kids, and still loves his wife. And by all accounts, she still loves him. But she can't be married to a man who runs a sports book anymore. The odd hours, the smoky rooms, the seemingly life-and-death decisions whose outcome rests on the bounce of a ball, the mind-set of a quarterback, the lingering effects of a cortisone shot or who was out partying the night before have taken their toll. Between his marriage breaking up and the possibility of a betting ban, Lupo's got the ticket for a losing parlay that has him taking stock of the life he leads.

Even 285 large in the bank can't change that.

Chapter 6

Hi Mom! My Bookie Called, Send Money

It's no coincidence that there was huge growth between our network and the coverage and interest in NCAA basketball at the same time. But, did we bring betting to college basketball or make it more common? I don't know if that's true. Did we bring a lot of games to people? Yes. Did we give a lot of information about every team? Yes. But, if you're gonna bet on college basketball, you don't need TV. People are gonna bet on cockroaches.

—BOB LEY, ESPN ANCHOR, BRISTOL, CONN., FALL 1999

In **1970,** former Maryland basketball coach Lefty Driesell had fans drive their cars onto a campus track and shine their lights on the field so his players could run laps beginning at exactly 12:01 on the first day practice was allowed. Now, nearly one-third of Division I basketball teams schedule their first workout, titled Midnight Madness, for exactly 12:01 on October 15, the official day college basketball teams are allowed to begin practice. Every school uses this opening as a pep rally for the fans, the team and the sport. At St.

John's University in Queens, New York, in 1999, students lined up outside of Alumni Hall on a bone-chilling, rainy night to get a glimpse of their team, even though a sign on the field house door read the event was sold out, and it had been for weeks. Inside, the school band played for fans who were filling the bleachers at 9 P.M., three hours before the practice was scheduled to start.

St. John's, like a lot of the high-profile basketball schools in the Northeast, has one of the most storied histories in college basketball. And the atmosphere inside Alumni Hall harkens back to the game's early days. Unlike the gleaming, 20,000-seat shrines most big-time programs have on campus, St. John's plays in an intimate box of a gym with backless wooden benches. The court is ringed by banners reminding everyone of its glorious past: There are several regular season Big East championships and conference tournament championships, a couple of Final Fours, and four NIT championships, including in 1944, when that was the postseason tournament that mattered.

"I would rather play here than at Madison Square Garden any-day," St. John's star point guard Erick Barkley says before the practice. In 1999, partly because of Barkley, the team finished 28–9, went to the Elite Eight of the NCAA tournament and ended the season ranked fifth in the country. Yet, the next season, despite having Barkley, two other starters, and a highly touted freshman on the team, St. John's was not a favorite to win the Big East, a conference their coach, Mike Jarvis, says, "is the best. If I could I would probably wager on that. But I can't, so I won't."

It's because of Jarvis and Barkley that the opening of the St. John's season is the place to be on this Friday night. Rappers Jay Z and Dr. Dre are watching from the sidelines. The St. John's athletic department charged the general public $20 for tickets and students $10.

In addition to the school band, there is a DJ spinning rap underneath one of the baskets. A group of junior high kids puts on an exhibition, which is followed by a game including St. John's stars of the past. There's a comedian to warm up the crowd and a prepractice race of students in flippers running up and down the court while dribbling a ball. One lucky student even gets a shot at free tuition for a year by making a half-court shot. He fails miserably, but the carnival atmosphere inside the gym is a success.

And it's a scene repeated dozens of times throughout the country on October 15. The crowd at a Midnight Madness practice is a benchmark for the passion fans feel for the program. At the University of Kansas, the Midnight Madness practice was so overwhelming that DeShawn Stevenson, one of the top high school players in the country who was in town for a visit, signed a letter of intent to play there within hours after attending the madness. (Stevenson eventually rescinded his signing and opted to turn pro instead of going to college.)

At Texas, students camped out for days before the event. At Duke, fans came dressed like it was Halloween. At the University of Connecticut two-thousand people had to be turned away at the door. At Maryland, where the Madness began thirty years ago, there were indoor fireworks and gymnastics routines. At Kentucky, head coach Tubby Smith was escorted onto the court by the newly crowned Miss America and Kentucky native, Heather Renee French. At Michigan State, head coach Tom Izzo rode onto the court on a Harley.

While ESPN didn't broadcast from any Midnight Madness practices, it was only the second time in the nineties that that was the case. In the same way that *Monday Night Football* pounded the NFL into our consciousness and culture, ESPN turned college basketball from a game of regional interest into a national phenomenon. Without wall-to-wall basketball coverage on that cable network, students would not be standing in the rain, money in hand, begging to get in to nothing more than a practice. Without dozens of games to watch, kids might not be so certain that their bet is a sure thing.

In 1979 Magic Johnson of Michigan State and Larry Bird of Indiana State squared off in the NCAA Finals. That game drew what are still the highest ratings for an NCAA Tournament game. Hot on the heels of that matchup, ESPN began broadcasting from Bristol, Conn. Originally intended to be a regional network focusing on sports within the state, ESPN quickly developed grander plans because, surprisingly, they would cost less. Founder Bill Rasmussen learned that it would cost a standard fee of $1,250 to use a satellite dish for five hours of broadcasting but only $1,143 to use it for twenty-four hours. That meant broadcasting games from the University of Connecticut wasn't enough.

While the jokes about the early days of what has become the most powerful brand in sports revolve around late-night airings of tractor pulls and Australian Rules Football, it was actually college basketball that helped the network sustain itself. At the time, the major broadcasters only showed about 25–30 college basketball games a year. What about the hundreds of other teams in Division I basketball? Didn't anyone want to watch these games? Rasmussen thought someone did.

While Rasmussen negotiated with the NCAA, he signed a separate deal with the University of Connecticut to broadcast twenty-eight events in ten different sports. Then Rasmussen telecast several Connecticut games nationally, commercial free. During the games he had a message scrolling on the bottom of the screen asking viewers to call in and give the location from where they were watching. People from twenty-six different states, including Alaska, called the Bristol home office. That was the push Rasmussen needed to prove to the NCAA that he could get it the national exposure for teams it was always assumed no one cared about. In late February of 1979, he signed a deal with the NCAA to broadcast regular season games and the early rounds of the tournament.

"It wasn't our master plan to build around college basketball or the tournament," says Bob Ley. "It was had for a song because no one wanted it. We had no vision this would be a staple. We just needed something on the air.

"In 1980, we had Metro Conference games which included Louisville and the Doctor of Dunk, Darrell Griffith. Everyone watched. That was the year Louisville won the National Championship. I mean we just stepped in it."

Like a sexy new girl on campus, ESPN had college basketball nuts spreading the word about its prowess. Fans begat more fans. Early on, Ley remembers doing a game in Iowa and students recognizing him as the guy who does college basketball on ESPN. And it wasn't just college kids who were noticing: Ley heard stories about people leaving hotels that didn't carry ESPN. In 1981, broadcast luminaries Dick Enberg, Billy Packer, and Al McGuire were driving from New York City to Providence to broadcast a Saturday afternoon game for NBC. En route during the week, they stopped off in Bristol to survey the offices and, of course, catch some college hoops on satellite. Six years later, in 1987, after the Big Ten decided not to broadcast games on ESPN to protect its schools' individual rights packages, conference coaches begged the conference to redo a deal with the network because not being on ESPN hurt their recruiting.

Barely six months after first broadcasting, ESPN telecast twenty-three games during the opening-round weekend of the NCAA Tournament, an effort that would earn the fledgling network its first significant amount of national attention. As the crew watched feeds coming in from across the country, Ley and the producers had an epiphany: Why not cut into games that were close at the end?

"It wasn't a master plan," recall Ley. "The idea just percolated. We would say if this game gets interesting, let's go to it. It was serendipity."

The idea became known as "the whip-around," now a staple in network coverage of college basketball, but back then it was totally unprecedented. The tournament itself became known as March Madness, a staple in every sports fan's season. And college basketball became known as the most exciting sport around.

With the rights to so much college basketball, the network picked at the carcass of the sport for every last scrap of programming. In doing so, it brought fans places they had never been or even knew they wanted to go. In 1980, it broadcast the first NCAA basketball tournament selection show, which has since mushroomed from being largely ignored to something close to a national holiday known simply as "Selection Sunday." The network aired postseason tournaments for small conferences like the Sun Belt and Big Sky. The do-or-die games for teams like the University of Southern Alabama were usually more intense than those of the NCAA tournament because these teams had one shot to get into postseason: winning their conference title. Last-second heroics not only made stars out of the small-college players and catapulted them into the big time, it did the same for the small-time network broadcasting the games.

"In many ways, the conference tournaments were more important," says Ley. "It is certainly where we earned our stripes for knowing our stuff. We spoke a language to the fan no one else was speaking. And we did it by accident. Out of necessity really because we had all this information and all we had for programming was college basketball. In the end we changed the mechanics of the game, from recruiting to the way it was played."

And in the way it was bet. To say ESPN is the sole reason for an increase in betting on college basketball is like saying the flapping of butterfly wings causes a hurricane. But the impact the network had on the interest in the game cannot be ignored. For bettors, this was a new dawn in the information age. Previously unable to distinguish teams like Siena from Hofstra, those games became as easily wagered upon as Duke vs. North Carolina. The info, and the medium through which it was delivered, also helped dramatically alter the landscape of who was doing the betting. The majority of people watching ESPN were college kids. Faced with the option of watching two obscure teams play college basketball on cable or cracking open a book the choice was a no-brainer. There was a good chance that a basketball fan could see a particular team play a dozen games over the course of a season. He'd know that team about as well as the reporter covering it on a daily basis. Armed with a thorough understanding of how the team plays, what its patterns are, which player is in the doghouse and which is playing well, why wouldn't the fan take a shot and make a bet?

According to surveys in Professor Paul Weiler's book *Leveling the Playing Field,* 85 percent of all college students bet occasionally and 23 percent bet every week. Two percent of those students bet as much as $100 a day. On-campus bookies are as ubiquitous as kegs of beer. And ever since cable, college basketball has been the bettor's game of choice. In 1986, the bookie *Sports Illustrated* spoke to for its report on gambling said the sport growing fastest among his clients was college basketball. Today, many operations on school campuses run by students rake in tens of thousands per week.

"It's scary how accessible betting is to college kids," says Dr. Ann Mayo, the director of the Sports Management program at Seton Hall University and a former administrator in the University of Nevada–Las Vegas athletic department. "The kids who used to fix games with a bookie now will do everything they need over the Internet. And just like a bookie who changes corners, an Internet site getting some heat will just change its address."

There's no better example of how popular college basketball has become than the rising costs of broadcasting NCAA basketball tournament games. A mostly ignored tournament that cost NBC just $726,500 in 1971 cost CBS $1 billion for seven years (or $142 *million* per year) to exclusively broadcast the games in 1991. And that $1 billion was nearly ten times what the network paid for broadcast rights just five years earlier, when it was sharing early-round coverage with ESPN. CBS overpaid for sure, but that is the market that ESPN had created with wall-to-wall coverage of the tournament earlier that decade. "We built a monster," says Ley. Of course, he wasn't just talking about the tournament.

Chapter 7

"A Dying Breed"

Alan Boston really is the last of a dying breed. The kind of guy who can still do it on instinct and would have been just as good 20 years ago as he is today. He just loves college basketball so much and in the end, no one can compete with that.

—DAVE MALINSKY, LAS VEGAS HANDICAPPER,
NOVEMBER 1999

Alan Boston fell in love with college basketball while watching the opening rounds of the NCAA basketball tournament on ESPN. During the early days of the network, and his early days as a bettor, he'd invite over buddies from college, cook a twenty-pound turkey, and sit in his underwear watching basketball for four days straight. The ritual indulged his passion for college basketball and rewarded his lifestyle. If he was still breathing and could afford to pay for the bird, it had been a successful season.

In the late 1970s and early 1980s, Philadelphia was a hotbed of basketball. St. Joseph's, Penn, Villanova, Temple, and LaSalle, considered the Big Five, put on a tournament every year that was full of the passion and intensity of a tribal war. This was blood sport for the basketball bragging rights in a town that as often as not, defined who you were by which of the Philly schools you went to. As a student at Penn, Alan and his friends would play hooky from class and catch games at the Palestra or at McGonicle Hall.

"It was awesome trying to win those games," says Alan. "We wouldn't bet a lot, just enough to make us nervous, $50 at the most. But the games were so competitive, we didn't know from handicapping, we just watched a lot of basketball and then picked who we thought was playing better. But I loved it. Then we would bet football all day Sunday. It was just about action.

"When I graduated and moved back to Boston, it was still all I cared about. I had no idea what I was doing. I was calling guys up in New York and just gambling. I loved it. Flying back and forth to New York, paying people off, making more bets, no cares in the world, living on the edge day to day.

"I would meet all these guys at the track who became my circle. Jimmy and Howie and Frankie, they were all Jewish except for Frankie. They took my bets on sports, but we all competed for winners on the horses. It was like a competition, it was great, really great, trying to pick winners. Of course, everything I won, I would turn around and bet with Jimmy or Frankie or Howie. And then I would bet what I didn't have. I kept losing, it was up to something like $11,000. And I owed another guy about the same. I couldn't pay that. But those guys were greedy and stupid for letting me bet like that. How was a young kid going to pay back that kind of money? One of them got mad and I did the easy thing and just left.

"I was a sicko, just betting everything, out of my mind. I didn't know if these guys were trouble, I was just a kid. One guy wasn't trouble for sure, but the other guy I wasn't so sure. So I left town and went to Manhattan. I lived on a friend's floor and went to work for Hammacher Schlemmer on Fifty-seventh Street. It was an easy job to get. They didn't have too many Ivy Leaguers looking for part-time work during the Christmas season applying there. Then one of the bookies tracks me down through a third party, I think it was Howie.

The third party tells me Howie says I can come back and work off my debt by working for him. I said fine, I just don't want to have any trouble.

"So I come back and work for the guy, and, within a couple of years, I pay the guy off. It didn't take long because I brought in some new customers and they were always losing, and their losses got deducted from my debt. He loaned me to other bookies and I just worked with them for a while. I'm just answering phones for this guy, I'm a clerk for a bookmaker so he doesn't have to work. I would take all the calls and tell him who he needed. It was easy work. I enjoyed it and I was good. It was just writing down bets and being polite and being professional. A lot different than it is now.

"And I love it, I mean these guys are real characters. I mean they are regular guys but in those days they came and went as they pleased, no nine to five, no boss, they did whatever the fuck they wanted to and for me it was action. They ate good and drank good and so did I. I would get free Chinese food and ate like a pig and wherever they went I didn't have to pay for nothing. I had no expenses. They paid for my apartment because that is where I took calls. I made about $300 a week, and gambled most of it back. I kept owing money, but the customers I brought in, I got most of the BU campus betting, kept losing so my debt got wiped out.

"Then my apartment got raided by the cops. But it wasn't because of anyone I was clerking for. It turns out I did betting with a guy the cops were after. I would call him up and say, 'What's the best I can get over on this *Monday Night Football* game?' He'd say, 'I can get you over forty-four.' I would say, 'Great, give me over forty-four for $500,' and he would do it. That was our entire relationship. When the cops came by, I had no idea why they were bothering me because I was a nobody. I was just a sports bettor. But this guy was just always at my house because I owed him money, and I was ducking him because I didn't have it. And I owed a lot. My friend Al was over because he was going to play the twin trifecta at Wonderland Park, and he didn't have any money and I was going to give him the little I had. The twin trifecta was up to something like $120,000. It was worth betting.

"It was fall and on a Sunday because the Broncos are playing the Raiders in a late game. And it's funny because I have some coke in my pocket, and if they happened to go in the car I had lots in the car, but they searched Al's car and not mine for whatever reason. Anyway I have this little bullet with coke in it and I am thinking, this is not good.

"So here I am sitting with this vial of cocaine in my pocket. They had just searched this garbage bag, which was sitting next to a chair and the one cop is sitting at the desk, with the phone, with his back to me, and the other cop is searching the other room. So I kind of plop into the chair and drop the coke into the bag they have already searched. They both turn around and all they see is me sitting in the chair. Now the one cop comes back out and says, 'Did we check this bag yet?' Pointing to the bag they had searched where I just dropped the coke. The other cop says, 'yeah, yeah.' They never found anything, just a couple of bets on paper and my racetrack programs and tickets, which I saved for tax purposes. I always wrote in the program how I was doing. The cops took all that and the football bets I had made for the day. And they took all my money. After that I called my lawyer.

"I went to Vegas shortly thereafter for a December poker tourney. I met this guy Jeff at the poker tournament at the Golden Nugget every year. I knew he had money and he said come on out to Vegas full time and bet with me and we will make money. He and I used to talk about *Jeopardy* so I knew he was smart. I was actually coming out west to try out for *Jeopardy* because I used to be smart, then I got stupid. When I went back to Boston the police kept harassing me and asking me about all these phone calls I made in Vegas. Eventually they arrest me for bookmaking.

"I'm afraid my phones are tapped after I'm arrested so I go over to the bank and ask if I can use their phone and I make airline reservations from there. I pay the lawyer who bailed me out $2,500, which isn't what I owe him but it is all I have. I go to New York to collect some winnings, and then I go to Florida because I owe someone money so I figure I would go pay him. I was doing a little college basketball at the time, I was just following a friend who did the handicapping and I would help him get down because I had access to so many lines. I was winning back then, but I had all my money in jeopardy at all times. That's the way I was and still am, I need the edge.

"That summer I was back in Boston, and I used to go drink at the Hyatt Regency all the time. One night, I took all the college football stuff from the year before, and I figured out my own ratings, from 0 to 100. After doing every team in the country, I read about the teams for the upcoming year and worked on those ratings even more. So I called the guy Jeff from the poker tourney up. I had decided I was going out to Vegas no matter what because I was just going to be harassed in Boston. I had no idea what he planned for me but I wasn't going to go out there cold, and I called him up and gave him my line for the six games that weekend.

"One of them was Washington State at Illinois. I had made the game pick, but the Vegas bookmakers had it Illinois minus-6. By the end of the week it was down to pick. So Jeff is all happy because he had Washington State plus-6 when it first came out because of what I told him. All the games moved in the direction I picked them to, so obviously I had done good work and he is all excited because he won.

"So the next week I start driving out. I stopped in Chicago to see a friend, this was late August or early September. At this point I am not betting any of my own money because I don't have any. I was driving the yellow Corvette. I stopped in Chicago to sweat the games I had given Jeff that week. A friend of mine there had a computer and was able to access the lines of the games that day. I could see how everything had moved in the way that I had predicted they should go and I thought, 'Hey, this is cool. I had an impact on how the lines moved.'" Jeff won again that week and I got out here a week later. Then he started giving me a cut of like $200 a game. He also got me a place to stay with a friend of his where I had to take care of his dogs.

"Then college basketball season started. I went over to a bookstore called the Gambler's Book Club and bought a book by Jim Fiest that had all his power ratings of college basketball teams from the year before. I worked those numbers, went to the Stardust to bet, had a feel for it, and that is how I started doing college basketball.

"Eventually I had to go back to Boston for my hearing. My judge was the same guy who did that baby-shaking case with the English nanny. The judge asked me my name, where I went to school, what I majored in, and he looked at me like, 'what are you doing here?' Mainly because the guy before me was some kind of murderer. The case was dismissed and the judge told the D.A. to never bring a case like this in the courtroom again.

"I flew back to Vegas and that is how it started."

Twenty-thousand dollars. That's as much as Alan will bet on any game during the entire season. And he chooses the first game of the year, No. Ten Duke vs. No. Thirteen Stanford in the preseason NIT, to plunk down that kind of change. Most bettors see themselves as businessmen, handling their bankroll as any CEO would handle his company's budget. Most bettors would no sooner put 20K on the first game of the year than they would let their daughter intern in the Clinton White House. It's too much to gamble too soon with too many factors yet to be determined. But, Alan's impulsive behavior supersedes any cash-management skills. He is first and foremost a gambler, in it for the action, not the money.

But the first game of the year? With two teams featuring freshmen as key players in the lineup who are playing their first college games in Madison Square Garden? Both teams will be tight. Neither team has faced live competition for more than seven months. They've officially practiced together for just three weeks, since the madness of that first midnight practice in October. There will be adjustments and cold shooting and nervous stomachs and anxious coaches and freshman mistakes. Some players will be overwhelmed by the crowd, others intimidated by their teammates, and the rest awed by the competition. The experts say they're the tenth and thirteenth best teams in the country, respectively. But at this point in the year those rankings are based on last season's results and this season's expectations. The numbers are as arbitrary as saying off-white is a better color for the bathroom than eggshell.

At least that is how it looks to the casual observer.

But to Alan picking the games is a science. For weeks before Midnight Madness began, Alan greeted the Maine sunrise like a rooster, scrambling egg whites, guzzling water, and settling in with reading material about college basketball. In November, shortly before the season started, he moved back to Vegas and did the same there, creating a cocoon at the desk in his living room that would be his incubator for the coming season. "As soon as the first college basketball preview came out," he says, "I started getting horny."

He didn't just bone up on the Stanfords and the Dukes, but on every team in Division I college basketball. Kent State, South Florida, the University of Denver. He studied more about Ivy League basketball than his subjects while attending an Ivy League school. People talk about team chemistry, and Alan conducted chemistry experiments: He broke teams down to their essential elements. The players coming back were the oxygen. The coach was the hydrogen. How they played down the stretch the year before was the nitrogen. How they played at home equaled carbon, and how they played on the road was calcium, the truest sign of a strong team. Into this brew mix elements like the conference the team plays in, the travel it has to do, its style of play, and the level of competition it will face.

The compound that comes together is the team's power rating, according to Alan. "I have to get into the heads of all these teams," says Alan. "I have to become one with every one of them. Obviously, as I get older, it gets harder to do that." That's because the teenagers that play college basketball, who are more than half the forty-year-old Alan Boston's age, don't live in a perfect world. Their lives and the games they play are full of X-factors that act as nitrate in Alan's potion. "In our lives we don't understand the people closest to us," says the handicapper Dave Malinsky, a friend of Alan's. "It's silly to think we can make judgments about complete strangers. But we do. I believe it. Alan does too."

Alan records all his data by hand in a black three-ring binder. He hires a young bettor—an intern—each year to write the name of a team at the top of a piece of loose-leaf paper, the kind students used to write term papers on before computers. The kid then writes the team's schedule for the upcoming season in longhand down the left side of the page. He does that for more than 300 teams, all by hand in blue ink. On each team's page, Alan writes down what he thinks their opening power rating should be, based on 0–100. The rating will be fluid, changing on a game-by-game basis.

Before every game, Alan compares one team's power rating to the team it is playing, and the difference is what he thinks the point-spread should be. That number goes in one column starting at the top of the page and moving down the schedule. In the next column, he records what the point spread opened at. Looking back at the daft moves made by bookmakers always give him a chuckle. After all, he reasons, if the oddsmakers were that good at picking games, they'd be gambling with their own money, not making book for some corporate-owned casino.

In the column next to the team power ratings he records where the spread closed after all the wiseguys, squares, and bookmakers got done fingering the number. Inevitably, the number moves his way, which gives him a boost of confidence and a sense of satisfaction in the work he's done. Every bettor will tell you that is what they strive for, the satisfaction of making a good number. If only a job well done paid the mortgage.

In another column, he puts the final score of the game. Finally, there is room for notes, random musings, and observations that Alan hopes to carry from one game, or one season, to the next. In an industry where every dollar you make is controlled by what someone else does, your observations and the relevance you attach to them give you something to hold onto, like the guardrail on a roller coaster. Sometimes he comments on how a coach managed the clock at the end of the game and at other times he adds his favorite quotes from a coach's postgame press conference.

Alan listed Stanford as a two-point favorite over Duke in his binder, figuring that as a veteran team it would be more disciplined early in the year than Duke, which prominently featured a host of freshmen in its rotation. At the Stardust, however, the game opened with Duke as a 4.5-point favorite. All over town, the books followed suit, giving the edge to the Duke team that, while it was the national runner-up the year before, still featured a freshman point guard running the show.

The name Duke carries a lot of weight in college basketball. For the squares making a play or two, Duke over Stanford by 4.5 is a gimme, whether it's Magic Johnson or Mickey Mouse starting at point guard. The money came in on the Duke side in droves, pushing the spread up from 4.5 to 5 and ultimately 5.5. Alan's live-wire eyes practically popped out of his skull. Having the game at Stanford minus-2 according to his ratings, meant getting it at Stanford plus-5.5 was a 7.5 point value. This was, to say the least, a huge gap.

To Alan, money on Stanford plus–4.5 was a good bet. At plus-5.5, his money is safer than being in a bank. He hadn't planned on putting so much money down on the opening game. But now he physically couldn't stop himself. He ran around town, putting $3,000 down on the game at various sports books. If he could, he would have put more, but ever since the early nineties, when large, risk-averse corporations took over the casinos, the limits in the sports books have been lowered to eliminate huge losses. While you could once get down

$10,000 or $15,000 or more on one game at one place at one time, now $3,000 is the limit. So, if you see a Stanford-Duke spread that will make you so much money your brain sizzles like a short-circuited computer, you've got to shop all over Vegas to get down your bet.

By game time, as they watched the spread go higher and higher, meaning Duke would have to win by more and more, Alan and his partner, Billy, had laid out $20,000 in cash by either walking into sports books or calling phone accounts at various books in Nevada.

"Ultimately, I have to bet a lot," says Alan. "Not just because I am betting for three. But because it's the only time I feel anything."

Sick to your stomach. That's the only thing you would feel as a bettor watching the Stanford-Duke game. The first half was a cacophony of shots clanking off rims and sneakers squeaking on a polished floor in a quiet gym. To the fan, the game was sloppy, with nothing to cheer about. "I tried watching the game," Alan says. "But it was so poorly played and I had such a big bet on it, I couldn't stand it."

In the first four minutes of the game, Stanford was up by ten points. With five minutes left in the half, it was down by three points. At halftime Stanford was up by two. At one point early in the second half, Stanford builds a nine-point lead. But, after taking a 60–55 lead with 4:26 left, Stanford goes cold. Over the next three and a half minutes, Duke outscores Stanford 11–0, taking a six-point lead with less than a minute left in the game. Suddenly, the bet that had been a sure thing to kick start Alan's season looks like it would cripple him instead. With thirty seconds left, Stanford cuts the lead to two. Then, after a bad pass by Duke's freshman point guard Jason Williams— thank god for the freshmen, Alan thought—Stanford tied the game, sending it into overtime.

The Duke-Stanford overtime takes on the same course as the game's first two halves. Stanford jumps out to an early lead—ahead by as much as eight—only to squander it late in the game. Lucky for them, Duke runs out of time, losing by one. Alan's prediction was right, and, in his first game of the year, it paid off to the tune of $20,000.

RULE NUMBER FIVE
Seniors may struggle, but freshmen will falter.

As much as winning the money, wiseguys get a rush from seeing bookmakers and bettors react to their bets. Alan is no different. Does the bookmaker change the point spread in response to his bet? When he puts his money down, how quickly do other wiseguys find out about his play and follow his lead? He can also use his reputation to manipulate lines to his advantage, called arbitraging. The bettor spies a game on the board and has an opinion about who will win, but the point spread is a couple of points off his projection. He'd like to move it closer to how he handicapped the game. He then lets it be known he likes one side over the other. Instantly, he'll recognize which book-makers are respecting his plays by how they move the line. Through the grapevine, he'll also find out which wiseguys are riding his coat-tails on the bet. Then, after baiting the books and the wiseguys with his first couple of bets, and seeing the line has been moved in his favor, he switches sides and bets more money going the other way.

One night after the Stanford-Duke game, Alan chose to play the Siena-Davidson game, a matchup that wouldn't get much public action but would be a favorite with the wiseguys. Siena opened as a ten-point favorite and Alan thought Davidson could easily cover that. But he wanted to bet big. And he wanted to bet sure. He'd be more comfortable if he could bet Davidson at plus-10.5 or 11. (While no team will ever win by half a point, line makers have always moved games in half-point increments or simply opened with half points included in the spread. This produces more winners and losers and makes a push—where they would have to return all the wagered money to both sides—impossible. Over the course of the season, being on the wrong side of half points can either make or cost book-makers and bettors hundreds of thousands of dollars.) Alan laid several thousand dollars on Siena, hoping the line would move to 10.5. Instead, he got beat to the bet by another wiseguy looking to lower the point-spread, because he liked Siena to cover. The game moved to 9.5 instead of 10.5. Alan then had to lay double the money on Siena minus-9.5 to push the spread back up to ten. Now he has nearly $10,000 riding on Siena to win by 10 and by 9.5. The game falls right on the number, with Siena winning by ten points, meaning Alan pushed on one bet and won the other. It's a win, but not the big win he was hoping for.

One way that bettors like Alan get their ego fix is by manipulating the lines and seeing bookmakers scurry. Another way is more time-honored, may cost less in the long run, and gets you a whole lot further. In his book *Casino*, Nicholas Pileggi wrote that, "Las Vegas is a city of kickbacks. A desert city of greased palms. A place where a $20 bill can buy approval, a $100 bill adulation and $1,000 canonization." The same rules that applied in the fifties, sixties, and seventies still apply today. For all the clashing styles in Vegas—flowered carpets that soak up wayward chips, Venetian palaces, Roman piazzas—the color that never goes out of style is green. Gamblers get paid in cash and use the money to buy respect all over town. That's why, on a night when the computer industry's Comdex convention is in Las Vegas, and there are more billionaires in one place than there are germs on a pinhead, it's free-spending Alan Boston who's treated like a king. He called Hugo's Cellar at 6 P.M., asking for a 7:30 reservation that night. He showed up at eight o'clock, and was seated immediately at a corner table in the back. There are 200,000 people in town for Comdex, and all of them seem to be in the bar at Hugo's. They are the players of the next millennium, discussing broadband, wireless, and business-to-business strategies. Everything they say requires nothing less than a confidentiality agreement. But, it's Alan who is given the table that affords him some privacy.

Hugo's is, appropriately, in the cellar of the old Four Queens Hotel in downtown Las Vegas. Long forgotten by tourists, the Four Queens is a local joint with casinos that open right onto Freemont Street, and hosts and hostesses dressed as kings and queens of a deck of cards. Unlike the civilized, almost gentlemanly nature of the upscale properties further down the Strip, the Four Queens feels like Mardi Gras.

Back when the mob ran Vegas, it's easy to envision Hugo's darkened dining room as the setting where deals would get hammered out, hits would get arranged, and kings of the underworld presided. Hugo's is not braised pork served with mango chutney on top of basil risotto accompanied by a glass of chardonnay. It's broiled lamb chops, goblets of blood-warm red wine, and waiters who have made serving this food their life's work. The lighting is dim, the tables are wood, and the atmosphere is heavy with history. The chef thinks Belgian endive is a tropical disease.

Hugo's is not the obvious restaurant of choice for an aspiring vegetarian. But Alan would no sooner turn his back on a Vegas tradition than he would leave his ticker at home. The waiter makes his salad without oil and cheese and the chicken with raspberry cream sauce without the sauce. He also takes the parmesan stuffed tomato garnish off of the plate so, "I don't have to look at it," says Alan. In a restaurant full of millionaires who are shaping the next generation of business, it is Alan who is treated like the player.

As they bring out his salad, sans dressing, Alan surreptitiously tips the waiter and leans back, incessantly checking his beeper. In addition to the Siena-Davidson game, he has action on Ohio State-Notre Dame, Utah-Arkansas State, and a big bet on Kansas State plus-18 against Arizona. What he can't check on his beeper is how his horses ran at Yonkers earlier that night and whether or not he won any of those bets. In total, what he's got in play tonight is what a lot of people make in a year.

Alan sees on his ticker that Arizona has taken a twenty-seven-point lead into halftime, which coincides with delivery of his stripped-down dinner. With tasteless chicken and a losing bet, he just got a double dose of pain.

"I fucking hate myself," he blurts out.

By the time dessert arrives, a complimentary plate of chocolate-covered strawberries and homemade pastries, Arizona is up by thirty-two. "We're not likely to cover," Alan says. "Lute Olson (Arizona's coach) is such an asshole, he'll keep his starters in the entire game. I swear to god, Duke and Arizona always cover if they are gonna win, they never let benchwarmers play."

A moment later, he checks his ticker one last time. Arizona-Kansas State falls nineteen. Arizona covered by one.

Alan loses.

"Oh fuck, that's funny," he says. "That's pretty funny."

By *Monday Night Football*, the pall cast by the pending antibetting legislation is washed away in a sea of soy sauce and Asahi beer. Lupo, Scucci, and Korona sit at the sushi bar at Hamada, a restaurant about ten minutes from the Stardust, chowing on spider rolls, spicy tuna rolls, and California rolls.

Lupo, a small-town midwestern kid whose dad bartended at race-tracks throughout Ohio, learned about the win, place, and show at the same time he learned his ABCs. He'd sit on sawdusted floors beside the bar when he was six years old and hear his dad's customers talk about the Browns being favored over the Steelers by seven and what a great value that was.

Scucci, growing up the son of a cabdriver in New Jersey and Las Vegas, learned about gambling while working as a runner between his dad and his peewee football coach. Every week, his dad would drop off Scucci for practice with a little extra padding in the form of cash.

Scucci would hand over the cash to his coach, who would give Scucci dozens of parlay cards for his dad to play.

Korona lived a privileged life as the son of well-off Wall Streeter. He traveled to Europe in college and on family vacations, which he gets razzed about constantly by Lupo and Scucci. "He'll try and drop the fact he studied in Switzerland at least a couple of times a week," says Scucci. But he also accompanied his dad on weekly trips to the Meadowlands Racetrack in New Jersey. As a result, Korona is an anomaly among his generation of bettors, a twenty-four-year-old kid as comfortable betting the sixth race at Aqueduct as he is the sixth game of the NBA Finals. It was his horse sense, which Lupo related to while remembering days spent at his dad's trackside bar, which clinched his hiring at the Stardust.

For all the numbers and research and consultants Lupo has at his fingertips, it's what he and his managers knew before they got to where they are, an instinct for bookmaking developed from a young age, that ultimately makes or impedes the sports book's success. He trusts his own instincts as well as Scucci's. And in Korona, Lupo and Scucci both see a younger version of themselves; an ambitious book-maker who, when he closes his eyes at night, still sees numbers moving up and down while falling asleep.

Korona would like to be running his own book by the time he's thirty and is interested in preserving the way his mentors think numbers should be made and sports books should be run. "But he's not there yet," says Lupo. "Sometimes I look at him and I have no idea what he's thinking."

For a while, Lupo didn't know if Korona was actually thinking at all. Korona is hard of hearing out of his right ear. Half the time, Lupo or Scucci will be talking to him and he'll be in a trance, his mouth slightly agape and his eyes fixed on a spot in the distance. For months they seriously worried that he was partially brain damaged—and they wondered why they didn't recognize this during the interviewing process—until Korona finally told them he couldn't hear.

While he doesn't know it all, Korona knows enough to realize he's been taken under Lupo and Scucci's collective wings and anointed a golden child in the bookmaking industry. He does the grunt work in the book, endures the hazing like a dutiful younger brother and seems to enjoy every minute of it. There are perks, such as the minor celebrity status that goes along with working in the book. On Sunday nights, Korona is the designated Stardust representative on the Stardust Line radio show. On Monday morning he'll usually see his name in the paper as the Stardust bookmaker along with a comment he made on the show the night before about which games were a good value. And publicity brings credibility.

As the Jets-Patriots game, playing on television across from the bar, nears halftime the trio of bookmakers begin thinking about a halftime line. Essentially, this means each team starts the half at 0–0, and the bookmakers make a new spread and new total based on the circumstances of what happened in the first half. It's a chance for thoe gamblers who are winning to push their luck even further or, for the unlucky souls who guessed wrong, to get themselves even. Their stomachs full of raw fish and rice, their bodies warm from a couple of beers, and their senses tingling from a weekend in which their craftiness made the book more than a quarter-million dollars, Lupo, Scucci and Korona weigh their options. The Jets, whose quarterback Ray Lucas has only started a handful of games, were underdogs when the game started. But, behind two Lucas touchdown passes, the Jets are winning 21–3 at halftime. This is extremely bad news for the Patriots. New England still has a chance to make the play-offs if it wins. Combine their probably desperate play with the chance that the novice Lucas will cool off in the second half and the Pats, although they are down 21–3, are—according to three buzzed bookmakers in a Japanese restaurant—minus-7 in the second half.

As Lupo dials his cell phone to the manager on duty in the book to deliver the spread, Scucci takes another sip of beer and begins to smile.

"What's so funny?" Korona asks.

"Well," Succi answers. "I just can't believe three guys in this bar made a line that can turn into millions of dollars in action."

Every morning at 8 A.M. during the basketball season—and on Sunday nights during football season—the Stardust holds a lottery in which the wiseguys draw cards to see who can get first crack at the fresh numbers. One-thousand dollars is the minimum bet. The lottery started in the mid–1980s, when sports betting began its rise in popularity and before the Internet and tracking software were so easy to use. Back then, dozens of hopeless bettors would crowd around the counter at the Stardust like cows grazing on a lone patch of grass, jockeying for position to crack the first lines. Young turks like Alan Boston could be found side by side with old-timers named Montana Mel and Dick the Pick in the last era of such comingling between two generations of bettors. Soon, the old-timers would become relics, unable to keep up with technology while the kids like Alan, who loved gambling for its Runyonesque stereotypes, would lament about how it was better in the old days.

For many years the Alan Bostons and Montana Mels would cram together when the lines were posted. One day, a bettor left his place to use the bathroom. When he returned and stepped back into his old spot, a gambler named Crazy Jim asked him what he thought he was doing.

"I was in this spot, I just went to the bathroom," said the bettor.

"I don't think so," said Crazy Jim. "Get to the end."

"No," said the bettor, staring down the diminutive Jim.

Then Crazy Jim pulled out a gun, pointed it at the guy's nose, and said again, "I don't think so."

"At first we just had guys sitting in the desks before they bet," remembers former Stardust bookmaker Richard Saber. "We'd announce that it's time for the lottery and there would be a mad dash, guys tripping each other to get to the counter first. This lasted two days before we realized someone would get killed. Then we had them stand in line until the Crazy Jim incident. After that we had the bettors draw numbers. One day I walked in and guys were betting how many guys would show up for the lottery."

Today, with so many offshore options, the significance of the lottery has dwindled. Most wiseguys don't bother getting up that early—that's why they pay runners—and the number of people making early bets is never more than 10 or 15. No one goes out for breakfast together anymore. Yet, as protectors of the sports book's traditions and out of respect for the romantic notion of the way things used to be, Lupo and Scucci still take it seriously. Every morning, Scucci drags his tired body into the book by 7 A.M. and runs through the same prelottery routine.

"First I have to turn on the two huge TVs, which is kind of silly when you think about it. You'd think they would leave these things on all night, but the problem is the $2,500 bulbs we bought only have 800 hours of life. So we have to turn the big TVs off at midnight everyday."

He's interrupted by a scraggly looking regular. "Hey Bobby," the regular asks. "Are there any college sheets yet?"

"That's what I'm working on," Scucci says in a voice that sounds like a parent responding to a child who keeps asking, Are we there yet?

"I have to manually input every game into the two terminals that track who bets on what and for how much," he explains. "It's mainly just data entry, but it's a pain in the ass early in the morning when you're rushed and people are asking you silly questions every couple of minutes.

"Everything is strategically geared towards making it easier on the bettor. Higher profile games and the daily schedule go directly above the counter. So, when someone is ready to bet they have what they need right in front of them. Sometimes it's like an impulse buy. They'll be coming on Friday to bet a Saturday event and a game that night will catch their eye. We just want people to be able to look up and see what they want immediately."

Normally by 7:30 Scucci is well into making the lines for the day's games. But only two of the five consultants contracted by the Stardust have filed their numbers. "It's the first day of college basketball on a full scale," he says. "No one is ready yet."

If he wants to be ready for the 8 A.M. lottery, Scucci has to trust his own internal power ratings which, this early in the season, take into account returning starters, last year's record, and strength of schedule.

"Hey man," a twenty-something kid asks Scucci, "When do you put the lines up?"

"Eight A.M. sir," Scucci says, gritting his teeth.

"They have no idea I am trying to make these lines right now," Scucci mutters, getting back to work. "They think they come up automatically."

At 7:55 Scucci stands at the counter shuffling a deck of cards. Before he makes an announcement that the drawing for the lottery will be in five minutes, bettors start huddling around him, like hungry puppies jockeying for position at feeding time.

At 8 A.M. the lines are up, this being the only place in the world currently posting odds on the day's basketball games. Although marquee teams like Indiana, Kentucky, Clemson, and Utah are playing, it's the Cal–Irvine vs. San Diego game, which has San Diego as three-point favorites, attracting everyone's attention. Each bettor in the lottery gets five plays before he has to cede his place at the window to someone else. Mike, a rotund runner with a gray beard who spends six days a week sitting twelve hours a day in the same seat monitoring the board, mooching drink tickets and sneaking out to the pay phone to report to his boss, makes the first play of the day.

"Gimme 742 plus 3 for $1,100," says Mike.

742 is the Cal–Irvine vs. San Diego game, which flags Scucci's attention immediately. Normally, the strategy is to move numbers slowly in the morning in case a bettor is trying to manipulate the lines.

But on this game in particular Scucci isn't going to risk it. He takes it down to San Diego minus-2.5. "I respect his play for one," says Scucci, explaining the move. "Also, we hate booking these games. These small games are the ones where the gambler has the advantage. So we are more conservative."

The act-and-react drama between the bettor and bookmaker is a constant mind game. He who flinches first pays the biggest price. Mike bet the $1,100 to see how quickly Scucci would move the number and how much he would move it. And Scucci flinched. Moving it quickly meant Mike knows that even Scucci thinks he's posted a soft number and that he has to hit it hard and fast before Scucci moves it again. With his second play, Mike puts two dimes on Cal–Irvine plus-2.5, which Scucci now moves down to San Diego minus-2. With his third bet, Mike takes the plus-2 for $1,800. In three minutes he's bet $4,800 on Cal–Irvine, and each move has sent Scucci jumping. In the real world, fans are thinking about the Utah vs. Kentucky game, a rematch of the 1998 NCAA Championship game. But in the sports book, two schools with little basketball tradition that won't appear on national television the entire season are the marquee matchup. When Cal–Irvine is a 1.5-point underdog, Mike puts another $2,000 on the game. Scucci is like a defenseless boxer in a match the ref won't call. In a last-ditch effort to stop the bleeding, he moves the game to "pick," meaning neither team is favored. Mike is laughing now as his last play in the lottery unfolds slowly. He looks at Scucci, staring him down before he peels more bills from his thickly folded wad, and the others waiting to make their bets in the lottery go silent.

"Seven...four...two...Cal...Irvine...pick...two dimes," Mike says, mocking Scucci's move.

Immediately the pace in the book picks up, like a movie scene speeding to normal from slow motion. Mike walks away licking his fingers and checking his tickets while Scucci gets on the sports book P.A. to make an announcement.

"Game 742, Cal–Irvine, minus-1," he says.

The damage is done. Mike made the book $8,800 heavy on a meaningless game and got the satisfaction of moving the line four points and changing the favorite by himself. Not only is the Stardust heavy on one side of a game it had little confidence booking to begin with, but now the bettors can pick at the bookmakers' insecurities like vultures on a carcass. Every bet they make will have the bookmakers on their heels. For all the cache posting the first line brings the Stardust, it is equaled out by the potential pounding it'll take on a game like Cal–Irvine vs. San Diego.

When the lottery is winding down at around 8:45 and Scucci has a chance to assess the damage, he notices that the Mirage finally posted its lines. Cal–Irvine is a one-point favorite over San Diego.

"Good for them," he says bitterly. "It must be nice to come in and hang lines at a quarter to nine."

Largely ignored in the sports book on Friday morning is the announcement being made on CNBC, which plays in the book, around the time the first hour of betting comes to a close. That morning, CBS agreed to pay the NCAA $6 billion over eleven years for rights to the NCAA Tournament, extending its coverage of March Madness through 2013. This payoff makes the tournament the most expensive, and in the eyes of at least one network, the most popular sporting event in the world.

In his house, Alan is bouncing off the walls and chanting like Dustin Hoffman in *Rain Man*. "Gotta bet, gotta bet. Traffic's not good, never gonna make it. Gotta bet, gotta bet." It's 3:45 and the first games on the East Coast start in forty-five minutes, at 7:30 EST. Alan had been trying to keep a low profile this season, not making big moves in public, not giving out tips to everyone that calls. But he just saw some of the small college spreads at the MGM flash across his screen.

Alan loves the MGM and what Richie Bacciellieri is doing with the book. "It's a great feat to research all these games and post numbers," says Alan. "It means he should be betting, not booking. For this I will give him my business."

Alan already has action on five games—Texas Tech plus-6 against Indiana, Virginia Commonwealth plus-7.5 against Louisville, Dayton plus-9.5 against New Mexico, Cal–Irvine plus-1 and plus-1.5 against San Diego, Drake plus-4 and plus-3.5 against Iowa State as well as Iowa State minus-3 over Drake. Drake vs. Iowa State was an arbitrage game that went his way, with him betting a lot on Drake at 4, then hitting it big again at 3.5, only to turn around and bet Iowa State minus-3 for even more, which is what he really wanted from the start. His biggest bet of the night approaching the $20,000 range is Cal–Irvine. He also laid out a lot of money on Iowa State vs. Drake, but the upside isn't that big when you factor in all the arbitraging. All counted, he's got nearly $50,000 riding on the night's games. "We tried to avoid the degenerate stuff," Alan says. "But I didn't know the MGM had the add on games, now I'm horny and discipline goes out the window."

Welcome to Alan Boston's Las Vegas.

An old friend once described Alan as appearing so tightly wound—his eyes darting and fists clenched—that his friend thought Alan might actually explode into a bloody mess. But when Alan is betting the pressure actually diminishes, releasing so slowly you can almost hear the hissing sound of air rushing from his body. Anything that impedes his progress toward making the bet pinches the release shut.

Alan bolts out the laundry room door that leads to the garage and jumps into his gold Corvette like some dashing TV cop. He's forty minutes and a waiting traffic jam away from the MGM. But the games start in thirty-five minutes. On the highway, Alan has one hand on the wheel as the other holds the phone, which rings incessantly. The speedometer approaches ninety mph as he weaves through tiny slots between the cars doing a more respectable sixty mph. The other drivers don't know the pressure Alan is feeling. Fairfield is a 27.5-point underdog to Kansas. Don't they get it? *It's free money.* Why isn't everyone heading to the MGM?

He changes lanes and the valve pinches shut. "I never choose the right lane. If I'm stuck the other one is moving. If I get in the moving lane it stops," he cries. "Do you know what it's like to never do the right thing?" Just like that, the uncontrollable ebb and flow of traffic has become a metaphor for Alan's bad judgment. In the game of chance, even your instincts for traffic patterns are cause for concern.

RULE NUMBER SIX
Everything is a game of chance.

Alan pulls into the jammed MGM valet line at 4:20. Stuck behind three other cars with the drivers waiting inside to get their tickets, he peers his head out the window. "Fuck me, I am the unluckiest person in the world. Fuck me," he mutters. He jumps out of the car and slams the door shut. The pimply teenager writing out a parking ticket three cars up sees Alan rushing toward him like a pit bull and, with an instinct for self-preservation, starts backpedaling.

"Hey," Alan screams at the kid, who does an innocent double take, as if to say, "Who? Me?"

"Where are you going?" Alan asks. "Stop."

Stuck in his tracks, fearing the worst, wondering why the angry bald man who left his car running in the valet line is going to kill him, the kid opens his mouth, but nothing comes out.

Alan reaches a clenched fist toward the attendant and the kid blanches, as if shielding himself from a smack across the face. Waiting drivers are honking, Alan's car is running, the games he wants to bet on start in less than ten minutes. When the kid opens his eyes, he sees Alan's outstretched hand, a folded $20 bill tucked between its fingers.

"Leave her somewhere nearby," Alan says of his car. "I'll be back in ten minutes."

The MGM sports book is tucked in the corner of the 171,500-square-foot casino, through the ornate lobby, past rows of slot machines, blackjack tables, and a restaurant. It's a good five-minute walk from the front door without obstructions. But on a Friday afternoon, when the entryway is teeming with guests checking into the hotel and checking out of reality, Alan might as well be running an obstacle course with moving targets.

He sprints into the book with a minute to spare, and Baccellieri is standing behind the counter. "Uh-oh, here he comes," Baccellieri says. "You got your grocery list?"

"The last time I had a grocery list it said bananas, oatmeal, and a life," Alan responds. "I picked up the first two."

The games are tipping off but, among friends, betting a minute or two posttip isn't going to make or break the book or the bettor. And, while the MGM's official betting limit for college basketball is $2,000 a game, it's at Baccellieri's discretion to let some bettors play more. At the Stardust, there's no chance Lupo would let Alan have more than two dimes on a game, especially an add-on game that no one else is putting on the board. But Baccellieri is a gambler at heart. These add-ons are his chance to separate himself from the pack. If you're gonna put them up, you might as well let the wiseguys play.

"Alright, Alan, I'll give you three dimes per game," Baccellieri says.

For all the competition between bookmakers and handicappers, there is an unwritten code of rules each side follows to keep their dalliances honorable. While each rule varies, the basic element is this: Don't get greedy. A bookmaker tracking a hundred different games on a given day may not hear that the star player at Podunk U. has been scratched. He won't adjust his spread accordingly, and the number will sit on his board like a golden goose for the wiseguys. Whoever gets to the number first is entitled to bet the game hard, getting down as much as he possibly can. But then he's got to tell the bookmaker his number's off so no one else can pile on. Greed bleeds the goose. And there should be plenty to go around for everyone if they play nice.

Alan puts down three dimes each on Clemson minus-14 over East Tennessee State, South Carolina minus-6.5 over Wofford and Fairfield plus-27.5 against Kansas, as well as $2,000 on Southeast Missouri State at minus-4 over Western Carolina. Since he's just bet more than $10,000 at one time, he fills out an IRS form before grabbing his tickets and racing back to his car.

"Basically, I shouldn't have done that," he admits on the way out. "I have too much work to do at home scouting the games. However I do think Richie deserves the business, so whether I win or lose is irrelevant."

Of course by the end of the night, when he's lost his five-figure bets like Indiana and Iowa State by one point each while winning his smaller bets like Fairfield and Southeast Missouri State easily, he'll be preaching a different sermon. Alan goes 6–3 for the night's games and still ends up on the losing side of the ledger, thanks to the Cal–Irvine vs. San Diego game. His hunches that San Diego was overrated—by whom is unclear since no one outside of San Diego covers the team—and that Irvine's coach was a genius turned Alan into a chump. (San Diego won the game 75–62, easily covering the 1.5-point spread.) While largely ignored by anyone outside of those two campuses, this is the type of game—small schools with competitive programs—that sends a charge through the Vegas sports books the moment the Stardust posts a number. And it's the kind of game that Alan just lost $20,000 on.

Chapter 8

The Devil's Deal

I mean, I still like the United States. I miss the amenities, I miss my friends. I do still live in a third-world country when all is said and done and I do have serious regrets. I missed my brother's wedding because I couldn't go back. I missed him having a kid. If I knew then that coming down here to work at the book would mean I could never go back, I wouldn't have come.

—HADEN WARE, COFOUNDER, WORLD SPORTS EXCHANGE, AN ON-LINE GAMBLING SITE BASED IN ANTIGUA

In 1990, the Boston College basketball team traveled up the road to Cambridge for a game against Harvard. The game opened with Boston College as nine-point favorites, and Alan thought that was a good value. He had followed both teams and felt that Harvard, by far the less athletic of the two, wouldn't be able to stand up to the constant defensive pressure B.C. would present.

Predictably, with a team from the Big East playing a team from the Ivy League, most bettors expected a B.C. blowout and the game moved from nine to ten. Shortly before tip-off, Alan got a phone call from a friend. Rumor had it, the friend said, that Harvard's best player had gotten hurt. He asked Alan if he could find out if the story was true.

At first, Alan blew off the tip, because he saw the spread on the game fall from 10 to 9 to 8.5 at the Stardust. Whispers throughout the book indicated that the Computer Group, the most successful betting syndicate in Vegas, was taking Harvard and the points and they were doing it loudly. The Computer Group had more info on every game than the tabloids had on Kathie Lee. They wouldn't bet heavy on Harvard if its best player was hurt.

But Alan was intrigued by the rumor. He called WNBR in Cambridge, the radio station that carried the Harvard games. He concocted a story that he was a student reporter on vacation who couldn't be at the game and needed to get some information. The game was about to start and the operator patched Alan through to a live feed of the pregame show. He was connected just in time to hear that, "There is some bad news for Harvard," the announcer said. "Its best player is out for the year after slipping on some ice on campus and breaking his leg."

The Computer Group had overbet on bad information. Alan took advantage and laid the 8.5, which ended up winning him enough money to fill his bullet with cocaine and keep him in action for another day.

A little more than a decade later, the subterfuge and investigative work Alan needed to flush out the tip would be unnecessary. Today, he—and every other wiseguy—would just log onto a late-breaking news Web site based in Boston to read about Harvard's bad luck. (And, he wouldn't have to be patched into a radio network via the phone because he could listen to the game on the Internet.) The Internet's incredible power to deliver information has made using your wiles to get the edge on a game a lost art. And the explosion of information available has meant the pool of gamblers has grown from a pond to an ocean, including not just hardcore addicts who dig for clues like Sherlock Holmes, but casual bettors looking to parlay their fanaticism for sports into cash. You needn't spend endless hours researching games to avoid making a sucker bet. You don't need a secret password and a bookie named Fingers. You don't even need to be in Las Vegas. If you're a rabid bettor and living in Cleveland, that's great news. But if you happen to make your living running a book or betting on the slightest disparity in the spreads, the Wild West days of bookmaking and betting are over. For the Las Vegas of Alan, Lupo, Rodney and the others, it is death by download.

Depending on who you talk to, Albert Corbo was one of two things: either a visionary cursed with bad timing who was unjustly accused of being a mob associate for having a vowel at the end of his name; or, the convicted bookmaker who ran card games in the basement of his Philly home. He was banned from casinos in Atlantic City and infamous enough to earn a listing in Nevada's "Black Book," which meant he was barred from entering any casino in that state as well. What's indisputable is that he knew the business of sports betting, and his vision for its future reshaped the industry, from Las Vegas to the Caribbean and beyond.

Corbo was born in Philly in 1934, the son of an Italian tailor. Although his formal education stopped when he was seventeen, he earned a graduate degree in making ends meet. He and his wife, Betty, raised three sons on Philadelphia's posh main line (his son Dana grew up to be a respected prosecutor who spent two years working for Janet Reno in the State Attorney General's office of Dade County) while running several legitimate businesses, among them a series of gas stations. He was the last chance for gas before Philly's city streets turned into the rolling hills of rural Pennsylvania. But while he could pump gas into his veins 24/7, it still wouldn't kill the gambling virus living in his blood.

"He liked betting, all kinds of betting," says his son Andy. "He kept close to the people who were betting on sports and making numbers. His motto was simple, 'Never buck the wiseguy.'"

A couple of nights a week, after Corbo locked up the gas station, he opened up the basement for impromptu games of craps. The games, played on a crickety table with scuffed dice and the diminutive Corbo barking out winners and losers, attracted everyone from the local sporting-goods salesman to the local mobster. Sometimes the games ran all night, with Corbo and his partner/brother unlocking the door from the inside to start the business day.

One night a player felt he got cheated. Corbo thought otherwise. "My father was the kind of person who would tell you if he disagreed with you," Dana Corbo once told the *Las Vegas Sun*. "He could be rough and blunt." Furious, the player risked a gambling conviction by admitting to police that people were playing craps in Corbo's gas station basement. The cops promptly went after Corbo. "Of course he gets convicted and known as a gambler," says Andy. "Afterward," Andy adds, "there is always talk of organized crime wherever he would go."

When the New Jersey legislature voted to allow gambling in 1977, Corbo naturally made a go at legitimately doing what he loved. Like a shepherd leading his flock, Corbo would take other hopeful gamblers on weekend junkets to Atlantic City, earning his living from the hotels that paid him to shuttle guests from Philly to their tables. But when the President's Commission on Organized Crime presented its report in the mid-1980s and Corbo's name was mentioned, the Gaming Board of New Jersey banned Corbo from every casino on the Board-walk.

As a result Corbo became a gambling nomad. Instead of trying to outrun his reputation, he embraced it. First he went to the Dominican Republic. The Dominican was, and still is, a wasteland of poverty. But to Corbo it represented the land of opportunity. It was warm and tropical, not that expensive, and easy to get to from the United States. If you could steer clear of the shantytowns, tropical diseases, and unpalatable water, it was almost paradise. Most important, gambling was legal there. And that was all that mattered to Corbo. In fact, gambling was a fledgling business that many beachfront hotels hoped would catapult the island from afterthought to tourist spot. Local hotels hoped Corbo's reputation and alleged connections might jump start the Dominican Republic's gaming industry. But Corbo saw a chance at making the big score himself. He could monopolize the industry down there, be the first one with any skills to organize it, set the standards for it, and make it his own.

"My dad realized that people didn't have access to calling Las Vegas unless they were in Las Vegas," Andy said years later. "But they could call over to the islands. A guy sitting in Chicago could call my dad in the Dominican and get $50,000 down on a game."

Nevertheless, according to the 1961 Wire Act, even though he was not technically in the United States, Corbo was transmitting betting information within the United States over telephone lines. That was illegal. A Tampa detective and the Broward County Sherrif's Department had been monitoring Corbo's behavior on the islands and knew there was nothing they could do about it until he was on American soil. After two years of running his multimillion-dollar book in the islands, Corbo came home for the holidays in 1990, where he was promptly picked up and arrested. He plead guilty to twenty-five counts of illegal bookmaking and one count of conspiracy in Florida and was sentenced to six months in prison with two years' probation.

Shortly after serving out his sentence in 1991, Corbo and his wife moved out to Las Vegas, where Andy was working as a blackjack dealer. One of the first people he met was a visionary named Don Bissett. Bissett envisioned a computerized line service that transmitted odds, eliminating the need for gamblers to have runners stationed at books all over the city phoning in the lines. Bissett had cancer and was looking to take on a partner. At the time, the service focused on offering local players all the Las Vegas lines. But Corbo knew which direction the industry was headed. Vegas itself was on the verge of being overrun by large corporations, turning old-time mom-and-pop hotels on the Strip into megaplex entertainment centers. The MGM would open in just two years, and the Mirage just a few years after that.

Corbo recognized that coming to Vegas would soon be no different than going to Disneyland, and the outlaw culture would have to adapt. He paid Bissett $50,000 for a piece of the business, which had only twenty customers in Las Vegas, none of whom were wiseguys.

By the early 1990s, following Corbo's lead, the number of sports books running out of Costa Rica and the Dominican Republic, and Caribbean islands like Antigua, had grown considerably. For the wiseguys looking to get down more money in one island joint than they could in ten Vegas sports books combined, the island books were both a more efficient way to bet and a good fix for their need to get big money down. Just wire a check, open an account, and bet, bet, bet. And since the action took place offshore, there was no need to fill out annoying IRS forms if you laid down more than $10,000 at a time. They might lack the cute waitresses and free beer, but when it came down to the most important details—betting vast sums of money— the Island books were the old time, Vegas sports parlors reincarnated.

Corbo knew first hand how influential the Island joints were becoming. He could see they were taking higher and higher limits while Vegas sports book managers started to cower under corporate pressure to lose less money. While ticket writers in Vegas were look- ing around for approval on a college basketball bet of $3,000, opera- tors in the Islands were asking customers who laid down $10,000, "Is that all?"

(In 1986, the Gaming Control Board had passed a law that required bookmakers accepting a bet of more than $10,000 to fill out a form and record that bettor's name, address, and social security num- ber and forward that information to the IRS. The impact on high rollers was immediate. The law was passed in May, and the January before its passage the Stardust took seven Super Bowl bets for more than $100,000. At the following Super Bowl, the Stardust didn't take a single bet of more than $10,000.)

Corbo convinced his Caribbean contacts to let him carry their spreads on his line service. Then he convinced some of the biggest players in Las Vegas that a service with a running feed that transmitted all the Las Vegas and Caribbean lines would be invaluable. They'd be able to shop for their numbers without ever leaving their desks. And, of course, have a chance to make some real money.

"My dad was living in the Santa Fe Apartments out here, working out of a room that was the size of a closet," says Andy. "I would come by after work and think, 'what is he doing with that computer?' He'd just be sitting there taking calls from the island guys and typing their numbers in by hand whenever there was a change."

For fifteen hours a day, Corbo hand-pecked data into his computer, driven like a young programmer by the notion that his vision would change the world. And slowly Corbo's service spread across the desert, collecting customers like a growing herd of tumbleweeds.

With the island listings added in 1993, Don Best—the name of the service Corbo bought from Bissett—saw its customer base grow from twenty to nearly a hundred. In 1995, using a cable signal to transmit the lines, the list grew from around 150 to nearly 500. In 1997, using the Internet, the customer base doubled at nearly $500 a pop. Now, with the explosion of the Internet and the island lines, Don Best has a cash-spewing monopoly on its hands.

But the impact of the service can't be measured in dollars. It was a catalyst in changing the entire industry. As soon as the Island books, previously thought to be disreputable joints years away from establishing any credibility, appeared on the Don Best screen they were instantly legitimized. The stigma of betting in the Caribbean lessened with every additional island book in the service. Meanwhile the Vegas sports books, under pressure to reign in the losses and run a tighter ship, could more easily protect themselves by watching which lines the other books were posting and deciding whether or not their lines were leaving them vulnerable. Wiseguys would have a hard time playing them for fools if every book on the Strip showed the same spread. The books loved the service.

"A sports book manager always has a defensive posture now," says sports-betting historian Peter Ruchman. "When a number moves it moves all across the world. In the old days, numbers would move based on money; now they move in reaction to other books."

Not everyone likes this new conservatism.

"It's pathetic," bemoans old-time bookmaker Jimmy Vaccaro. "I saw what it was like in the 1970s and this is a shame."

The hoodlum legacy of Las Vegas has been scrubbed clean by sound business practices and strictly enforced laws. But the cleanup has weakened the stranglehold Las Vegas once had on the betting community. Why use your phone account to make a college basketball bet for $2,000 at the Stardust when you can bet on the same game for $7,000 at Costa Rica International Sports? Why run down to the book to make a $10,000 bet on the NFL and then be bothered with IRS forms when you can bet $20,000 offshore and never even report it?

In 1996, two Internet sites accepted sports wagering on-line. At the end of 2000, there were nearly 500. The money wagered on-line has grown from $60 million in 1996, to $600 million in 1998, to $1.2 billion in 1999. According to a 2000 report on the industry by the investment bank Bear Stearns & Co., it's expected that $3 billion will be wagered on sports on the Internet in 2002. "People are spending more time on-line, they are becoming more comfortable with e-commerce, and they love games of chance," said Jason Adler, a Bear Stearns gaming analyst.

In Great Britain, where betting has long been as common and accepted as afternoon tea, the local betting shops are embracing the Internet. Easybets was based in Dublin, Ireland, and established a chain of parlors throughout the city in the 1970s. In 1997 it morphed into easybets.com, closed all but one of its land-based stores, and relocated to Antigua. "We had an annual turnover of $700,000 in our traditional shops," said easybets.com CEO Tim Lambe. "In our first year of operation on-line (1998), we had $38 million. Nineteen-ninety-nine's turnover was $60 million." Lambe said he expected turnover in 2000 to reach $150 million. In Australia's Northern Territory, instead of fighting the trend, the government regulates on-line gaming and will collect taxes from the virtual casinos. Lasseters, a land-based Australian casino, was the first government licensed on-line gaming venture. With little advertising, the site drew more than 35,000 gamblers and took in more than $2 million in wagers over its first two months.

Stateside, the government has given the same mixed signals about what's right and wrong about Internet gaming that it has about all other forms of gambling. In November of 1999, the Senate passed the Internet Gambling Prohibition Act, named the "Kyl bill" for its sponsor, Republican Senator Jon Kyl of Arizona. While the law makes it a federal crime to operate virtual casinos and sports books on the Internet, it exempts sites who offer horse and dog racing, state lotteries, and fantasy sports leagues. It also does not target individual bettors for prosecution. Because of all the holes in it, the bill was mocked in Congress as the "Swiss Cheese Law" by opponents and proponents alike.

At the state level, there is confusion about how to handle the potential threats the Internet poses. In 1997, Nevada Governor Bob Miller signed a law making it illegal for anyone in the state of Nevada to bet over the Internet to a site that is outside the state. However, the law allowed for licensed gaming facilities to *accept* bets over the Internet from anywhere in the world. Even with this license, the increasingly conservative sports books have dragged their feet; none accept on-line wagers, according to the Nevada Gaming Control Board. "If you could call the Stardust or Mirage from out of state and make a bet," argues Vaccaro, "people would do it. But they don't have that choice. The masses accept sports betting, but the people making laws can't lose the stigma. I mean if Britain can do it, why the fuck can't we? We are missing the boat, really missing the boat. I mean sports betting, are you crazy? Are you fucking crazy? We could close up the off-shores in half an hour."

"Clearly, the greatest benefit of wagering on the Internet would be from sports," says Bill Bible, "You look at blackjack or poker or slots on the Internet and those are games you can't be sure aren't rigged. But sports is determined by forces outside of the site, which makes it conducive to sports betting."

"To be honest, the only chance of betting that has any chance on the Internet is sports betting," adds Chuck DiRocco, publisher and editor of *Gaming Today*, a weekly newspaper. "Anyone who goes and bets poker on-line, where some geek has a chance to write some program that determines the outcome, they deserve to get clipped."

Cyberbettors can shop hundreds of different sites looking for values and high limits. And, unlike twenty years ago, they don't have to move to Vegas if they want to make a career out of it. Instead of wearing fedoras and chomping on cigars, today's pros wear backwards baseball hats and chew gum. Betting on-line is more sanitized and less visceral than doing it in the sports book, but the rush of winning is exactly the same.

"As crack cocaine changed the cocaine experience," says Howard Shaffer, "I think electronics and the Internet is going to change the way gambling is experienced."

Jay Cohen didn't see black or white or the impending racial divide while watching the O. J. Simpson criminal trial verdict. The only color he saw was green. The options trader from San Francisco was on the floor of the Pacific Stock Exchange, taking bets from his trader buddies on the verdict. Already a hotbed of betting activity because of the nature of the business, the trading floor crackled with action during Super Bowl week, the NCAA tournament and even the O. J. criminal verdict. And Cohen, acting as the local bookmaker, envisioned an income from full-time bookmaking that could make the $500,000 a year he made trading seem like chump change.

In the mid-1990s, San Francisco was ground zero for the Internet revolution. Surrounded by true believers who were reshaping the way business would be done, it was impossible to ignore the Web and the far-reaching effects it could have. For Cohen, the Internet was the perfect vehicle through which he could outline his plan to revolutionize sports betting. His experiences taking bets from ebullient traders in the pits, and all the pedestrian money he saw flowing into the stock market, convinced him that a virtual stock market of sports wagering would be the next wave of gambling. In the pits where he and his friends traded, they didn't just put money on one team over another. They purchased options in teams and then bought and sold those options based on speculation of how the team would do. Working options is the most complicated and technical form of trading done on Wall Street, but Cohen was willing to bet that, when applied to sports, the construction foreman would take to it as quickly as those he worked with.

But even under the guise of being a stock market of sports rather than an Internet sports book offering straight bets, Cohen's idea would push the boundaries of the 1961 Wire Act. Ultimately, even if people were technically trading teams instead of betting on them, Cohen could be transferring information used for sports wagering via telephone lines. But Cohen was committed to the cause. He had heard of offshore books popping up all over the Caribbean and he realized, even in a city full of anarchists flouting conventional wisdom and reshaping the world, his idea didn't fit.

In Antigua his idea and his money were welcome. As quickly as the United States was trying desperately to outlaw Internet gambling, the Antiguan government was embracing it. By the summer of 2000, there were ninety licensed Internet gambling sites in Antigua, and Antiguan officials boast that Internet gambling is one of the few growing sectors of the country's economy. In the face of pressure from foreign governments hoping to regulate the industry, Antigua actually rejected a plan to install monitoring devices on gaming sites within their borders for fear it would anger the web operators.

For $75,000 Cohen, along with fellow traders Steve Schillinger and Haden Ware, whom Cohen had convinced to come to the Caribbean with him, bought a sports-gaming license from the Antiguan government. For $200,000 the trio installed state-of-the-art software that could process 250 bets a second. They called their company World Sports Exchange, a.k.a. WSEX, and opened as the world's first free market for buying and selling athletic teams as though they were stocks.

And then, nothing. No calls from clients. No money rolling in. Once the euphoria of revolutionizing an industry wore off the reality of doing business in a third-world country settled in. Ware had to share road space with goats. For the first month they were in business they had no computers or chairs because their equipment was held up in customs.

But there were two other problems. One was their lack of experience in the industry. Most bookies running offshore books had traveled to the Islands because they had to, not because they wanted to. The police had tapped their phones, raided their apartments, or thrown them in jail overnight one too many times for their liking. They were industry veterans with healthy client lists who did most of their business over the phone. It didn't matter if they were on the corner or on the beach. As far as their clients were concerned, what difference did it make if they called a local or an 800 number to make a bet? But the WSEX guys didn't have a client list. They were just three guys with no reputations running a sports book from a third-world country. Potential players have to be convinced they'll get paid if they win before they put their money down. And the word of Cohen, Schillinger, and Ware wasn't enough.

A second, more pressing problem was that no one understood the premise of trading teams. Cohen had misjudged that the nation's growing lust for the stock market would translate into a passion for betting on sports in the same way.

So, after two months, like any nascent Internet operation, WSEX changed its business plan. The trio of traders started taking straight bets, with Ware booking by doing whatever the Stardust did. Then they started taking interactive bets, where bettors could bet on the next play or the next pitch. (Some people have wagered as much as $2,000 on whether or not the next pitch in a baseball game would be a ball or a strike.) Slowly the business grew, as did its reputation. By word of mouth, and by paying out winners, WSEX developed an active client base of nearly 10,000 bettors. By 1999, the company accepted $200 million in wagers, with 95 percent of those coming from clients in the United States. In 2000, that total was expected to double. Profits at the thirteen-employee betting shop reached around $7 million, also a figure expected to double in 2000. And, once the public had taken to their site and the straight bets, Cohen, Schillinger and Ware started pushing the options style of betting on their customers. This time, it took. That aspect of the business now accounts for 15 percent of the action.

"I think of myself as a twentieth-century bookmaker," says Ware. "I'm not feared or connected. I'm just an entrepreneur."

As the guys from World Sports Exchange teed off and counted their cash, in the United States a war was waging over Internet gambling. Nevada passed its bill. Missouri indicted, prosecuted, and eventually forced two offshore sports book owners using a Missouri bank to launder their earnings to plead guilty to impairing the IRS and violating the Wire Wager Act. In Florida, where Miami is connected to Antigua by a fiber-optic cable (making for high-speed T1 access) the state partnered with Western Union to stop money-service transfers to forty offshore books and sent letters to media outlets asking them not to advertise offshore establishments.

By March of 1998, John Kyl had introduced his anti–Internet gambling bill. And on March 4, Attorney General Janet Reno declared that while the laws concerning parlor games were still murky, the 1961 Wire

Act was clear: It is illegal to transmit sports-wagering information over telephone lines. And since the Internet uses telephone lines, anyone running a sports-betting Internet site and sending that information to customers in the United States was guilty of violating the Wire Act. The announcement was timed for maximum effect, coming just one week before the start of sports betting's silly season, the NCAA Basketball Tournament. "[This] sends a message to Internet betting operators everywhere," Reno said at the press conference announcing the indictments. "You can't hide on-line and you can't hide offshore." Fourteen sports book operators were indicted for conspiring to illegally transmit bets over the Internet and telephone, including Steve Schillinger and Jay Cohen from World Sports Exchange.

Ware, who was also eventually indicted, and Schillinger are prisoners of their own castle. "I'm only twenty-four years old and still in denial about the whole thing," says Ware from the islands. "Kids my age are going to Europe or hiking in the Himalayas and feel like their life is ahead of them. I can't go home without being detained." But Schillinger, in his early 40s, remains the zealot. Nothing can diminish his enthusiasm: Not the fact that his mother didn't tell him his father died until five days after it happened out of fear he would come home for the funeral and be arrested. Not the fact he can't kiss his wife, who is still living in San Francisco, or coach his twelve-year-old daughter's basketball team and his ten-year-old son's baseball team. And certainly there are no regrets about the fact that he is a fugitive from justice, trapped on an impoverished island where $1,000 is as good as $1,000,000. "To be honest, I still would have done it," he says. "In the end, it will probably be a good career move and be very lucrative." It's the ultimate devil's deal: He's got all the money in the world and nothing to spend it on.

Of the twenty people eventually indicted by the Justice Department, ten pled guilty to the original charges, three others pled guilty to related charges, and six, including Ware and Schillinger, remain fugitives. One person came back to be tried. That was Jay Cohen.

Chapter 9

"This Life . . . Is Starting to Make Me Sick"

My lifestyle is always the same. I get up at 6:30, work on numbers, and read about games until I go eat breakfast. At breakfast I have a bowl of oatmeal with nothing in it and six scrambled egg whites. I go to Jamms to eat. Then I go work out at Gold's Gym. Then I go home and read. And then I bet.

It's still early in the year and this life, which used to work for me, is already starting to make me sick. I can't stand it much longer.

—ALAN BOSTON, DECEMBER 1999

uring one of his last weekends in Maine, Alan Boston came back from the races one Saturday night and discovered the show *Freaks and Geeks* on NBC. Instantly it became a priority in his life. In December, after the poorly rated show had been off the air for nearly a month because of sweeps, Alan called NBC in New York demanding to know when the show was going to be back on. "It's wrong to take it off the air," he told them. "I relate to it, and I can't relate to anything. That means it has to be good." While the NBC secretary said she appreciated his comments and certainly shared his pain, her hands were tied. There was simply nothing she could do to get the show back on the air.

Alan had a habit of venting to unsuspecting secretaries. When the University of Tulsa fired its football coach, Dave Radar, Alan called the Tulsa Athletic Department, told a secretary the school had made a big mistake, and that he couldn't in good conscience support the program anymore. Of course he had never sent the school money or been to a game, but his internal sense of what is right and wrong, even though it may be warped to the outside world, is so acute that the slightest imbalance can trigger an altered state.

While angry at the pure injustice of taking *Freaks and Geeks* off the air, Alan is more enraged about the lack of decency some wiseguys are showing their fellow gamblers. Their betting patterns—when they bet on games, how much they bet on games, and which games they bet on—leave the board looking like the remnants of a terrorist attack. Once they're done, there is nothing left to bet. They're betting early, often, and indiscriminately, trying to take the best early season games off the board and making life tough on the rest of the wiseguys. Alan, who traditionally likes to bet later in the day, when lines aren't as volatile and his bets aren't as easily tracked, now has to think about making moves earlier in the day.

"It has already cost us a lot of money," says Alan. "Those motherfuckers are letting everybody know what they are doing and then the idiots who don't know what's up start following their lead. Then the line gets too far away from where we want to do anything with it. They are greedy and stupid."

Most handicappers recognize their limitations. Instead of digging deep on all 318 teams in thirty-two Division I conferences, the wiseguys narrow down the field, focusing on a few teams and conferences that will be their bread-and-butter bets throughout the year. Then, the pros will consider how the roller coaster ride that is a team's emotional state can play into its schedule. For example, a team on the road for three straight games coming home to play a big rival is naturally going to be fired up. But will that same team have a letdown when it's playing a weaker opponent? Then, there are certain teams that always play great at home, regardless of their time away. While the average fan might only know Ball State as the school where David Letterman went to college, the bettor knows the Cardinals were 40–6 at home between 1996 and 2000.

Another theory followed almost religiously early in the season is that teams with four or more returning starters that are underdogs represent good values. More than any sport, basketball relies on teamwork and cohesiveness. At the college level, where the athletes aren't nearly as good as the pros, the players' reliance on each other is intensified. Early in the year, teams that have played together for at least a season know each other's quirks and habits. Running the plays is second nature to them, while a team of newly formed pieces is still learning its way around the court. This is the principle Alan followed early in the year when he made his big bet on Stanford to beat Duke.

"But these fuckers," says Alan, referring to a rival syndicate, "who knows what they are thinking when they bet? They don't follow any of the rules. They just seem to want to bet a lot and stick out their chest so everyone knows what they are doing. Normally I'm very solid in the beginning of the year, but these guys have disrupted my system. They aren't even doing it right. Let's say a game goes up from minus-4.5 to minus-5 and every wiseguy in the city sees that it's going up to minus-5.5 because of public money, these guys are still taking it at minus-5. I'm embarrassed for them."

He's also getting beat by them. Bad. In two days he's lost three big bets—nearly $60,000—by half a point. All three were games in which this competing syndicate pushed the line just a notch above the high end of where Alan wanted to be. But bettors bet. At some point discipline, values, bankroll management, and professionalism all succumb to the addiction. And when it's early in the college basketball season and the lines are soft and this is your chance to get some easy wins, you take a few more chances. Besides, any bettor who thinks he can't will his team half-a-point has no business making numbers to begin with.

Alan can ignore only so many games he likes because some loose cannons are beating him to the punch. On November 30, like a drunk reaching for the whiskey, he decides he can't hold back anymore. Alan put low five figures on New Orleans plus-9.5 against Southern Mississippi and the same amount on then sixteenth-ranked Illinois, who were 2.5-point underdogs against seventeenth-ranked Duke. Both games were a half-point higher than his original numbers, 9 and 2 respectively, but in both cases the bets made by the syndicate he'd been tracking kept the numbers from getting any lower than where they closed. Alan was the first to confess that he'd bet against his better judgment.

With little fanfare, the New Orleans vs. Southern Mississippi game tipped off at 7:30 EST in front of 3,643 fans at the Reed Green Coliseum in the sleepy hamlet of Hattiesburg, Mississippi. Meanwhile, Illinois vs. Duke started at 7:30 EST and was the showcase game of the Big Ten/Atlantic Coast Conference showdown, an early-season tournament at the United Center in Chicago. More than 20,000 fans would file into the United Center that night, and hundreds of thousands more would watch the nationally televised game on ESPN. But to Alan, whether the games were played in a college town or boom town, whether there were 10 people in the stands or 10,000, didn't matter. A beautiful pass, a monstrous dunk, a devastating block—none of it mattered. The final score was all that counted, and waiting for it was agonizing.

Alan sat at his desk in his cavernous living room, blanketed in darkness except for a soft pillow of light coming from a desk lamp that shone on his cleanly shaven head. He was surrounded by a bank of equipment that included a fax, a phone, a computer, a ticker, a remote for the television, a remote for the CD player, and a cell phone. With the television on mute, the loudest noise in the room was the hum of the computer. In near silence and darkness, Alan read about tomorrow's matchups and incessantly checked his ticker for updates in the two games he had big bets on.

Nothing goes right for him early in the New Orleans vs. Southern Miss game, as UNO is trailing by thirteen at halftime. But Illinois is living up to its Fighting Illini nickname, thumping Duke for a 40–35 halftime lead. When Illinois pushes the lead to six with 17:25 left to play and New Orleans starts the second half strong to cut the Southern Miss lead to ten, a slight smile creeps across Alan's face. *Those greedy bastards can't take me out of my game*, he thinks, *no matter how early they bet.* But, as surely as stink follows a skunk, dread follows smugness. All Alan can think next is, *Please let these games end now. Please let them end now.*

But they don't. Southern Miss remains comfortably ahead of UNO the entire second half, which is great for the fans in Hattiesburg but painful for Alan and every other wiseguy who took UNO plus-9.5. Meanwhile Illinois, which was comfortably ahead by six points—which equals eight if you are playing the spread—gets outscored 17–4 over the next six minutes and is down by seven points with just over nine minutes to play. The once raucous crowd of 20,000 fans at the United Center is silent. The once-smug crowd of one in Las Vegas is losing it. "I'm such an idiot. I deserve a cancer. I'm an unlucky prick," he says. "I should have known better."

In Hattiesburg, Southern Miss runs out the clock on a ten-point win, beating the spread, and Alan's bet, by half-a-point. In Chicago, Duke wins 72–69. After the game, Illinois coach Lon Kruger says, "It was a good game for us to learn from."

For Alan, it was an expensive lesson. "If you make a good bet, there shouldn't ever be any random finishes like these," he says. "Normally I am so strong in the beginning of the year, but these guys have disrupted my routine. I'm doing all this fucking work and making good numbers and not getting rewarded because of these guys and their bets.

"I need to check my ego at the door and start making good decisions again. Because bad plays like tonight can just mushroom."

So can good ones, no matter how you come by them. It's early December and, as Alan is spending countless hours researching, hypothesizing, and "getting into the heads," as he says, of nearly every team from Virginia Beach to Rodondo Beach. Rodney Bosnich is just betting. He's as worried about syndicates, patterns, and early-season theories as he is with getting a real job. Which is to say not at all. What he knows is that his professional betting career is off to a much better start than his careers in construction and security administration. He finished the college football regular season by winning three $600 parlays for $1,800. With the bowl games not starting for another three weeks, and $30,000 in his bankroll, Rodney sees college basketball as the mother lode.

In addition to moving into a new apartment with Missy, which necessitated that he find new places to hide his cash, and making a resolution to find employment, Rodney has taken on a new approach to betting for college basketball. Out are the parlays that paid so handsomely all fall. In are straight bets. "Two reasons: One, I think I had been getting too lucky with the parlays and had to cut myself off. Two, basketball is my game."

Unlike Alan, who would like to bet every game on the board if not for a tiny spec of self-preservation, Rodney chooses his games with prudence. On December 1, there are twenty-five games listed in the Don Best rotation. Rodney puts money down on one game: 2–2 Florida State minus-2 over 3–3 Northwestern, at Northwestern. And again unlike Alan, Rodney's wager isn't the result of analysis and power ratings.

"That stuff is all bullshit," says Rodney. "I got this as the tip of the day off of one of the Internet newsletters I subscribe to. It said Florida State is a lock over Northwestern at minus-2."

The juxtaposition of Alan's tortured life as a bettor, a pendulum of moods dictated by his own well-crafted lines and his ability to capitalize on them, and Rodney's carefree demeanor could fill a shrink's notebook. Anyone who could commit themselves to a profession where the outcome is so arbitrary that 24 hours of work will give you no better chance of making money than a random choice plucked off the Internet must be certifiably delusional. "The gaming of humans is different than any other form of betting," says Howard Shaffer. "People who do this think it requires a skill of some sort, and they all think that sports betting is the skill they have. That is what gives them the illusion of control.

"Of course understanding the game does not mean you can pick a winner. And that is what sets you up for problems."

To have bet and lost feels better than never having bet at all. At least that is how Rodney sees it. Which is why he decides that his normal $200 bet won't do. Alone in his prefabricated apartment, with unpacked boxes littering the floor and the video game system tangled on the ground in front of the television, Rodney finds the shoebox full of cash that he has yet to hide. He pulls out a $5,000 brick of one-hundred dollar bills held together by a rubber band, and he counts off $700, more than triple the amount he's wagered on a single game since he's been in Las Vegas.

"I am only betting what I can afford," he says. "Then again, I am not really worried about money right now."

He's still not when the night is over, after Florida State easily beats Northwestern 60–46. With his choices that night narrowed to collecting his loot or getting high and unpacking, Rodney drives 20 minutes to the Stardust and cashes in his ticket. As he walks out of the book and into the dark parking lot, $700 richer, he thinks to himself: Can it really be this easy?

At 8 A.M. on a mid-December Saturday morning in Las Vegas, a crisp chill still hung in the desert air. The sky canopied the Strip in an icy blue, enjoying its finest hour before the sun and heat and pollution blanched its color. Four hours earlier, Las Vegas Boulevard was bumper-to-bumper on the street and sneaker-to-sneaker on the sidewalks. But now it feels as though the town itself is sleeping off its hangover.

The biggest disadvantage to being on West Coast time and being the only state in the Union where sports betting is legal is the early morning start times of the East Coast games. While most of Vegas sleeps, the diehards have crawled out of bed, out from under a bar stool, or come straight from the airport to get action down on the nine o'clock games. The gambling-away-your-life-savings-on-a-hunch scenario plays better when it's 4 A.M. and you're drunk then when you are stone-cold sober and the sky is a bright blue.

Walking into the poorly lit, windowless, airless rooms before breakfast feels like you're following Alice through the hole into Wonderland. One minute you're warming in the morning sun and desert air; the next you're surrounded by television sets, the smell of cold sweat, and a group of people that remind some of the bar scene in *Star Wars*. "You are not dealing with a country club set here," says bettor Dave Malinsky. "Walk through the book and there are a lot of degenerates. I mean, we are really only one or two levels away from being subhuman. We're damn near close to being circus freaks."

In the 1980s, the Hilton Hotel on Paradise, one block east of the Strip, aimed to be the circus freaks' most welcome big top, building what it called the Race & Sports Superbook. The only thing "super" about the book has been the criticism against it. Like at most books, the majority of the space in the Hilton's football-field-sized room is dedicated to horse racing. But, unlike most books, the Hilton hasn't adjusted the seating ratio to reflect sports betting's growing dominance. Only about one-quarter of the amenities—including chairs, televisions, and betting windows—accommodate sports wagering. And, instead of a wall-size board listing all the games available for betting, the Hilton's lines scroll across several small television screens behind the betting counter, which leaves players herded like hungry cattle near the TVs, waiting impatiently for the number they're interested in to roll by.

As nine A.M. approaches, tip-off time for the day's first game, Stanford visiting Georgia Tech, a quartet of college-aged guys stumble into the book. Wearing standard-issue prep uniforms—khaki shorts, backward baseball hats, T-shirts—they sit in the combination chair/desks neatly arranged in rows in front of the book's banquette of small-screen TVs. They're sucking on bottles of Budweiser, and, with their game notes spread out on the desks, pens in hand, and bloodshot eyes, they look like they just rolled out of bed for an early morning class. Behind them the bar is stacked high with sandwiches while, nearby, a makeshift picnic table serves as a beer stand, where a fresh keg is constantly being tapped. It may be morning in Las Vegas, but it's late enough for a beer somewhere.

For the uninitiated, watching sports early in the day is unsettling. Even noon may be too early, exemplified by the sparse crowd at Atlanta's Phillips Arena, where the Stanford vs. Georgia Tech game is being played. There are so few people in the stands that the game between two of the biggest programs in college basketball looks and sounds like a public access broadcast of a local high school matchup. Viewers can hear every sneaker squeak, every scream uttered by a coach, and every groan exploding from a player's mouth. The early start time seems to have thrown the players off their game. At two different points in the first half, Georgia Tech goes five minutes without scoring and then—after making one shot—back to four minutes without scoring. They shoot a meager 36 percent from the field; lucky for them, Stanford, ranked third in the country, shoots just 31 percent, and 16 percent from three-point land. At halftime, Georgia Tech actually leads 24–23; a nightmare for people who bet Stanford, the 6.5-point favorite, of which there appear to be as many sitting in the book as there are fans in the stadium.

Goldfish have a memory that resets itself every thirty seconds, which means every thirty seconds they forget they've eaten. Any fish flakes floating at the top are fair game, occasionally causing the fish to burst from overeating. Ultimately, the beauty of watching games in the sports book is how easily nightmares like the Stanford vs. Georgia Tech first half are immediately replaced by more pressing issues in other contests. That's because, except for the smell of smoke in your clothes, nothing sinks in. There are so many games—so many flashing graphics—the brain's synapses are constantly firing, erasing any short-term memory.

Seasoned pros like Lupo and Scucci, however, are immune to the goldfish syndrome. And they can't forget the first half of the Stanford vs. Georgia Tech game, the $2,000 the Stardust has on the Stanford side, nor the nearly $10,000 that will remain in play because of parlays if Georgia Tech covers. "Basically, this is the type of game that kills you," says Lupo. "Whether you are a bettor or bookmaker. Too many freshmen, too early in the season. It's just no good."

With four minutes left and Stanford down three points, freshman Casey Jacobson leads the Cardinal on two fast breaks. On the first, Jacobson drives by two Tech defenders for an easy layup. On the second, he threads a bounce pass between two Tech players, a play that belies a freshman's instincts; a savvy move pulled off in a pressure situation by a kid in his first month of college basketball. When the run is over, thanks to a three-pointer following one of the fast breaks, Stanford is up by three with 3:26 left.

"This is when it gets karmically tricky," Scucci says. "When it's close like this you start thinking you are gonna be the one who forces destiny today."

With time running out, a Stanford freshman fouls a senior who hasn't missed a free throw all year on a three-point play, giving the underdog a chance to tie it. Suprisingly, the senior chokes and, as the game winds down, Stanford is up by four with 27.5 seconds left. Of course, being up four points isn't enough for most who bet on the game. How, they wonder, can Stanford keep Georgia Tech from scoring, get the ball back, score themselves, and then do the same thing again in the next 27.5 seconds? It will be especially difficult given that, presumably, none of the players care if they score another three points to cover.

"Basically," says Scucci. "The only chance we got is overtime."

And, on a miracle three-pointer by Georgia Tech's Tony Atkins to tie the game with one second left, that is what Scucci gets.

But, in OT, Scucci's will seems to lose some of its magic. Neither team scores for the first 2:17 of the 5:00 extra session. With a little more than a minute left and only up by one point, Stanford still has a shot to win, but those who need the favorite to cover will finish out of the money. When Georgia Tech's last two shots rattle in and out in the waning seconds, Stanford walks away a winner. Lupo and Scucci walk away feeling cursed.

For the first month of the season, this has been a familiar pattern for the Stardust. All the good work done during the college football season is being eaten away by missed free throws and miscalculations on their part. "We'll make 90 good lines and 10 bad ones," says Lupo. "But the wiseguys will always find the 10 bad ones and pile on." It's still the small-college games that cost the Stardust the most. "We win Arizona vs. Michigan State but then we get beat on Kent and Wisconsin Green Bay. Are you kidding me?" Lupo says. "Most people can't tell you the nicknames of those two teams. Forget that, they can't even tell you where they are, even if you spot them Wisconsin and Green Bay. But they know who was favored. That kills me to lose that game."

The losses are miniscule, only $10,000–$15,000 a game at the most, compared to $50,000 a game on football. But on college football, there are so many games getting big action, the books can make up the loss in one game. With college basketball, only the wiseguys laying down thousands bet the small-college games. The public plays it safe on teams they know like Arizona and Michigan State. And in the big games the house usually comes out ahead. But a $5,000 win on a big-name game doesn't eliminate a $10,000 loss on the teams no one knows. Five-thousand-dollar losses coupled with $2,000 losses like Stanford can strip away profits like acid on skin.

"We are expected to win less in basketball season," says Lupo. "But right now we are not winning at all."

The Stardust reached its zenith with Lefty Rosenthal (later played by Robert DeNiro in the movie version of *Casino*) in the 1970s and had been declining since he was kicked out in the early 1980s. Bookmakers Scotty Shetler and Richard Saber helped turn the book around, adding features like the world's first, and only, sports-handicapping library that posts stats and scores from games around the country. Even now the library is consistently packed with novice handicappers looking to find the edge. But when new owners took over, they felt the Shetler and Saber reeked of the old regime and old Vegas. They were too friendly with the wiseguys, too loose with the numbers, and too quick to take a quick bet. The two bookmakers were fired.

It didn't behoove Alan to have a couple of corporate-appointed bookmakers come in and ruin the wiseguy-friendly atmosphere Shetler and Saber cultivated. He made a T-shirt mocking the executive in charge of the Stardust sports book named Stan Roth. For that stunt, Alan was asked not to bet at the Stardust anymore. Years later, when Scucci and Alan crossed paths while shooting pool one night at a local dive, Scucci commented on how much he liked Alan's purple Corvette. Alan said, "Thanks. Tell Stan thanks, too, since the Stardust paid for it." (When Scucci told Stan about Alan's car, Stan responded, "At least he got it in the Stardust's colors.")

As the gloaming descends on Las Vegas that same Saturday as the Georgia Tech vs. Stanford game, Alan stands at his gray marble kitchen counter wrapping Chanukah presents for his family. He will also send his father, mother, and sister $2,500 each. "What am I gonna do with it? I'll just blow it. That's why I never have any money even though I make so damn much," he says. "Besides, they can use it more than I can."

While a Washington State vs. Utah game plays on television he hears how badly the books are doing today, and he lets out an undeniably wicked chuckle. "Everything is falling on the number today," he says. "The books should get killed. Outsmarting them is a snap, I have no fucking sympathy for them."

The five o'clock games are minutes away and, with the lights dimmed, the big screen TV's volume on high, and Alan incessantly screaming about this bet or that, the plush and cavernous living room feels eerily like a sports book, only this book is built for one. The phone is his ticket window, open twenty-four hours a day.

"Three dimes, five dimes, seven dimes, eight dimes, whatever," he barks into the speaker. "Fine, three dimes at 1.5 and 8 dimes at 1 everywhere else for Southern Miss over UL Lafayette."

Alan already has $12,000 on the game. But on a Saturday afternoon, in the rush of the moment, holding back is harder than pulling a tugboat in with twine. "It's a lot," Alan adds. "But it's exam time, so homecourt won't help Lafayette. What the fuck, do they even *have* exams in Louisiana?"

Minutes later he puts $6,000 on University of Arkansas–Little Rock at plus-30 against Oklahoma. Alan is going for the middle here, since he already has $6,000 on Oklahoma at minus-26. If the game lands on 27, 28, or 29, he wins $12,000.

But the game that most piques his interest is Baylor vs. Marquette. The bet is nominal, a few dimes at the most. But Alan felt great about the handicapping. With the only tangible reward in betting being financial, and because the games are so fickle, good work can go unpaid as easily as bad work gets rewarded. Sometimes personal satisfaction about making a good number can be as fulfilling as winning a bet. Marquette closed the game as a two-point favorite, but Alan actually had Baylor power rated as one point better. Checking his ticker he noticed that Baylor had gone up by four with a minute left in the game. Normally, he'd wouldn't watch, but compelled by the satisfaction of actually seeing his prediction ring true, he turns on the game.

When Baylor goes up by 4 with 20 seconds left, he thinks he's won. Then Marquette hits a three-pointer, to cut the lead to one. Baylor answers with two free-throws, extending the lead to three again. With 2.6 seconds left, Alan is convinced that the betting gods are against him. Marquette may only be hitting 27 percent of its three-pointers in the game, but it's a guarantee they'll hit this one to tie it. And, with no time left, they do.

"How can they let a guy get a shot off?" Alan complains. "Go fucking mug him. It's disgusting, fucking disgusting. You know they are gonna shoot that."

Alan picks up the phone, screams out an account number, and, out of disgust, bets $3,000 on Southern Cal to beat Loyola Marymount.

He slams the phone down and says, "That will be a table smasher if we lose that one." Even the sight of Oklahoma being up by twenty-seven over UALR with thirty seconds left, which puts Alan in position to win his $12,000 middle, can't change his mood. "Nothing matters now. This is so pathetic. Real great psychologically going into OT."

Alan can't bear to watch the OT. Baylor however, seems completely composed. It jumps out to an early lead. When Alan reads on his ticker that Baylor is up by five with six seconds left, he finally feels comfortable enough to watch his bet come in. And, in a sign that not every karmic soul is conspiring against his bets, Oklahoma wins by twenty-seven points.

"This," he says. "is full torture."

One of Alan's rules about his gambling: Never bet on a game in which a team you've lost two bets in a row on is playing. That's why, as he cruises down the highway at 80 mph, he's disgusted with himself after hanging up his cell phone. "I can't believe I just did that," he says.

"Fullerton State has killed me their last two games, but I just bet UC–Santa Barbara plus-5 against them. I should get a cancer for betting that game."

Alan's every action has an equal and contradictory reaction. For all the talk about getting sick, hating himself, and wanting to quit, Alan's purest form of happiness comes when he is sweating out a game. He'll berate himself and the human race one second, then hand out gifts to musicians he barely knows. He'll spew hurtful words at anyone engaging him in small talk, but greet the owner of the Thai restaurant he eats at three nights a week in the language of the owner's homeland. He's not selfish, but his skill lends nothing of value to society, which makes him appreciate even more those whose do. Those who contribute good music, good food, good movies, and good books to the world have his undying devotion. He once tracked down Roger Ebert in a hotel lobby to thank him for recommending the film *Gates of Heaven*. He loved reading a betting column in *New York Daily News* by a writer named Jim McCarthy because of his pithy wordplays. When he first started listening to jazz, he showed up at the WBUR radio studios in Boston around 3 A.M. to give the host of the Jazz program "All Night Long," James Isaacs, a tape he made of James Moody at Sweet Basil in New York City. He's a bettor annoyed by his own greed and awed by anyone who has a gift they can share.

"I'd love to retire, go back to school, get another degree, and teach high school," Alan says. For a second he takes his eyes off the sports pager and loses himself in the thoughts. "But I can't, I'm too dumb. My mind is mush. I've got nothing to give. I'd love to save more and not bet my balls off on the Stanley Cup and NBA Finals. But I need to make as much as I can because I want to live in Maine for the summer and keep my house out here and drive a Corvette and buy horses. That's my lifestyle."

As is the uncertainty of knowing whether you'll be broke when its over. That's what he likes best of all. The Fullerton State vs. UC–Santa

Barbara is his swing game: If UCSB covers the five-point spread, he'll win for the week. If not, he'll be a loser.

With each second that passes he begs the ticker for an update. "Come on, come on," he says. "Turn over." When he sees some new scores scrolling down, he positions his thumb over a portion of the tiny screen where final outcomes are listed. This way the suspense factor is in full effect. When he sees the names of the two teams, he'll pull his thumb back to reveal the scores. This thrill brings him back again and again.

"I love sweating the games," he says, ignoring his spicy tofu.

Finally, he sees the names "UCSB" and "Fullerton State" on the ticker. He pulls his thumb back. A smile creeps across his face. He pops a piece of tofu in his mouth, and full of satisfaction, announces the score: "Fullerton State 67, UCSB 63."

He's a winner. Today.

Chapter 10

Take Me Home

It wasn't a good day. Tech almost gave me a heart attack. Duke almost gave me a heart attack. South Florida did give me a heart attack. And then there was the stupid Texas game.

I'm getting gray hair because of this. I'm twenty years old and I have gray hairs from half-points. I'm too young to have gray hairs, it's ridiculous. And I actually won $750 yesterday.

—RODNEY BOSNICH, DECEMBER 1999

odney Bosnich made the call for help in December, a mayday from the middle of the desert. He wanted out of Las Vegas and out of the morass his life had become. He and Missy were fighting all the time because, while she worked thirty hours a week and went to school, Rodney ignored the Sunday want ads she begged him to read. Mostly they fought because he was lonely. The gamblers' mantra is that they want to do what they want when they want to do it. They don't want office jobs, bosses, or even security. But adhering to that independence comes at a cost. An unwillingness to make sacrifices for a relationship doesn't endear you to those who are. That's what Rodney is learning.

He has chewed his fingernails so low that puffy chunks of skin balloon over each massacred nail. His stomach is rounder by twenty pounds than it was six months ago, and his preternaturally cherubic face is fuller. He has stopped playing basketball completely. While Missy is at work or studying, Rodney sits alone in his apartment, smoking dope and playing with his cats. On Friday nights he'll watch the show *Sabrina the Teenage Witch*, which features a talking feline. While watching, he'll sit on his couch in a marijuana-induced haze, convinced that his own cats, Sammy and Ike, are speaking to him. During the day, he'll get high some more and throw a ball, watching Sammy and Ike chase it down like a mouse. "If not for the two cats," he says. "I would be bored to death."

But on the day Rodney calls for help, he is stone-cold sober. At the other end of the line his mom can hear the fear in his voice. For months he had been telling his parents how great life had been. His friends keep asking him to lay down their money on whatever he bets. He is up nearly $30,000 since moving. A hard day at work means watching three college football games and a couple of college basketball games. But, other than his cats, his social interaction is limited to the "who you like tonight" chitchat with sports book ticket writers, a job he can't even get. With the holidays three weeks away, he sees that his life is empty.

When he left Munster in May he did it to break away from the monotony of life in a midwestern town that's best days went the way of the Industrial Revolution. Had he stayed, his path would have been crystal clear. He'd be a cop, or a teacher. He'd spend all his time with his high school buddies at the same bar. If he wanted to bet he would need a bookie, and there's no guarantee that he'd ever get paid. "I'd rather be thought of as a degenerate in Vegas than stuck doing that all my life in Munster," Rodney once said. "Those people need to get a life."

Now, he's wondering if he needs to do the same.

"Ma, I don't want to be here anymore," he says. "Me and Missy aren't getting along, and it's stupid for me to stay if it's gonna be like this."

Rodney left college because he was tired of working at it. He left Munster so he could bet without having his parents hassle him about getting a job. Now his mom was hearing him say it was too hard to live with his girlfriend and he wanted to come back. Before he moved to Vegas she told him it would be hard for him and Missy to sustain their relationship because they were both so young. Six months later, her son is finally hearing her.

"Honey, you can come home," she answered. "But you're gonna have to get a real job if you wanna live here. You can't just gamble."

That stung like salt in a wound.

Rodney's mom told him to think about coming home for a week. But it didn't take that long for him and Missy to have another blowout. That night Rodney packed his bag and, at 3 A.M., set out for Indiana. Twenty minutes later he was back on the Strip, playing cards and weighing his choices. Driving thirty hours starting at 3 A.M. wasn't an option. Working wasn't an option either. He liked gambling and the gambling industry. As the sun came up four hours later and Rodney had run through the $200 he started with, he stepped away from the table and drove back to his apartment. He needed some rest. There would be games to bet on tomorrow.

There's no time that's so sacred it can't be spent in the sports book. No time that it's inappropriate to think of getting a dime down on the New Orleans Saints vs. Dallas Cowboys. No time when settling into a not-so-comfy seat to have a not-so-cold beer with guys you know not-so-well could be better spent with family. Especially when the guys in the book—the runners, the bookmakers, the cocktail waitress selling lighted souvenirs—are the closest thing you've got to family. They're the people you see everyday, who you trade laughs with when you win and cry with when you lose. As Christmas Eve approaches, a meaningless football game winds down on TV, the

Strip is lulled to sleep by Christmas carols, and the dozen or so creatures nestled into the Stardust sports book stay put. They've got nowhere else to go.

"I actually can't believe they are here," says Lupo, who's sitting at his desk going over the December and year-end numbers. "There are a lot of lonely people out there and this is their life, their family. The sports book is all they know. It makes me sad. And a little scared."

When Scucci arrived at 6:30 in the morning there were already ten people lined up waiting to get money down on the Saints vs. Cowboys game. The year before on Christmas Eve Day, gamblers showed up out of habit, even though there wasn't a single game scheduled. They kept asking Scucci, who opened a couple of windows so people could bet on futures, when he was going to post the day's lines. Finally Scucci copied the December 24 page from the rotation that read, "No Game Scheduled." "They ran from the bathroom for the sheets," remembers Scucci. "Like it was food or something."

Every year during the holidays, the regulars bring Lupo and Scucci gifts. Lem Banker, one of the most renowned wiseguys in town, offers cheap brass rings and fake gold bracelets. Others drop off bottles of wine and baskets of cookies. This year, the week before Christmas, a bettor asked Lupo and Scucci if he could take them to lunch. "We can't say no to anyone," says Scucci. "But we had no idea who this guy was. Joe finally just asked him his name."

Sympathy for the pathetic souls sharing nachos and hot dogs the night before Christmas comes easy to Lupo because his life is so full. He's a father with a steady job that brings in good pay and, in Las Vegas at least, is well respected. When his day is done he'll see his kids tear into a warm Christmas Eve meal and watch them fight off sleep because they're anxious to open their presents. But, he's still in the midst of a divorce, partially brought on by his dedication to the sports book. What does he have? A solid line, a close win, credit—and cash— for beating the bastards across the counter, the bond formed with

Scucci and Korona everyday as they make the lines. Contempt for the pathetic souls sharing nachos and hot dogs the night before Christmas comes easy to Lupo because he's so close to joining them.

The holidays are an especially nervous time of year for Lupo, as familial responsibilities collide with budget pressures brought on by the end of the month and year. Unlike October and November, which are plump with winning opportunities because of college and pro football, December's handle isn't as high. Except for the bowl games, college football is over. And college baskets won't get serious play from the public until after New Year's. "You need every penny this month. It's vital we hit our mark at this property," says Lupo. Things are even tougher, he explains, because "there has been such a decline across the board in the rest of the hotel's business." The pressure manifests itself physically in neck and jaw cramps. By November, a year's worth of strain has Lupo's head on a swivel, as he twists and stretches his neck every couple of minutes, as though his tie is strangling him.

Christmas Day is the hardest. Because the bowl games start so early, there's no time to settle in, have a cup of coffee, pick at Christmas dinner leftovers and open presents. That first game is critical. Win it and the rest of the day is a joy. Lose it and the cramps take hold like a vice. The kids might say something funny and make him forget for a minute, but only for a minute. He'll be making small talk with relatives and all the while be itching to turn on the television. Outwardly he looks and sounds normal. But he wonders why no one notices how uncomfortable he is, how he's fidgeting on the couch like an addict in withdrawal. Inside he feels like demons are looking to make a break for it through his throat.

"My in-laws once noticed something wasn't right, and they asked me what happened," says Lupo. "I told them we just lost $100,000 on a game. Immediately, they start worrying that I am gonna lose my job. I once made the same mistake with my mom, telling her we lost $200,000 on a New Year's Day. She called the next day all nervous.

They don't have a concept of the money we are dealing with. You lose and you get depressed.

"I don't want to be preoccupied at Christmas. I want to pay attention to my family. But it's hard when we have so much money riding on these games."

This year he may get lucky. Unless they suffer a fluke losing streak the last week of December, the Stardust is on pace for it's second highest hold total ever—possibly more than $4 million. Considering the book lost money on the Super Bowl, underperformed during the baseball season, and has had a losing start in college basketball, the output is remarkable. It's a testament to the attention Lupo, Scucci, Korona, and the other bookmakers paid to even the most meaningless games.

As he sifts through the budget printouts, a football game plays silently on TV and the frosting on a Krispy Kreme donut on his desk slowly melts. The normally stoic Lupo allows himself a smile. Maybe this Christmas, there won't be any games posing as the Grinch.

At the sports book in the Desert Inn the players are so desperate for action they are watching Alpine ski races with disabled skiers. (This is truly a new, perverse definition of handicapping.) The quartet of guys in front of the televisions sit mesmerized by the one-legged and one-armed athletes swooshing down the slopes. They should be so active.

The DI is a classic Las Vegas monument, and, for an old-school gambler like Alan Boston, it's a shrine to the way Vegas used to be. Legendary gangster Moe Dalitz opened the place in 1950 and, along with the Sands, the Sahara and the Flamingo, it catered to the Hollywood hotshots, Mafia kingpins, and powerful politicos whose convergence in Vegas during the 1950s and 60s helped make the town worthy of the name Sin City. Howard Hughes loved the DI so much that, in 1967, rather than vacate the top floor of suites so Dalitz could accommodate his big players coming in for the holidays, he bought the entire property.

But today, the DI's mainstays are the same people who stayed here during the glory days of the 1950s and 60s. On a Saturday night, the floor of the casino is no more crowded than it is on a Monday morning. Located too far down the strip for overflow from the Bellagio or Caesars Palace, and too antiquated to attract a younger crowd, the DI might as well be an abbreviation for dinosaur. (In fact, Vegas mogul Steve Wynn closed the hotel in August of 2000.)

While Alan rails against the notion that no one appreciates the legacy and history of a place like the DI, on this particular weekend it suits his needs perfectly. Like he does every Christmas, Alan's dad, Norman, has made the trek out to Vegas for what he says is a much-needed week of gambling. In reality, he comes out to watch his son the wiseguy get treated like a big shot around town. He's certainly not disappointed at the DI and the complimentary suite he gets, courtesy of his son's large line of credit with the hotel. When Alan went by to pick up his father shortly after his arrival, he called up to the room and there was no answer. The suite was so big that each room had a different phone number. Norman would hear the ringing in one room but he kept answering the wrong phone.

The two gifts Alan cherishes most—his love of horses and his need for gambling—are inherited from his father. Norman never made much money in his work as a manager at a Framingham, Massachusetts, lumberyard and as a Boston cabdriver, but there was always something left over for the track. Nothing irresponsible, just some action for a little interest, a good sweat on the horses at Foxboro. When his son was just two years old, Norman took him to the track and helped him place a $2 bet. As Alan grew older, Norman brought him along to penny-ante card games with the boys. The games of risk became so common that the lines between what was acceptable and what was downright stupid blurred into one. At 10, Alan and some friends took his mom's car from the garage and headed for the track. Even now Alan's mom, Phyllis, is thankful for the fender bender that stopped her son from blowing his life savings on the ponies. In high school, while his parents were away, Alan took a jaunt to Atlantic City. He came back $500 in the hole and had to borrow money from his parents' friends so he could pay off some debts without his parents finding out.

"I truly believe if not for his father," says Phyllis, "Alan wouldn't be doing this at all."

"I take responsibility for it," admits Norman. "I gave him that gene. I took him to the track, talked to him about horses and how they should be trained and driven."

After graduating from Penn, Alan moved back home and lived with his mom. His parents were estranged and on the way toward divorce. "He wasn't working at all, which I thought was weird," says Phyllis. "I think I suspected he was doing something like gambling, and he wasn't paying rent and times were tough. Then he told me and I was shocked. A kid from the University of Pennsylvania who wanted to go to medical school ends up gambling?

"Put yourself in my shoes. My son goes through an Ivy League on scholarship, and then I find out he is gambling for a profession. I said to him, 'how could you?' I told him either get a job or get out."

Even his sister, Linda, whom he read to when she had trouble in school, was ashamed of her brother. "I wasn't surprised because it had been with us our whole lives. I went to the races in my mother's belly," says Linda. "But I had a real hard time telling people. I found myself prefacing everything by saying he went to an Ivy League school. I was kind of ashamed to say he was a gambler because everyone thinks gamblers are such degenerates."

The one person who understood was Norman. His son's career choice wasn't a waste of an Ivy League education, it was a validation of the elementary education earned at his father's knee in the classrooms at Foxboro. His son wanted into his world and he was flattered. Alan could be everything as a gambler Norman never could. While Norman shook with nervousness if he laid down more than $25 at a time, Alan tossed around money with abandon. The father always bet knowing he had a family to support. The son would bet with no conscience, like a burglar unafraid of the consequences.

Years after Alan had established himself as a player, he took his dad to shoot some craps. As the chips piled high and Alan talked trash, his dad stood quietly by his shoulder. On a ten-minute roll with the dice, Alan's chips, and thus fortunes, moved up and down like an EKG. When he turned around to check on his father, Norman was pasty white and shielding his eyes. He couldn't bear to watch his son blow it all. He couldn't believe what he had created.

Norman's room at the DI, courtesy of his son the player, is bigger than his apartment in Boston. The bar seats four comfortably, speakers are built into the wall, the dining-room table seats six and—"Check this out," Norman says sounding like a kid with a new toy, "the blinds are mechanical." The jacuzzi and steam room even has a phone in it. "I barely touched the jelly beans, fruit and nut basket that they just gave to me," he says. "That was just too much."

"My dad loves that I'm a gambler," Alan says. "He's proud that I'm successful and respected in the industry. To him that is the best you can do."

He pauses at the door of his father's two-bedroom penthouse suite and looks back at the digs. "My mom learned to accept it also," he adds. "After I got her a room like this one at the Mirage."

But even Alan's dad, as much as he wanted to spend time with his son the gambler, was wary about coming to Las Vegas during the college basketball season. "I want to do what I want when I want, which is why I have stayed away from relationships to begin with," Alan says. "It's also why I don't like having my dad here. But he likes to come, so what can I do? But even a ten-minute distraction from my routine can be difficult for my betting." Even a minute lost from doing research, missing a change on the ticker that might give him insight into the game's flow, can cause his already tense body to tighten up even more. The tension spills out in fits of rage against himself, against visitors, against anything or anyone that wreaks havoc with his focus.

Alan's first apartment in Nevada was a one-bedroom rental in Henderson, a posh suburb about twenty minutes from The Strip. He had lived there for three months when his sister Linda was passing through town on the way to a ski trip. "I can remember he didn't have any furniture at all," says Linda. "All he did was sleep and go to the book. He hadn't bothered getting any furniture or cups or glasses. I couldn't drink anything for twenty-four hours because he didn't have any cups." Even today, in his spacious new house, the amenities are irrelevant. A foldable card table and aluminum chairs fill the kitchen, a punching bag and exercise bike greet visitors in the expansive foyer. Except for the beds in his room and the guest room, his desk in the living room, and one black leather couch and matching chair, the house is devoid of any furniture. It's designed to accommodate as few guests as possible, eliminating any potential distractions.

Fortunately for Alan, there was a relatively light schedule of games while his dad was in town. "As disgusting as the NCAA and college basketball are these days," Alan says. "They still can't fuck around during exam times." The last week of the year also gives wiseguys a break during the grind of the college basketball season. Schools are on vacation, and, in addition, there are fewer games as teams get in the final weeks of practice before they start their conference schedules. For the bettors and athletes alike, conference games present the biggest challenge. This is when the big mismatches and easy pickings of Oklahoma vs. Arkansas–Little Rock gives way to the slim pickings of Oklahoma vs. Kansas. Alan joked during the summer how he'd bet that when Indiana and Purdue played the next February, no matter what their records going into the game were, neither team would be favored by more than four. He won't stop thinking about the games—

that would be like the Pope taking the day off from worshiping God—but he can shoehorn in a dinner or two with his dad. At the very least.

On Christmas Eve, Alan arrives at the DI to pick up his father a little early and settles in at a $5 blackjack table. He changes several thousand dollars and gets back some green $25 chips, black $100 chips, and purple $500 chips in return. Arranged in front of him, the chips look like a bruise. Every bet he makes is for $300 or more, and it seems every one is close. For nearly an hour Alan goes one-on-one with the dealer, who apparently knows him well enough not to be offended by the insults and razor-sharp one-liners slung his way whenever Alan loses a bet. At one point, the dealer shows a face card and, as is customary, asks Alan if he'd like insurance against the chance the dealer has blackjack. Accepting the insurance would limit Alan's loss if the dealer does draw 21. "I don't have health insurance, auto insurance, or home insurance," replies Alan. "I don't need blackjack insurance." And then he loses the hand.

Alan cashes in $1,000 more for chips and loans $300 to a friend named Kenny in town with Norman. Over the next four hands, Alan puts $500 in bets down each time, tossing out the chips like they aren't even worth the plastic they're made of. And each time he draws a twenty, only to lose three of those hands to the dealer's twenty-one.

"Thank God my dad didn't watch this," Alan says as he leaves the table. "He can't stand watching me gamble. Ironic, huh?"

While changing Alan's remaining chips for twenty $100 bills, the older woman behind the gold-plated, metal security bars at the register absentmindedly asks him how he's doing. She's kind-looking with large, octagonal, violet-colored glasses, and a brassy blonde hairdo. Her tone of voice welcomes winners and losers to trade their chips for cash and hardly betrays that she's cheerily asked dozens of customers today how they are doing. She genuinely seems to care.

"I'm ambivalent," Alan answers.

"What do you mean?" she innocently asks.

"Basically, I'm a little sick in the head and don't always feel so great," he says.

Trying her best to be polite—she is after all in the customer service industry—but visibly uncomfortable, the sweet old lady, smiling and counting out Alan's cash, says "You look okay to me."

"Well," he responds. "How do you know? I'm not taking my medicine." With a flourish, he pulls himself up by the metal bars and, like Jack Nicholson poking his head through the bathroom door in *The Shining*, sticks his face through the grates, and growls.

Christmas morning, a Saturday, breaks like any other weekend day at the Stardust. That's what makes the scene even sadder for Scucci. By 9 A.M., husbands and wives sit at the sports book's desk, filling out parlay cards with their pencils, looking like students taking the SATs. As usual, the line when Scucci opened an hour earlier stretched eighty feet from the counter to the back of the book. The Stardust waitress in her black skirt and tray of lighted souvenirs makes her rounds, barking "cigarettes, lighted souvenirs," and toying with a yo-yo while she walks. Her dexterity—the ability to see through the lighted roses standing tall in her tray, dodge the drunken fools in the book, carry a heavy load and keep the yo-yo moving—is remarkable.

How could nothing be different on Christmas Morning, Scucci wonders. Why don't these people go be with their families? On Christmas Eve it was so slow that Korona put on a tape of the first Evander Holyfield–Lenox Lewis heavyweight championship that took place the previous March. During the prefight breakdown, the few people loitering in the book asked Korona if they could get a bet down. *Come on people*, Scucci thinks. *It was a tape.*

Just then a man in his midthirties walks into the book with his six-year-old son. He's on his way to his in-laws' house, his wife and daughter still in the car. He needs to get a bet down on the Aloha Bowl between Wake Forest and Arizona State later that day. He says his son wanted to see the sports book, but, rather than flout the laws, which don't allow minors in the book, the father leaves the boy in the back, pats him on the head, wags a finger in his face admonishing him to stand still, and walks up to the counter to make his bet.

What's so disconcerting to Scucci is that there are no games on TV this early on Christmas Morning. Not even pregame shows. Not even races at any of the tracks simulcasted in the book. All the televisions usually dedicated to racing are showing Saturday morning cartoons. The screens usually showing games have a rerun of Sportscenter's year-end special. The most heartbreaking moment of the show involves the story of the Columbine High School football team. That December, seven-and-a-half months after the massacre in which two Columbine students went on a shooting spree that took the lives of nine students and one teacher and themselves, the Columbine Rebels won the Colorado State Football Championship, the school's first state title. The piece focuses on the one player who was lost that spring, Matt Kechter, and the tattoo bearing his initials that his best friend and teammate, Zach Rauzi, had embedded in his skin. The customers in the book silently watch. For a moment, they have found perspective.

It's fleeting.

The silence is shattered by the crackling static over the PA system that preludes any change in the lines. "Game 106, Lions, minus-4.5," Scucci announces apologetically, knowing he ruined the moment. Then he shrugs and adds, "Don't think Christmas or anything else is gonna stop people from betting."

There are two NBA games to bet on Christmas Day, one NFL game, two college bowl games and a meaningless college all-star contest called the Blue-Gray game. At one point during the day, someone saunters up to the counter and asks Scucci, "You gonna post a halftime on the Blue-Gray game?"

"I'll tell you what," Scucci says, leaning his elbows on the counter so he can get closer to the bettor. "If you can name one player on either team, I'll do it."

The bettor walked away.

"We need the underdogs from here on out, every bowl game until the end of the year. Even this Blue-Gray game," says Scucci. "Guys like this one [pointing to the one who just walked away] will see Gray is favored by 2.5 points and lay the points. They don't know anything about the teams, they just want to bet."

There is a lot of money floating around in the world, and a lot of sports-crazed young adults in their 20s with disposable income. For those who grew up watching ESPN, started their careers at the dawn of the internet revolution, and cashed in, the sports book is an idyllic vacation spot. But from Scucci's perspective behind the counter, that of a former gambler gone bust, they are human cash registers. "I've got no respect for the people who wager a lot of money and get cocky just because they are betting that money," says Scucci. "They are making horrible bets and that's when I get cocky and look 'em in the eye and say, 'What do you want? Anything at all, tell me how much you want to bet.'"

But Scucci can't be too cavalier. Over the phones a bet comes in taking Wake Forest plus-3 for $1,000 against Arizona State University in the Aloha Bowl. The bet, from a wiseguy whom Scucci respects, piques Scucci's curiosity. The number on that game hadn't changed in two weeks, why would someone call in with a bet on the underdog just a few hours before game time? Checking the offshore books he sees they are all listing Arizona State as the one-point favorite. He moves the number down Arizona State minus-2.5, thinking there are probably some jittery bookmakers working the holiday shift on the islands and they overreacted. Meanwhile, he can't find any information about the game concerning players being out. Then another phone bet for a dime comes in on Wake Forest. Scucci moves the number down to 1.5, where it stays until game time.

"Finally, in the pregame show, minutes before the game starts, they report that ten guys on Arizona State got food poisoning and wouldn't be playing," Scucci says. "Thank God it wasn't a regular Saturday, we would have been wide open and that guy would have had his runner in here betting nearly $10,000…" Scucci stops in midsentence, his eyes widening like an owl's at midnight. "What the fuck is…"

His voice trails off as the sound of footsteps, sprinting frantically toward the book, becomes audible. From the casino side entrance, past the Wayne Newton theater and the Handicapper's library, a black man in jeans and an untucked short-sleeve button down shirt races into the book. His arms flailing, cheeks puffed with air, and head jarring forward every time his feet hit the floor, he's running from no one.

The bettors in the book stand frozen, unable to react. If the man were carrying a gun and taking aim on stationary targets, no one would be left standing. Less than an hour ago, everyone in the book watched the Sportscenter piece about the Columbine football team's triumph after the deadly tragedy. How are they any less vulnerable right now than those students? Some people remember the talk back in November of putting armed guards on the casino floor after the killing at the Golden Gate casino, but today there's no veneer of protection, just a frightening looking man sprinting through a well-populated sports book filled with people scared stiff.

If the man were in trouble, running from the law or security or some gambler he just ripped off, he would have made a beeline for the door. The wide berth between the sports side and the race side that leads most directly to the exit was clear. Instead, he kept going straight, running full speed in between a row of chairs bolted to the ground and the built-in desks on the race side of the book. There's about eighteen inches of space separating the two. A normal-sized person walking slowly would have a hard time navigating the row without banging a hip on a chair or desk. The runners, most of whose stomachs preclude them from even trying to move between rows, spend most of their days camping out on the end seats. For a disoriented man running full speed, escaping the row unscathed is as unlikely as leaving an all-you-can-eat-buffet hungry.

Remarkably, he eludes three chairs, but the fourth takes him down like a linebacker. He hits the ground hard. He stays down for a minute. Two minutes. The people in the book slowly start moving toward him, as though he were an alien. Though of all the places an alien should choose to land, the sports book might be where he would feel most at home. Scucci grabs a phone to call security. And then, just as suddenly as he ran into the book, the fallen sprinter pops up with his arms raised high in the air, imitating a gymnasts dismount. The small crowd that had gathered around him jumps back. Faint cries of "ouch, shit, damn," erupt as they bang elbows and knees on the desks and chairs while running for cover.

Security still hasn't come. But the man appears too dazed to do any harm. He slowly walks into the center aisle, brushing himself off and nodding his head at all the eyes catching his every move. His jeans are halfway down his butt, showing the checkered-patterned boxers he's wearing. No one dares move toward him. Slowly, he walks out of the book, without even making a bet.

"Fucking motherfucker cocksucking Jaguars!" The hatred spews from Helen Finkle's mouth like oil from the Exxon *Valdez*, polluting even the raunchy air at the Stardust. Finkel is famous at the book for two things: one, being one of the few women who hangs around and knows anything about betting sports. Two, she's got a mouth that embarrasses even the lifelong sports book inhabitants. She's a classic dog lover in the Vegas sense: she would always rather bet against the favorites. "If everyone is on my side," she says, "then I get scared."

Finkel grew up in Brooklyn and spent twenty years working for Met Life insurance. One day they told her she was being transferred to New Jersey which, for a lifelong New Yorker who doesn't drive, was the equivalent of being sent to China. Instead, she took a severance package and talked her husband, a postman, into getting transferred to Las Vegas.

She had loved betting on sports since she was a teenager when her brother, then and still a bookie in Brooklyn, turned her onto it. Now her husband works weekends and she spends every Saturday and Sunday in the back row of the Stardust, betting on and swearing at every team in college and professional football. During the baseball season, she gets money down everyday. It's never more than $200 or $300 a game on football or $500 on baseball, but it's enough to keep her interested, or make her angry.

A round woman with pasty white skin and unkempt hair that crawls down her neck, Finkel always has a hard-luck loss story to tell and a fanny-pack full of cash strapped to her waist. But it's her mouth that endears her to everyone from Lupo and Scucci to the other regulars. When she's angry she has no qualms saying what everyone else in the book is thinking. It's as though she's afflicted with a case of Tourette's syndrome that shows itself only when she's losing her bets. One afternoon her tirade became so offensive another gambler sitting near her glared angrily and said, "Helen, please. There are women around."

Rodney walked into the Stardust the Sunday after Christmas—following five days at home in Indiana—and heard Finkel giving the television an earful. He sucked in the nasty verbiage like it was pure oxygen. It's good to be home, he thought.

Three weeks ago he had been on the phone with his mom, near tears, begging her to let him come home. She rebuffed his pleas unless he could live by her rules, which meant working—not betting—for a living. Wicked fights with his girlfriend were commonplace. Getting high alone was not. While he had reconciled with Missy and won enough bets to repress his homesickness, it wasn't a given he'd come back after his trip home for Christmas. Once he was home, however, he remembered why he had left.

Of the five nights he spent in Indiana, four were spent getting drunk with his high-school friends at a local dive. Unanimously they filled his ego with praise, telling him how lucky he was to be on his own, living in Vegas, making a living as a bettor. They were envious and they asked his advice because they wanted to be him. Back in high school he was the sharpshooting guard without a conscience who could bury the three with two hands in his face. Now, home again, he was the wiseguy with ice in his veins, unafraid to gamble on a meaningless college basketball game what a friend would make in a week. All his friends were gamblers. They all asked him what they should bet on. Several asked him to take their cash and bet for them in Las Vegas, keeping a percentage of the winnings for himself. The working stiffs in Munster revered the wiseguy in Vegas.

Even his parents, fatigued by the distance between them and their only son, loosened up. "My feeling now is he might as well do it when he is younger," says his father George Bosnich. "And maybe he can be successful at it. But the only guy I know of who was good was Jimmy the Greek. Eventually, he'll have to get a job with insurance and stuff, but for now it's okay."

His friends' reverential treatment, his parents growing acceptance, the fact it was just as hard to make a bet in Munster in December as it was when he left in May, made Rodney lean heavily toward going back to Las Vegas. Christmas dinner at Missy's parents house sealed the deal.

The conversation started pleasantly, as Missy's Aunt and Uncle made chitchat with their niece's boyfriend. After inquiring about Missy's school and where they lived and how they liked the weather, Missy's uncle asked Rodney how he was earning a living.

"Gambling," Rodney answered, stone-faced.

"No," the uncle laughed it off. "Really."

"Really," he repeated, suddenly imbued with confidence while defending his lifestyle. "I'm gambling."

"After that they didn't talk to me the rest of the night," Rodney says. "I could see in their eyes what they thought of my livelihood. Loser. Scum of the earth. That's fine. I'm still making money. And I'm still living with their niece."

For better or for worse, during his trip home, Rodney had gestated from a kid unsure of his choices to a young adult convinced he'd found his calling. He flew back to Las Vegas on a 7 A.M. flight the Sunday after Christmas. When his plane landed at 9:30 Las Vegas time, he headed straight for the Stardust, where the NFL games were just getting under way. The sound of Helen Finkel cursing a blue streak at the Jaguars, the stench of stale cigars, and the whiff of beer felt like a baptism.

"I had gone five days without betting," he said, taking a seat down the row from Finkel. "I was having withdrawal symptons."

Over Christmas, Rodney Bosnich had been reborn as a gambler.

Chapter 11

"We Believe Anything Is Possible"

Some people are gonna make $692.98 a week and get their paycheck every other week, and there is no fluctuation in it. You get your vacation two weeks out of the year. There is no motivation to get to work early, no motivation to stay late. As bettors however, we are constantly supplied with motivation. As we go to bed Friday night, we know Saturday morning that watching the first few plays anything is possible. We just have to stay positive and catch a couple of breaks.

We know what is probable. But we believe anything is possible. Watch the first couple of plays and see your team jump out to a lead and there is just such an emotional surge that happens. I don't know what I could ever replace it with.

—DAVE MALINSKY, JANUARY 2000

Through the first week of the year, Alan actually felt comfortable with his work thus far in the season. He survived the first three months of college basketball, and, heading into the New Year, his bankroll was up such a considerable amount that he was sure he and his partners would surpass their winnings from the year before. The conference schedules lay ahead and the three-day respite over New Year's and the first few days of 2000 had helped him regain his focus. That January morning, as the sun rose over the mountains and broke through the window shades in jagged shadows on his white carpet, Alan calmly went over the day's early college basketball games and an NFL playoff game, Buffalo vs. Tennessee. The NFL game had been the bettor's choice all week, with Tennessee opening as the 4-point favorite. Going over his bets on Saturday morning, Alan realized he was heavy on Tennessee by about $25,000. He needed to lay off some money fast.

The books all over town raise their limits during the playoffs and bowl games, therefore it would be just as easy to get even on the game as quickly as he got heavy on it. Alan picked up the phone and started making some calls to get money down on Buffalo.

"Gimme whatever the limit is on Buffalo," he'd say.

"How much you want?" the book would respond.

"You can't say enough," Alan would answer.

At three different books, Alan tried to shave off some of his baggage. But as soon as he bet at one book, the number changed all over town, and he couldn't get enough money down to truly feel comfortable.

"That one is gonna hurt me today," he says to his partner, Billy, who called in on the speakerphone. "But if we keep the bets down on college baskets, just stay disciplined, we should be okay."

"There are a lot of games," Billy answers. "We can win 'em all if we bet small."

But Alan doesn't bet small.

Before the games began, he already had:

> $20,000 on St. John's minus-4.5 over West Virginia;
> $2,000 on UCLA at minus-8.5 over Washington State;
> $13,000 on Virginia at minus-6 over Georgia Tech;
> $4,000 on Miami plus-4 against Syracuse;
> $2,000 on San Diego State plus-11 against Pacific;
> $19,000 on Georgetown minus-5.5 over Seton Hall.

Alan turns on the Georgetown game. Seton Hall is up 6–1 with less than two minutes played. "I'm a stupid fucking son of a bitch," he says and switches the channel after a Seton Hall steal. "We lost this game."

Next, he flips to St. John's vs. West Virginia, which St. John's is leading 8–5. "Alright, I like our chances better in this game."

On to Syracuse vs. Miami, where Syracuse is already winning 11–1. "That's great," Billy says sarcastically over the speakerphone. "Another good game for us."

They both realize that the Wisconsin vs. Illinois game is about to tip-off. Frantically they start working all the phones at their disposal. Cell phones, fax phones, second lines. Wisconsin is Alan's type of team, playing a fundamentally sound game that relies on defense and passing the ball until an open shot is available. Those teams are the best bets. With time winding down, Alan and Billy manage to get $20,000 down on Wisconsin at minus-1 and minus 1.5.

He checks back on the Georgetown game and the Hoyas throw the ball away. He skips to the Miami game for a few minutes and they are down thirteen. A flip to Wisconsin for a tortuous, scoreless seven-minute spell in which the Badgers go from up two points to down ten. He's losing every early game—$43,000 worth of bets—except for St. John's.

"This Illinois team is awesome," Alan says. "Just awesome. I don't know how they lost to Duke."

"I'll tell you how," Billy chimes in. "We bet on them."

And as games get ready to start at 10 A.M., 10:30, and 11:00, they will bet some more.

They're on the phone throwing out numbers like auctioneers, reacting every time the Don Best software on their computers denotes a line change.

"DePaul minus-10 for seventy dollars ($7,000)."

"Auburn minus-15 and 15.5 for twelve dimes."

"Michigan State for whatever he wants at minus-6."

"UMASS minus-6.5 for fifteen dimes."

"What do we got on DePaul?" Alan asks in the midst of the action.

"Seven dimes," Billy says.

"Alright, let's get down another 130 dollars ($13,000) and get out of the way," says Alan.

"Oh, fuck, look at this, Georgetown is only down by four," screams Billy.

"Want me to get the game on?" asks Alan.

"No, you fuck. We're much better without you watching the game."

St. John's beats West Virginia 86–74, easily covering the spread. Immediately, Alan feels bettor's remorse, thinking he should have bet more. Just as quickly he reminds himself it's good to have a little self-control.

Meanwhile, the three other games he had been keeping tabs on, Syracuse-Miami, Georgetown-Seton Hall and Illinois-Wisconsin, are all within reach with less than a minute to play. Miami is only down five, Georgetown is tied, and Wisconsin is down by one. Alan has three games on the line, two of which he's a point out of the money, and he hasn't even eaten breakfast yet.

"If we win this Miami game it's a steal. We would be stealing someone's money," says Alan.

He won't have to worry about it. Over the next forty seconds of the game, Syracuse goes on a 5–0 run, pushing their lead to ten. "They fucking play with your mind, getting that close," says Billy. "But I wouldn't want to steal anyone's money." Syracuse wins 67–55. Alan and Billy lose $4,000.

But Illinois-Wisconsin has grabbed their attention. Wisconsin had been up five with 1:31 seconds left. But two, three-point plays in a row gave Illinois a one-point lead with thirty-two seconds remaining. "Oh my God," Alan wails. "This game was a lock. This is unbelievable."

Following the second of the three-point plays, by Illinois freshman guard Frank Williams, Wisconsin slowly brings the ball up court. With eighteen seconds left, senior forward Mark Vershaw comes off a pick at the top of the key, just beyond the three-point arc. The pass is perfectly timed, and he gets the ball in shooting position. Only one problem: It's not a position he's comfortable in. He hasn't tried a three-pointer in any of Wisconsin's fourteen games. "No, no, not him," Billy screams over the phone. "Yes! Yes! Yes!" Alan screams even louder after Vershaw nails the shot. Wisconsin goes up by two, covering the spread. After a couple of missed Illinois free throws followed by Vershaw making two free throws of his own, Wisconsin wins the game 63–59. Alan and Billy win back $20,000.

"I don't know how we won that game," Alan says.

"Come on," Billy pleads. "Another easy winner for us."

"Oh yeah, we are real fucking geniuses. We could have had a million dollars on that game. We have the worst fucking luck," Alan says. "I need to eat some breakfast."

Click. The phone goes dead. For now.

By nature, a bettor is going to be inwardly optimistic but outwardly a curmudgeon. They never get the call, they always get screwed, nothing good ever happens to them. They turn self-loathing into such an intense feeling of self-hate that Hunter S. Thompson would seem chipper by their standards. But on the inside they are eternal optimists, steadfast in the belief that their greatest asset is their good luck. How else to explain the fortitude it takes to bet day after day on games that are impossible to predict? And Vegas is a town whose foundation is built on positive thinking.

On Saturday, January 8, the *Las Vegas Review-Journal* ran a front-page story titled "Positive Power," which was about the transitive impact of positive thinking. A sidebar to the story featured a quiz with questions geared to determine whether or not you are a glass half-full or half-empty kind of thinker. Right now, Alan, checking the score of the Buffalo-Tennessee NFL playoff game on his ticker and seeing that Tennessee is ahead by two with 1:48 to go, is the glass half-empty type. "I haven't got a chance in this game," he says, slamming his ticker onto an empty plate of scrambled egg whites. "I'm bet to my balls at Tennessee minus-4."

Alan takes the *Review-Journal* test, answering questions like "I hardly ever expect things to go my way" and "I rarely count on good things happening to me," by saying he strongly agrees with those statements. He scores a nine out of twenty-four possible positivity points. Another check of the Buffalo-Tennessee game, which shows Buffalo ahead 16–15 seemingly for good after kicking a field goal with sixteen seconds left, verifies that he's cursed. "I knew there was a rat in that game."

As he slips into the Corvette, thinking the money he made this morning on St. John's and Wisconsin has been wiped out by his Buffalo-Tennessee loss, the cell phone rings.

"They're not gonna overturn it," Billy screams before Alan can even say hello.

"What?"

"The touchdown, they are not gonna overturn it."

"Who scored?" Alan asks.

In the time it took Alan to leave a tip for the waitress and walk to his car, three minutes tops, Tennessee had engineered one of the greatest comebacks in NFL history. On the ensuing kickoff after Buffalo's field goal putting them ahead 16–15, Tennessee tight end Frank Wycheck found himself with the ball at his own twenty-five-yard-line. With the Buffalo special teams converging, he lateraled across the field to wide receiver Kevin Dyson, a last-minute replacement on the play for an injured teammate. Dyson sprinted down the sideline untouched for a touchdown, giving Tennessee the lead 21–16 with seconds left. Barring two miracles in a row, Alan has gone from pessimist to optimist, test scores be damned.

"Well forget about holding back now," he tells Billy as he guns the

Corvette while merging onto the highway. "Open it up because we can bet anything we want."

Like Arizona plus-6.5 against Stanford for $13,000. A win.

Or Missouri plus-10 against Iowa State for $20,000. A win.

Then there's $20,000 on Arkansas State plus-6 against South Alabama. A win.

And $13,000 on Western Michigan plus-5.5 against Northern Illinois. A win.

When they lay six on Dartmouth over Harvard for $12,000—a loss by the way—Billy facetiously asks, "Do we get some kind of bonus if we bet $1 million in a day?"

Before he can answer, Alan sees Michigan State has moved from a six-point favorite to six-and-a-half point favorite against Iowa. "Let's lay it for another three dimes," he says.

"Look at the *macher* winning the big football bet and throwing his money around," Billy says.

"Come on," Alan pleads. "We're winning over here."

They bet like a couple of contestants in a game show who have been put in the money booth. They have one minute to grab as much cash as they can. "The goal is to win every game," Alan says as the sun sets over the mountains. "But if we did it might not be fun. It would be like that *Twilight Zone* episode where the guy has women and money and everyday is great. He finally snaps and says he can't take it anymore.

"In the end, he's banished to hell."

RULE NUMBER SEVEN
You bet your life.

From the back rooms, January 1 at the Stardust looks like any office open for business just hours after ringing in the New Year. Bags of greasy hangover cures litter the floor. Party-food leftovers like deviled eggs, chocolate cookies, chips and salsa, and chicken wings sit in grease-stained doilies on a folding table in the hallway. Scucci is dragging as he makes his acquaintance with the bathroom. "It's one of the best days of the year," Lupo says. "We book, puke, then come back and book. Lots of action."

While technically it's the first day of a new year, January 1 is the last day of the old one at the Stardust. And with four bowl games on tap, they need to win $140,000 to finish with the second-best year ever. Going into the Rose Bowl between Stanford and Wisconsin, the book has already cleared $120,000. There is $40,000 on Wisconsin, which opened as a ten-point favorite and closed as a fourteen-point favorite, which means Lupo and Scucci have never loved a team more than they do Stanford.

And their affections are returned. Stanford loses just 17–9, easily covering the spread. For the Stardust, the win put the book over the $4-million mark.

Lupo enjoyed the moment for less time than it takes Scucci to scarf down a deviled egg. On Monday night, January 3, he called the staff into his office. He quietly told them how, although handle was down 15 percent, to just $105 million this year, the Stardust achieved its second-best year in history. Then, doing his best Michael Corleone impression, Lupo switched to a deliberate and angry tone, taking the air out of the room. He wanted to intimidate with intensity. He may have led the book to a great year, but the line moving was erratic and inconsistent. They were giving away value everyday. Even if it was just $1,000 a day, that could be worth $365,000 a year, more than 10 percent of their hold. His speech was motivated as much by fear as it was by expectations. Because of future bets placed in August on the 200–1 long shot St. Louis Rams to win the Super Bowl, they were facing a potential bill of $1 million at the end of the month. Lupo needed to save every dollar he could between now and then to avoid bankrupting the book.

"You're going to start moving the lines the way I want them moved or you can go somewhere else. We wanna book first halves on every college game. We wanna be aggressive and we wanna bet. You can't be a robot moving lines, just following the Caribbean or moving when some asshole puts down a couple of dimes. Don't cheat. Don't be lazy. Every situation is different. Who is betting? Is it a key game? What number is the game on already? Some of you have been around for four or five years and still have no clue what you are doing. The supervisors aren't doing their jobs. They are spending too much time talking and being lazy about moving the lines. You can't take for granted that just because the island moved the line and we move the line we are going to win. Just because they lose doesn't mean we have to.

"It comes down to wanting to do this right every single night. Scucci and I can't always be making every move, you have to use your intuition more. You need to learn how to do this. There is a lot more pressure on us because our book has to be the kind of moneymaker that the blackjack pit is at the Bellagio. It's critical that our decision making is good and we are on top of every line we move. We cannot give away value."

A couple days later, Korona is in Lupo's office recapping the speech for a visitor. "Remember that scene in *Glengarry Glen Ross* with Alec Baldwin. He comes into the sales meeting where Pacino and Jack Lemmon and some other guys are. He goes off on them telling they have no balls and they are losers. Then he tells them there's gonna be a sales contest. The winner wins a car. The losers get fired. That's kind of what Joe's speech was like."

Lupo was worried that the year could have been a fluke. They got by on talent and luck, but they needed to build fundamentals upon which their skills would flourish. Tiger Woods broke down his swing after winning the Masters, fell apart for a year, and then used his talent and a newfound form steeped in fundamentals to become the most dominant golfer ever. Lupo's speech was intended to help his staff establish itself in a similar way.

So, the first week after New Year's the staff stepped lightly when Lupo was around. Instead of jumping on a line move following a big bet, they'd peer around the corner, trying to read his mannerisms and figure out what he wanted. He looked on placidly, betraying nothing of what he was feeling inside.

What he was feeling was frustration. "I'm paying for that little speech now," Lupo confessed, somewhat superstitously. "We got killed on *Monday Night Football*. Killed in the Florida State Championship game. Right now, 1999 feels like it was four years ago and our great New Year's Day feels like it was last February."

It was the last-second loss in the Buffalo-Tennessee game that had hurt the most. While Alan had celebrated the miracle win with an unprecedented betting spree, Lupo still feels as though he needs medical attention. "I felt like I had been kicked in the stomach and then spit on when my head was on the ground. It was like it happened in slow motion. You are sick, just sick. I was sick when I came in this morning and I am sick now. It's so frustrating when you put all that work into it and you lose on a fluke play that people will talk about for years. It will make you sick everytime you hear it."

The game itself only cost $5,000. But throw in the parlays that won because of Tennessee, and the book lost $160,000 on the game. And there is still the priceless pit in their stomachs that grows every week St. Louis advances in the playoffs. Thinking of the Rams winning and covering the Super Bowl, well, that makes Lupo feel more nauseous than the morning after New Year's.

Scucci remembers the story that finally drove him out of betting. He had $5,000 on the Oakland A's in a regular season baseball game. Dennis Eckersley, probably the best reliever in the late 1980s, comes in to save a 4–2 game with two outs in the bottom of the ninth. He walks the first two batters he faces. The third hits a three-run homer, costing the A's the game and Scucci his bet.

"It ended so fast, I was stunned," Scucci says. "The game was running late and as soon as it was over, the network started some nature show. I couldn't even speak. I was flat broke and just watched about the plight of the Canadian elk. That's what it was like in here yesterday after the Buffalo-Tennessee game. What can you say?"

As Scucci tells his sob story, another one is unfolding on TV. The book needed the Cowboys to cover against the Vikings, and Minnesota is starting to blow the faded stars off the Dallas helmets. "Good," Scucci says in disgust. "I hope everyone out there wins across the board and we lose everything and no one has anything to bitch about."

In the meantime, Lupo and Scucci have to work through the pain. Unlike the wiseguys, who can lament a loss and allow the grieving to run its course naturally, the bookmakers have to shove the anguish in their back pocket and immediately start thinking about the next game they have to post, which is Tennessee at Indianapolis.

"I think we hang Indy minus-6.5," says Lupo.

"That's high," says Scucci.

"Tennessee shouldn't have won the last game, they're not that good."

"But now that they did, they have momentum," says Scucci, always accounting for karmic forces.

Korona walks in and Lupo grills him. "What's the highest you have the Colts?"

"Six-and-a-half," Korona answers quickly.

"I think we hang 6.5 because if we put up 6 it's gonna be a free-for-all with people laying it. Then we're at 6.5 anyways. Let's just start there and save some money," says Lupo.

"What do you do when Mike [the runner] lays 6.5 right away?"

"For him, we move to seven, then we stay there," says Lupo.

The Stardust hangs Indianapolis as 6.5-point favorites over the Titans. They are the first ones up with the line, and, in their book, it's like they dropped a piece of raw meat in a school of sharks. As the squares line up at the counter to drop a dollar, two dollars, or maybe a nickel on the miracle-working Tennessee Titans, Lupo and Scucci drop the line from 6.5 to 6. They've chosen the right bait for the public. It feels like a small victory during a week in which squares and wiseguys alike picked apart the book in bowl games, college baskets, and the NFL.

Twenty-four hours from now, those might seem like the good old days.

Chapter 12

"I Got a Winner, Huh Cuz?"

One of the things I find so funny as an observer of the Las Vegas
scene is I run into more guys who are at best, average sports bettors.
But, they have all this information that makes them think they can win.
It reminds you of a guy who can't drive a car very well but he drives a
Ferrari. He is gonna kill himself. You know they are gonna kill
themselves.

—JOHN. L. SMITH, COLUMNIST, *LAS VEGAS*
REVIEW-JOURNAL, JANUARY 2000

Johnny Cuz walks into the Stardust sports book early on a
Sunday morning dressed like it's still Saturday night. Part
pimp, part player, he saunters down the middle aisle of the
book wearing a rumpled white linen suit, black T-shirt, and,
dangling from his neck like a shield, a gold cross. He has a woman of
questionable reputation on his arm and cash in his pocket. Cuz likes
making an entrance and a six-foot blonde with a sexy case of bed head,
bright red lipstick smeared on her face, and a spaghetti-strap red dress
carelessly thrown on is a bigger surprise in the book than Elvis. The
ragtag group of bettors in ill-fitting clothes part ways and stare like
envious high school freshmen at the well-tanned, well-built Cuz and

his lady as they sashay toward the counter. They are caricatures of the swaggering hipsters that roamed Vegas when the mob was in charge, Sinatra played the town every night, and limits were for other people.

It's the day of the AFC and NFC Championship games and Cuz, who runs an escort service outside Vegas, wants to put $5,000 down on the Jacksonville Jaguars to beat Tennessee in the AFC game. "It's a nothing bet for me," says Cuz who, like so many people in Vegas, has adopted his nickname as his last name. "I'm taking in thirty grand a week with my business but I'm spending forty grand at the tables and in the books." Normally, he reserves a suite at the Venetian on the weekends and, other than the time he spends entertaining in his room—"I've got to give all my girls a test-drive, you know what I'm saying, cuz?"—Cuz camps out at the baccarat tables. Scucci and Lupo have seen him run up winnings of $75,000 at a time only to walk away empty-handed. "Gambling is my one vice," he says, excepting of course, his chosen profession. "I don't drink, I don't smoke, and I work out everyday." He whips off his white jacket and reveals a softball-sized bicep. "Feel my arm, cuz. Come on, feel it."

But for sports betting, Cuz makes his plays at the Stardust, much to Scucci's chagrin. He loves taking money from Cuz, who is nothing more than a square with cash to flash, but he isn't altogether comfortable with how much Cuz confides in him. Scucci has relatives from Cuz's old neighborhood in the Bronx and knows a lot of the guys Cuz grew up with. Every so often Cuz will spend part of the day reminiscing about old friends, some of whom are living in jail or dead in the ground. Inevitably, this leads to Cuz revealing a little more about his lifestyle than Scucci cares to know.

As he places his bet, Cuz looks over at his date and asks, "Who do you like, sweetheart?"

"Who do you like?" she coyly asks.

"I like the Jaguars."

"Well then, gimme the Jaguars."

Cuz puts down another $2,500 on the Jaguars and hands the

blonde her ticket, which she folds neatly and tucks in her handbag, before turning tail for the bathroom.

"Hey Scooch. What do you think of my new girlfriend?" Cuz says when she's out of earshot.

Struggling to find the right words, Scucci says, "She seems nice. How did you guys meet?"

"I stole her from some punk who wasn't treating her right," Cuz says. "I kind of like her."

Cuz walks away to read up on some stats in the Handicapper's Library when Lupo appears at the counter, looking a sickly gray. "Scooch," he says. "This Rams game is a M-O-N-S-T-E-R game for us."

In the NFC Championship game the Rams, 200–1 shots to reach the Super Bowl when the season started, are now 14.5-point favorites over the Tampa Bay Buccaneers. So much money, both public and wiseguy, has come in on the Rams to win that the spread has jumped from 13 up to 14.5. Not only will the book lose nearly half a million if the Rams make the Super Bowl, but they'll lose an amount equaling the low six-figures if the Rams cover. The potential catastrophe that all the books face as long as the Rams keep advancing has become a huge local story. "Basically, this one game is worth an entire month of regular season college basketball," says Lupo.

But, while on the inside he may be crumbling, on the outside Lupo looks dapper in a black mock turtleneck and brown herringbone jacket. That's because ESPN has sent camera crews to track the bookmaker's every move. By the end of today, he and Scucci will have posted the spread and the total for Super Bowl XXXIV. Within minutes that line will get picked up by all the other books in Vegas and the islands, and the information will be disseminated to every corner bookie, office-pool coordinator, and even nuns in a St. Louis convent. Betting on the Super Bowl is truly a national pastime in which, federal agents predict, nearly $5 billion will be wagered both legally and illegally, all based on the line Scucci and Lupo come up with. "I'm curious to see his mind-set once the Rams game is over," says Korona. "I'd like to see if he takes into consideration the liability we have on the game and tries to protect us. Because there is also a responsibility to the industry since we are the first ones putting the line out." In one week, the Super Bowl will generate the same amount in bets as 23,000 McDonald's franchises in 109 countries do in sales over the course of two years.

The Jaguars and the Titans are about to kick off when Johnny Cuz's blonde makes her way back to the counter, unable to find her man. "Has anyone seen my boyfriend?" she asks no one in particular. Lupo, who hadn't seen her come in, thinks she's lost and looks to Scucci for help. "You mean Johnny," Scucci says.

"I'm not sure that's his name. You know, the guy with the white suit, he liked the Jaguars," she says.

"Yeah, he went that way," Scucci answers, pointing toward the Handicappers Library.

Scucci looks at the befuddled Lupo and says simply, "Johnny Cuz." Lupo laughs knowingly as he walks back to his office.

Cuz and his girlfriend walk out of the library arm in arm, laughing like a couple of newlyweds. He hands her his car keys, his ticket from the five dimes he just bet on the Jaguars, a Stardust pen, and a thick wad of cash. "Write your name on here, baby," he instructs her while pointing to the ticket. "That way if you get in an accident in my car I know who you are. Alright?"

When she's gone, Cuz starts waving the ticket with both the Jaguars pick and the girl's name on it, and he screams to Scucci, "Hey, Scooch. I got a winner, huh cuz?"

It's unclear if he's talking about the girl or the bet.

"Yes! Yes! Yes!" A mousey-looking man with glasses and a Member's Only jacket does his best Traci Lords impression in the middle of the book as his horse comes in at the fourth race at Aqueduct. Simultaneously, on the other side of the book, Johnny Cuz is on his knees, pounding the Stardust carpet. "No! No! No!" he's screaming, clearly not concerned about getting his white pants dirty, as Jacksonville quarterback Mark Brunnell throws an interception from the Titans' six-yard-line.

At the time, the game was tied, with the first three possessions for both teams yielding identical results: a punt, a touchdown, and an interception. At halftime, with the Jags ahead 14–10, Lupo is already bracing himself for a long day. The Jags were seven-point favorites over the Titans, and the total opened at thirty-nine and closed at forty-one. Lupo needs the Titans to cover and the score to fall under the total to make a dent in the losses he's already facing because the Rams are in the championship game. On his desk lies a copy of an iron-on T-shirt decal that reads, "Jacksonville Jaguars vs. St. Louis Rams, Super Bowl XXXIV." He holds it up, not only as an example of the worst case scenario for the book, but as exactly what he expects to happen. He's so convinced the Jags and Rams will both win that he's taking early numbers from his consultants on a potential Jags vs. Rams Super Bowl.

But beginning with just over nine minutes left in the third quarter until there are just more than five minutes left, the Titans score 16 unanswered points to go ahead 26–14. The Jaguars, who had been controlling the game, never recover. The consultants, as well as Lupo and Scucci, switch gears and start researching the spread in a game between the Rams and the Titans.

There's no secret formula to making the line for the most bet on, most publicized, most scrutinized, biggest stakes football game of the year. Over the course of their careers working together, Lupo and Scucci have refined the process to focusing on factors like common opponents, whether or not the teams in the Super Bowl have played each other during the season, and if they did where the game was, what the line was, and how each team did. They also consider how the public perceives each team and how the teams are playing heading into the game. When they sit down to hammer out the line, the work is seamless, with one starting a sentence and the other finishing it. An entire industry of bookmakers and, subsequently, $5 billion worth of bets will follow the decisions made in Lupo's office over the next couple of hours. With the ESPN cameras tracking their every move and the specter of seven-figure losses hanging over their heads if St. Louis does indeed advance, they'll rely on the instincts they've honed together now more than ever.

"The fact the Titans beat the Rams earlier in the year..." Scucci starts to say.

"And that they beat Jacksonville three times..." Lupo continues, "is huge."

"We opened the Titans and Rams at 45.5 over/under, it closed 44.5," says Scucci.

"And the game fell on 45," finishes Lupo.

Korona walks in as the two are debating the game and offers a crucial point that should factor into the decision-making process. "The game should be higher because this is going to be on turf, which favors St. Louis's speed. I'd go with forty-eight."

Lupo nods approvingly and smiles. "Oooh, that's nice Jim."

"If we made the Rams three-point favorites in Tennessee," Lupo continues.

"Then they should be higher on a neutral site on turf," Scucci says.

"So they were three at Tennessee, they'd be six at a neutral field plus they are on turf," Lupo says.

"The public has to really believe in the Rams right now," says Scucci. "I could really see us opening as high as 7.5 and them laying that. The Titans gave up 24.4 points the last five games of the year. The Rams will easily score twenty-seven on them."

Scucci's theory about the public loving the Rams right now is confirmed by the fact that, over the last four weeks, every Rams game has seen them getting four times more money on their side than their opponents. In the NFC Championship game (which hasn't even kicked off as Scucci and Lupo debate a Rams vs. Titans Super Bowl) there is $30,000 on the Rams money line—essentially a straight bet picking the Rams—and not a single dollar on the Buccaneers.

Years of experience have taught them that openly wishing for the ball to bounce your way is tantamount to the bit player in a horror movie saying he'll be right back: It never happens. And wouldn't you know it, during the NFC Championship game, the Rams explosive offense that set NFL records for scoring during the year imploded, scoring just five points in the first half. Meanwhile the Bucs offense fared no better, matching the Rams' five points with just three of their own. At halftime, it looked more like a baseball score than the midway point of the NFC Championship game.

Lupo and Scucci were flabbergasted as the game progressed and neither team pulled away. Lupo, who can be so volatile during a game that he once threw a hockey puck at the wall hard enough to leave a baseball-sized hole, was confined by the fact he had an ESPN wireless microphone attached to his waist and a camera in his face; the network was filming a segment on sports betting during the Super Bowl and Lupo had traded his privacy for some face time. Now he was feeling constricted. When Tampa Bay's rookie quarterback, Shaun King, threw an interception with a little more than eight minutes left in the game, Lupo pursed his lips tightly, started to throw his ubiquitous Cleveland Browns football, and then pulled back when he heard the camera's lens zooming in on him. Instead he went to his computer and launched a clip of Al Pacino as Michael Corleone in *The Godfather* saying, "What the hell is this?" Meanwhile, Scucci kept getting up to adjust the thermostat, convinced someone had turned off the air-conditioning in the office.

Six plays later the Rams, now down 6–5, completed a thirty-yard scoring pass, giving them an 11–6 lead with four minutes left. With the flick of Rams quarterback Kurt Warner's wrist, the Bucs' chances at a Super Bowl were gone, as were the Stardust's chances of climbing out of their Super Bowl hole.

But there's little time for grieving. The consultants who had been calling in with Super Bowl spreads favoring the Rams over the Titans by 10.5 or 10 before the Rams game began to adjust their numbers. A dismal performance by the Rams in a big game against a good defense—similar circumstances they would face in the Super Bowl—showed they weren't invincible. They adjusted their spreads down to 8 or 8.5, but Lupo and Scucci had taken a potential Rams collapse into account with their earlier number.

"I think even eight is too high," Scucci says, after hearing what Las Vegas Sports Consultants recommends.

"I agree, let's put up the 7.5 and 48.5." says Lupo. "We can move either way pretty fast. And if we go to seven, it will take a million dollars to get off that number."

Seven, three, and ten are all key numbers in pro football. Thirty percent of the games fall on those numbers, which means if the books can get bettors to put money on them chances are good that they will do no worse than a push.

They post the spread minutes after the game ends: St. Louis minus-7.5 over Tennessee, total 49. Two minutes later, with $500 worth of wiseguy money on Tennessee, the line is down to seven. The chess match between wiseguy and bookmaker is playing out exactly the way Lupo and Scucci planned it would. They posted 7.5 knowing the wiseguys, and the public, would like St. Louis. But they also knew the wiseguys, fearing the books would move to 7 quickly, would want to get as many hits at minus-7.5 and then at minus-8 as they could. One of them bluffed that he wanted Tennessee, but his bet was so small that Scucci and Lupo knew he was tipping his hand. They quickly moved the line to seven, and have no intentions of getting off that number for the entire week. It won't make for interesting bookmaking, but it will help them reduce their losses if the game does land on seven. And after the line is posted, Lupo and Scucci see the island books and Vegas books slowly following their lead, like troops falling into line. One by one, sevens pop up on the computer screen at different books, indicating that none of the books plan on taking many chances this week.

"It's almost a relief to have it over," says Scucci of St. Louis advancing to the Super Bowl. "We have been dreading it for so long now, and we survived and it's not so bad."

"Bullshit," Lupo says, pounding his fists on the Browns commemorative football. There is no Corleone catchphrase he can play with to ease the tension in the office. Spinning around to check the computer that tracks all the bets, he brings up the future bets on the previously 200–1 long shot to make the Super Bowl St. Louis Rams. The average bet on the Rams to make the Super Bowl was a measly $60. The whole scenario is eerily reminiscent of when Lupo was first hired as manager in October of 1996. The first fight between Evander Holyfield and Mike Tyson was that same month. All the public money came in on the long shot Holyfield, but the average bet was only $45. Tyson was considered such a sure thing that most of the books didn't bother laying off the huge liability they were taking on with all the money being bet on Holyfield. Besides, the bets were so small, no one noticed.

When Holyfield won that night, the Stardust lost nearly $500,000. "I puked for one month straight," says Lupo. "Then I just dry heaved." His first month on the job and he was at the helm for the biggest catastrophe in the sports book's history. He could take solace in the fact that every book on the Strip lost nearly the same amount, and the MGM lost even more. But unlike the MGM, which not coincidentally happened to have one of its best nights ever at the tables after the fight, the Stardust's pit action didn't cover up the loss. The book was headed down the same path with the Rams.

"The bulk of our bets, $26,000 worth, are at 10–1 and below," Lupo says, tapping the up and down arrows on the keyboard. "But, we took ninety bets at 200–1, $1,000 worth of sucker bets, so we thought. That's $200,000. That is our liability right there."

The book's ability to win or lose money on Super Bowl Sunday is predicated on more than just the outcome of the game. Every play, every pass, every touchdown, field goal, turnover, or quarter is a little battle between bettor and bookmaker. It's the one game of the year where no bet is off-limits and the bookmakers can flex their creative muscles. Will David Duval shoot a lower score on Super Bowl Sunday than the total number of rushing yards the NFC team allows? Who will have higher completion percentage: Reggie Miller at the free throw line or the AFC quarterback passing the ball? They're called "prop bets," or "proposition bets," and they are the circus freaks of the betting carnival that is Super Bowl Sunday.

Lupo, dressed in a white shirt and splashy Italian tie, and Korona, wearing a royal blue shirt and gold tie, started working on the props early on Monday morning after the conference title games. Both of them showed up wearing suits today to impress the ESPN cameras and, even after sitting hunched over in front of a computer debating annoyingly minute details like whether three field goals is too high a number for a field goal total, neither has undone their ties. "When I got up this morning I had this whole plan of an olive-colored suit and blue shirt," says Lupo. "Then I thought to myself that Korona was going to wear the blue shirt. I'm a thinker that way. Then I show up at work and he's got on the blue shirt. He knows it looks good on TV."

At 3:30 that day, the props still aren't posted. Lupo is rubbing the tension of yesterday's games and the impending doom out of his temples, working on the Super Bowl prop sheet. "It's a big fucking hassle," Lupo says as he goes over the list. "I hate these fucking props." These bets give bookmakers fits. They are too gimmicky to make an educated guess on how people will bet, and they are up for so long it gives wiseguys a chance to research which props are soft. Essentially, the bookmakers are sitting ducks hoping no one betting is a very good shot. Subsequently, instead of rooting to win, they're rooting not to lose. Some of the props are truly random. In 1999, one of the props was whether or not backup quarterback Bubby Brister of the Broncos would take a snap against the Falcons. At the end of the game, Brister was on the field, but the cameras followed quarterback John Elway dancing victoriously on the sidelines instead of the play. No one knew until the play-by-play was released later that night whether or not Brister actually took a snap. It delayed payouts on props for hours.

The Super Bowl prop bets are a phenomenon that became popular over the last fifteen years as the audience for betting on the game grew from wiseguys to the general public. The first props weren't even on the game but on wacky events that seemed to take hold of the nation's interest. Jackie Gaughan, a bookmaking and hotel-owning legend, posted one of the first prop bets in Vegas in 1979 on where Skylab—a failing American satellite—would eventually fall to earth. Some random samples included one of the five oceans which, packaged together, went off as 5–1 favorites, the then Soviet Union had odds of 12–1, California was at 100–1, and Rhode Island went off at 2,000–1. He even offered 10,000–1 odds that the satellite would fall on the El Cortez, one of the properties he owned. Ultimately, it was the 30–1 long shot Australia that came home the winner.

The most famous prop wasn't on sports at all, but on the television program *Dallas*. In 1980, the entire nation was captivated by the soap opera's cliffhanger ending in which a shadowed assailant shot the show's evil star, J. R. Sonny Reizner at the Castaways took advantage of the hoopla and created a prop asking the question on everyone's lips by posting odds for every character on the show. A day later, the Gaming Control Board forced Reizner to remove the prop because, it reasoned, someone working on the show already knew the answer and could take advantage of the bet.

Lupo and Korona don't get nearly as creative with their props. Their best effort is whether or not Shaquille O'Neal's free throw percentage in the Lakers Super Bowl Sunday game against the Rockets will be higher than the number of points scored in the Super Bowl.

As Lupo signs off on the list and Korona brings the final sheet to the counter, Ray Spaulding, a stick-thin, cherubic-looking twenty-nine-year old supervisor, who just happens to be an ex-marine, walks in with the ESPN producer in tow. "I just wanted to let you know we're shooting outside," says the producer.

Perking up a bit, Lupo asks, "Do you guys need me for anything?"

"No," the producer answers. "Jim is out there. He's our star for the afternoon."

As the producer walks out, Lupo mutters to himself, "I knew I should have worn the blue shirt."

Both the high that Rodney Bosnich's trip home brought him, and the confidence that he could build a life as a gambler, carried over into early January. His friends came to visit from Indiana and one of them begged Rodney to take $1,000 of the friend's money and build a nest egg out of it so the friend could move to Vegas. "Not a chance I'll do it," says Rodney. "The kid would be in the gutter in a month. He's just bad luck. I think I lost three bowl games just because he was sitting next to me."

He's gone from being unsure of his own skills to being qualified to judge someone else's. And his winning streak has continued. He's still betting around $400-$600 a day, hoping to make around $200 a day. But occasionally he lets the gambler in him take over. The day of the AFC and NFC Championship games he had $200 on the Titans to cover, $200 on Tampa Bay to cover, and $200 on the number-one ranked Cincinnati Bearcats to beat Marquette by 9.5. He then put $100 on a parlay on the same three bets. At the end of the day, he'd won all three bets and was $1,200 richer.

But, as sure as he is that gambling is his lot in life, his practical side—rearing its head when Missy shoves the want ads in his face—forces him to make at least half-hearted attempts at getting a job. There are some impediments to the interviewing process. He's been sleeping until noon, hoping to shorten the time he's awake until the college basketball games start at 4 P.M.; because of that, morning meetings aren't an option. He hasn't stopped getting high, so the day before every interview he has to bloat himself by chugging a marijuana-masking agent—at $40 a bottle—that tastes like chalk and makes him nauseous. Still, making $500 a week doing a menial job he doesn't care about would cover his monthly expenses and let him spend the rest of his lucre making bets. He'd also like the company, since his only friends are the guys Missy works with at Abercrombie & Fitch, his cats, and whoever is taking bets that night.

The loneliness is why, at one P.M. on a Monday afternoon when there are no sports on television, Rodney decides to spend his afternoon at the Stardust sports book. At least he knows some people there. The guys behind the counter might say hello or the degenerate gamblers watching the horses will get in some argument that entertains him for a while. Once there, he sits idly in the book. He pulls at a pen cap with his stubby fingers, trying to separate the long part of the cap from the hollow top. He bites it, twists it, bends it, and gnaws at it again as though it is the object of a thousand frustrations. He may be winning, but he can feel the toll sweating the games has taken on his nerves. There's a reason most gamblers never sustain a relationship. The bet is the only mistress a bettor needs.

RULE NUMBER EIGHT
Everyone else is a potential distraction.

"I'm always crabby because it's stressful, and if Missy starts talking I'll just snap because she always seems to talk when the team I bet against is making a 10–0 run," says Rodney.

Professional athletes' wives often complain that they are essentially abandoned during the season of the sport their husband plays. The focus, intensity, and mental energy it takes to be just average in the high-pressure world of professional sports leaves precious little time for mates or kids or carpools or even taking out the garbage. But when you live with a sports bettor, there is no offseason. Baseball

begets football which begets basketball which takes you back to baseball. Your partner in life never travels, yet he's never really home.
Since she arrived in Las Vegas, Missy's been a nineteen-year-old bettor's widow.

"He does well at it, and our lifestyle isn't affected and bills are
paid, so I guess it's going okay," Missy says. After spending most of
the afternoon alone at the Stardust, Rodney made a $200 bet on Syra-
cuse minus-3.5 over the University of Connecticut and headed back
home to catch the opening tip. When he got there, Missy was grabbing
a quick snack and changing from the shorts and T-shirt she wore to
class into her work uniform of jeans and an Abercrombie & Fitch
sweatshirt. As she flits about the apartment in the twenty minutes she
has to regroup, Rodney pulls a hardback chair close to the television
and turns on ESPN.

"Back home," she continues, "it wasn't accepted that he was gambling all the time. My family especially is into the whole work hard,
blue-collar thing. But out here it's the lifestyle so nobody looks at it
funny. It would be nice if he had a job and gambled on the side, you
know just for insurance and stuff like that, something to take his mind
off the games once in a while.

"I'll call from work and can tell immediately in his voice that he
was either sleeping or losing. But if he's winning, he'll come to work
and see me or spend time on the phone talking to me. On Saturday
morning I'll sleep in and he'll be up at 9 A.M. If he's winning he'll come
wake me and want to tell me every detail of the game. But if he's losing
he's yelling at the TV and wakes me anyways.

"On Fridays I'll want to go out at night and he'll say no because he
has to be up early to watch games or has a game on that night. I'm
always asking, Why can't we go out and you can watch games after
dinner? and his only response is, 'I have to watch a game.' He's missing a link in his life right now. You need people other than the ones
you see only when you are sitting in a casino or on TV."

Rodney sits back in his chair, his hands clasped behind his head, listening to his girlfriend's review of his lifestyle. Normally as affected to criticism as an elephant is to a mosquito bite, Rodney feels stung by some of what Missy said.

"Gambling is what I came here to do," he responds somewhat defensively. "I came here to bet. I didn't come here to work in a sports book. I have to gamble everyday."

Missy's unruffled by the ire in his voice, brushing it off with a smile.

"I'm not lazy. I think laziness is the worst disease in the world," says Rodney. "I'd rather be an alcoholic, or a gambler, than lazy. Although, I guess if you have to gamble everyday like I do you are addicted to it."

"I think it's a hard life," Missy says ruefully. "He just studies the games on the Internet and watches that stupid blue ticker on the bottom of the screen on ESPN. I actually hate sports, and our life revolves around the game. We go out to eat, but only after the game. We can't go out Saturday during the day because of the game. I wanted to make him a haircut appointment and he told me not to make it for Saturday, Sunday, Monday, Tuesday, or Wednesday because of games. He can't even get a haircut because of the stupid games.

"Is that a life?"

RULE NUMBER NINE
You don't control the game, the game controls you.

As the haze settles in the valley and the sun sets behind the mountains near Alan's house, it reflects a bright orange color, giving off the effect that the entire range is on fire. For the first time all week, so is Alan. He sits shirtless on his stationary bike, frantically pedaling to nowhere. He's got a cell phone on his ear and the Imperial Palace prop sheet in his hand. Back in 1995, IP bookmaker Jay Kornegay assumed the 49ers vs. Chargers Super Bowl—a game in which the Niners were double-digit favorites—would be so boring he needed something to attract some bets. Now, while the Stardust puts out one page front and back, the IP—known as the Prop Palace— puts out ten pages of 140 different props like: Will the Rams score more points than the NHL's Chicago Blackhawks have shots on goal that day? As Lupo said earlier in the week, props are a bookmaker's nightmare and a bettor's fantasy. With four days to research, even the silliest bet can become a good value. And Alan could use a good value or two.

Sitting on the black leather sofa in Alan's living room is Artie. He's a sixtysomething down-on-his-luck gambler whose journey to Las Vegas from Brooklyn twenty-five years ago started after a stint in jail. His sweet, grandfatherly disposition belies the crappy hand he's been dealt in life. And, given the unlucky pattern he has no right believing he'd have any success earning his living playing poker. Yet he persists, playing everyday wherever he can get a game, sometimes traveling to California and back in a day to play in a single back-room tournament.

Alan knows all this, yet his penchant for rooting for the underdog, whether it be lame horses, unknown college teams, or animals on the verge of extinction, extends to him befriending the otherwise friendless. As someone who incessantly laments his lack of relationships but is unwilling to be flexible enough to accommodate one, Alan finds the perfect match in those who are disenfranchised. He doesn't have to change for them, and they aren't in a position to make him.

RULE NUMBER EIGHT
Everyone else is a potential distraction.

Alan compensates for his inability to give anything of himself emotionally with an overcompensating genius for gift giving. He paid for his sister's posh, Saturday-night wedding in a Boston hotel. He bought his father a $3,000 leather toiletries bag from Armani and still sends several thousand dollars a year home to his mother. When his favorite kick-boxing instructor was arrested and detained for an expired green card, it was Alan who grabbed $3,000 in cash from his desk drawer to bail him out. He did the same with Artie, staking him $25,000 for a poker tournament in Connecticut when Artie had no money, hoping to help him rebuild his bankroll and his self-esteem.

Since then, Artie has tried repaying Alan in unflinching loyalty and support. He'll be at Jamms everyday when Alan gets there. He'll listen to Alan's rants and Artie will tell him that, despite the fact his team finished out of the money by twenty points, it was still a good bet. He'll call him from the Bellagio poker room and give him updates of who's there and who's playing well. And lately, he'll show up at Alan's every Friday afternoon, so he can help Alan do the one thing that makes living in Las Vegas worthwhile.

Every Friday is like a gambling baptism for Alan, who's made a ritual out of running around to the books and taking his chances with the late-afternoon point spreads. The weekend starts fresh with new lines, new chances to bet, and newfound hope. Going from book to book, smelling the cigarette smoke, seeing the boards, and watching the runners takes him back to when he first arrived in Vegas. Although they were fighting each other for every half-point, the wiseguys shared the common bond of being addicted to the rush. That's all they were really after.

Running around the books used to be a tradition for wiseguys, but with computers and offshore books becoming so much more prevalent, fewer and fewer wiseguys need to make the effort. They just point, click, and bet. But Alan still runs around like a kid in an amusement park, scoping out lines, collecting tickets, seeing old friends, and giving bookmakers a hard time. And he loves it. It's easy to envision him in thirty years as the old curmudgeon who outwardly doesn't have a kind word for anyone but inside is softer than taffy.

And everywhere he goes Artie is with him, spurring him on or acting as a sounding board as Alan decides on which games he is going to bet. They're an odd match. Artie, with his potbelly, hangdog face, ruddy complexion, and droopy skin and Alan with his toned, razor-sharp features and milky-white coloring. While Alan would rather not always have the company, Artie's presence has helped on Fridays. Time is of the essence when a line he needs is on the board. If Alan likes it, some wiseguy at his computer will like it. And then it's a race to see who can get there first. With Artie waiting in the idling car, Alan can get in and out of a book fast, without having to go through a valet or the maze of a parking structure underneath the vast properties' underbellies. There are also the occasional places where Alan's bets are no longer welcome; Artie can walk in and get bets down without raising any suspicions.

The MGM, however, is not forbidden territory, and that's where Alan walks in and calmly pulls out $20,000 in cash from his pocket, spreading the loot around on six different games at three dimes each. Neither is Caesars, where he puts $3,000 on four different games and $2,000 on another. He's an ATM to every book in Vegas. At the Bellagio he once again proves his distaste for idle chitchat by lashing out at a runner who recognizes him as he walks by.

"Hey Alan," the runner says enthusiastically. "Whatcha doin'?"

"I'm betting."

"You wanna stake me?"

"What?" Alan asks incredulously.

"You wanna stake me?"

If the runner dares to talk to the bettor, he should be deferential. And, kidding or not, he should never talk about being staked in such a public forum. Even in a sport with as little decorum as betting, it's unseemly to talk business so openly.

"A, I've got nothing to stake you with," Alan says, drawing a crowd with his tone. "B, if I did, I'd never stake you. You cry too much and anyone who cries that much shouldn't be playing. It's unprofessional."

What had started as a friendly attempt at banter by the runner has turned into a scathing attack on his guts as a bettor. The runner, surrounded by his other friends, is clearly embarrassed and tries to shake it off with a laugh. "It's because these guys are always torturing me," he claims.

"Then don't bet when they're around—you're a fucking crybaby," Alan responds.

Emasculated, the runner takes a seat, his friends howling and pointing in his face. "Yeah," says one of his friends, laughing. "You got it Alan. You got it and he don't."

Alan walks up to the window and pulls out another thick wad of cash to make his bets, cruelly and inevitably teasing the envious runners. While he looks flush with money, Alan wasn't kidding about not having the dough to stake anyone. Normally the Friday bets are a primer for the weekend, Alan betting just enough to lay down a foundation that gets his juices flowing and gives him newfound hope for the weekend. But, this Friday's jaunt has taken on added significance. Since his and Billy's masterful maneuvers and lucky breaks earlier in the month, their bankroll has dwindled precipitously. Bad breaks, bad bounces, and, ultimately, bad bets have turned a potential record-breaking season into one that could force him into retirement in a matter of weeks. The uncanny nature of the way the games have fallen against the sharp money prompted the *Las Vegas Review-Journal* to comment on what a difficult year the wiseguys are having—specifically in college basketball, a sport that usually favors the wiseguys against the book.

Fucking eighteen-year-olds, Alan thinks. They have no sense of obligation. No sense of duty. They rollover when they are supposed to win and play like heroes when everyone has counted them out. Where's the justice, Alan wonders. Don't these kids know their place? The one game that truly crushed his spirit was on January 22, when St. John's played Ohio State in New York. The game opened at St. John's minus-4 and Alan ran all over town the night before laying the points. The next morning, the game was still at St. John's minus-4, so Billy and Alan decided to take advantage. As if in passing, one of them says to the other, "I think we should take a shot at St. John's. Things are going well there." A torrent of bets follows.

Five dimes.

Three dimes.

Ten dimes at St. John's minus-3.5.

The game moves down to St. John's minus-3 and Alan bets five dimes more. Then another three dimes.

Then two dimes.

Then five dimes.

They're gorging themselves on bets, intoxicated by the potential. Like a couple laying down for an illicit affair, they don't think about the damage they'll do, just about how good it feels right now. No matter what it costs.

Alan's eyes widen as he sees on the screen the game goes back to minus-3.5. Some schmuck is betting Ohio State. Big. Alan starts betting again, trying to reel the line in with more and more cash.

Five dimes at 3.5

Three dimes at 3.5

"My god," he says. "This is crazy."

Then it's over, and Alan and Billy settle in as though they just braved a wicked storm. They're too scared to survey the damage. There's no doubt it's their biggest bet of the year but even they won't tally up the total. "It had been a tough week and we weren't going to bet a lot today," says Alan. "But we went overboard on the St. John's game. My theory was this: Ohio State beat St. John's in the tourney last year. Then they beat Michigan State earlier in the week. They should be out of gas and thinking about the Big Ten season right now, not some team they've already proven they can beat. They're out of gas, that's it. But, what the fuck, overbetting is part of the fun of it."

Alan has the television on mute and a Sammy Davis, Jr., greatest hits CD in the stereo. Mr. Bojangles is playing softly, battling the wind whistling through the open patio door and the ticking grandfather clock for sound supremacy in the house. It's nearing 3:15 in the afternoon, about the time the St. John's game should be ending. Up until now, Alan hasn't checked the score since breakfast at Jamms with Artie. At the time it was 17–9 Ohio State. "I'm glad they're running out of gas," Alan muttered sarcastically between bites of his egg whites.

When he turns on the game, St. John's senior Bootsie Thornton hits a three-pointer to put the Red Storm up by 10 with 2:49 seconds left. Essentially, that's a six-point lead for Alan and Billy. For a top-twenty team playing at home with an All-American point guard—which St. John's has—there's no reason to think they can't control the tempo and the ball down the stretch. Unless of course you've "bet your balls like we did," Alan says. As if on cue, St. John's starts crumbling like three-day-old cake. A layup by Ohio State cuts the lead to nine. No biggie, if St. John's can bring the ball up, take some time off the clock and—"MOTHERFUCKER!" Billy screams into the phone as Erick Barkley, the St. John's All-American point guard, turns the ball over and Ohio State converts another layup. Suddenly the lead in the game is seven, the lead on the spread is three. The biggest bet of the season is on the verge of becoming the biggest loss of the season.

"Christ all fucking mighty Jesus fucking Christ," Billy yells. "It's the miracle of all fucking miracles." St. John's does not score for the last 2:49 seconds of the game, blowing a ten-point lead at home. Yet, the players taciturn looks walking off the court pale when compared to the sickly look in Alan's eyes. Normally he'd be defiant after losing a game like this, but now he just looks defeated. If he can't win this game, what can he win? What is he doing? This isn't just a financial crisis. This is something existential. It's not about a game, but *the* game.

"I should not be doing this for a living," Alan says, gently dropping his ticker on the desk and turning off Sammy. "This is a waste of a life, it really is. I fucking hate myself for what I've done." His head is in his hands as he tally's up the figures for all the other games he's bet so far today. Up until the St. John's game they were 5–5 on the day, with a lit-tle more lost than won. "$13,000 lost on UIC," he says, while humming "Mr. Bojangles." "Oh yeah, another loss, This is a very bad day." By day's end, they will have won ten bets, lost fourteen, and pushed on three. On a day when there are seventy-nine games on the board, betting only twenty-seven of them is an indication that their confidence and bankroll is dwindling. As Alan tallies up the wins and losses in his Don Best rotation book, he flips a page and finds two more betting tickets for St. John's that he had completely forgotten about. Bets made the Friday before the game when optimism was high.

"Six more dimes on St. John's minus-4," he says, laughing. "What good customers we are."

Chapter 13

"It's Just Another Day"

Give the casinos credit. They saw that more requests for rooms
were coming in on Super Bowl weekend and they started catering to
the people who came into town for the game. The casinos have
marketed the weekend as a party and now the hotel is filled. To eighty
million viewers, this is a chance to bet as a social event.

But the event players, the people who bet a lot on big events, those
aren't the wiseguys. Wiseguys don't bet more on the Super Bowl just
because it is the fucking Super Bowl. That is what you see in the
movies. The money that wiseguys bet has stayed the same and if there
is value in the game, they will bet what they have been betting all year.
No one tries to make back their losses in the Super Bowl.

—JIMMY VACCARO, SUPER BOWL WEEK,
JANUARY 2000

They call **Super Bowl** weekend the Gambler's New Year's
Eve. The game itself, once a clever marketing idea from the
brain of former NFL commissioner Pete Rozelle, has blos-
somed into the biggest sporting spectacle in the world. When
the Rams played the Titans in Atlanta on January 30, 2000, 88.5 million people watched. More than a handful of them had money on the
outcome.

Professional football had always been a game for the betting masses, but the Super Bowl itself did not garner the kind of attention it reaps now for nearly twenty years. A combination of the immense media coverage and the subsequent celebrity that surrounded the Chicago Bears in 1985 inspired not just knowledgeable football fans, but almost anyone who had turned on the TV or picked up a magazine that season to make a bet. The Bears were not just beefy players, but cartoon characters: "Iron" Mike Ditka, William "The Refrigerator" Perry, and Jim McMahon—the quarterback who never took off his sunglasses—and it was impossible not to know just a little about them, possibly root for them, and maybe even make a bet. "That was the first year I can remember that it was really extravagant," says Vaccaro. "I was at Bally's and they had me in all the marketing meetings, explaining to the finance guys why it was worth it to spend some money on this weekend. We ended up having all these parties for high-rollers and betting stations set up in conference rooms where people could watch the game." It was then the sports books realized the Super Bowl could be even bigger than the bowl games.

In 1992, Michael Gaughan, boss of the Barbary Coast and the Gold Coast, offered up a Super Bowl prop bet that earned him statewide acclaim for his bravado and foolishness. The Washington Redskins were favored by seven over the Buffalo Bills and action on the game had been slow. Nearly 7 percent of all NFL games are decided by seven points, which narrows a bettor's chances of making a buck on the game considerably. Subsequently, action on 7-point games is always slower than a game that is listed at 6.5 points or 7.5 points. Gaughan, the son of Jackie Gaughan and CEO of one of the few remaining privately held casino corporations in Las Vegas, needed to drum up some business. He posted a prop that offered players the Redskins at minus-6.5 and the Bills at plus-7.5. For the savvy bettor, it was a natural middle. Play both sides and you'll cash in twice if the game lands on seven. For the Gaughan-owned hotels, it was a death trap. "Our liability on that game was something like $23 million," says Gaughan.

Bob Stupak had come to Vegas twenty years earlier and instantly gained renown for a daring lifestyle even by local standards. He transformed a rundown property in the middle of Vegas slums into a $100 million casino called Vegas World. He once ran for mayor and actually won the primary before getting slaughtered in the general election. A motorcycle daredevil during his childhood in Pittsburgh, Stupak often rode his bike around the Vegas streets at recklessly high speeds, once crashing so badly he lay in a coma for five weeks. He once bet Donald Trump $1 million to play a board game, became a regular at the World Series of poker, and once bet $1 million on a card game.

A master of publicity, Stupak knew his reputation as a player in a town full of them would be solidified with a high-profile bet on the highest-profile betting event. When the Redskins-Bills Super Bowl spread stuck on seven, it presented a showman like Stupak with the perfect opportunity to grab some of the spotlight. Walking into Little Caesars with $1.1 million in cash in a brown-paper bag, Stupak put $550,000 on the Redskins at minus-7 and $550,000 on the Bills at plus-7. At worst, he'd be risking the $50,000 vigorish.

The Redskins won the game 37–24, but Stupak's bet and Gaughan's risky spread added to the reputation of the Super Bowl as *the* betting event. That was underscored again in 1995 when the San Francisco 49ers played the San Diego Chargers. Financier Carl Icahn, looking to have some fun with an extra $2.4 million he had lying around, called Jimmy Vaccaro at the Mirage. "He called me up and asked, 'Jimmy, what's the money line on the Niners?' I can't tell him that over the phone, it's illegal since he wasn't in Nevada. So I told him he would have to come down to the book. The next day he shows up with a silver briefcase full of cash and asks me again, 'Jimmy, what's the money line on the Niners?' I look at him and then I look at the briefcase and I say it's 8–1. We go in back where he can have some privacy, he lays out $2.4 million, and I give him a ticket. The bet only paid $300,000. But still."

The Friday before the Super Bowl at the Stardust, Scucci sits in his cramped, rectangular office, plotting strategy for the weekend. With so much attention focused on the football game, with nearly every play on the field having ramifications in the book, it's easy to lose focus on the other events that day. There will be so many tourists in town that every favorite will be heavy with square money. A $200,000 win on the Super Bowl can disappear real fast if you lose track of the money coming in on college basketball, pro basketball, golf, and horse racing on the same day. In 1993, someone playing the ponies at Garden State Park in New Jersey won more than $25,000. No one noticed that he was betting $20 a pop dozens of times, at a different window every time.

Meanwhile, with two days left until the game, there's been $61,300 bet on the St. Louis Rams and $61,000 bet on the Tennessee Titans. The myth is that bookmakers aren't interested in betting, they want two-way action and are happy to earn their salaries in juice. That's actually not the case. "That's a common misconception," says Scucci. "Two-way is nice but that is not how we are going to win the big money. We want to be heavy on one side and we want to win. It's still very competitive." Scucci is forgetting for a moment that they are heavy, to the weight of nearly $1 million in futures bets, on the Rams.

But, even with all the high rollers expected in town, handle on the Super Bowl in general is expected to decrease for the second year in a row. Bookmakers blame the paucity of interest in the two small-market teams and a seven-point line that no one wants to challenge. But that's more like wishful thinking. Having a bigger impact than the bookmakers would like to admit is the Internet. WSEX's Steve Schillinger expected offshore books to easily surpass the $76 million Las Vegas handles in Super Bowl wagers. Intertops.com, based in Antigua, expected to take more than 92,000 bets in a single day before and during the Super Bowl.

Without the action during the week to counteract the futures bets made during the fall, this Super Bowl Sunday is shaping up to be worse for the books than Black Sunday in 1978, when the books lost millions on the Steelers beating the Cowboys. At the high-rollers party on Saturday night, an event the Stardust and every other hotel on the Strip throws to honor their best customers who flew in for the game, Lupo sees his boss and casually mentions his dilemma. "I've been planting the seed that we are going to get killed on the Super Bowl since November," says Lupo. "But I wanted to mention it to him one more time before the walls come crumbling down."

The image of the empire crumbling is apropos considering the Romanesque setting in which Lupo delivers his warning. The high-roller parties are legendary for their bacchanalian feasts, Vegas style. Instead of a forum with marble columns, the Stardust party is in one of its football-field-sized conference rooms and features ice sculptures of the St. Louis and Tennessee logos. Instead of servants feeding guests grapes from the vine, the Bud Girls, dressed in tight spandex replicas of Budweiser cans, offer deviled eggs on silver trays. The Roman gods are replaced by second-tier gridiron greats such as former punter Ray Guy, former linebacker Jack Ham, and ex-quarterback Craig Morton, each getting around ten grand to appear. And Caesars' often-copied style had nothing on the hairdo Mr. Las Vegas, Wayne Newton, sports as he greets the masses.

The Stardust spares no expense to entertain their high-end guests this weekend, all with the sole purpose of engendering so much goodwill that the gamblers are compelled to pump some money back into the casino. They've supplied an endless array of party games for the guests to try, like the armchair quarterback toss, where the player sits in a chair and tries to hit a target with the football. There's also the Budweiser bottle ringtoss and, the most irresistible game for any knowledgeable bettor, Super Bowl trivia. "I helped out on that one," Lupo says proudly.

For the Stardust, a downmarket hotel struggling to compete, the display is especially extravagant. Scucci and Lupo, used to the dungeonlike atmosphere in the book, feel like they've wandered into some secret society of the well-guarded rich. At one point early in the evening, a beefy security guard dressed in all black recognizes Scucci and walks over to say hello. Feeling as out of place as the bookmaker, he winks at him as if to say, "Look what we pulled off!" Scucci, surveying the folly of the whole scene, can't help but mock it. When the security guard says to Scucci, "What's the word, Bob?" Scucci pulls the taller guard down so Scucci can whisper in his ear and says, "The word is 'bumblebee.'"

Later in the evening, the dread of Super Bowl Sunday dulled by a couple of vodka gimlets and free filet mignon, Scucci lays out one of his goals for the future. "I swear to God," he exclaims. "One of these days when I am out of this business I am going to come back to one of these things as a client."

"You mean as a whale?" Lupo mischievously asks.

"Yeah," Scucci answers. "Metaphorically, of course."

By 7:30 A.M., the Stardust sports book resembles the dining room at a fraternity. Dozens of college-aged guys in sweats and backwards baseball hats stand in line sucking on beer bottles, discussing their Super Bowl bets. The props are going at clearance-sale speed, getting all the attention in a game between two teams no one knows and a spread that's nearly impossible to beat. The ticket writers all wear "Super Day" T-shirts, a nod to the big game without infringing on the NFL's trademark of the phrase Super Bowl. Meanwhile Lupo, who has ESPN coming in for the last day of shooting, wears a red polo shirt, matching the red in the Titans logo, to be in sync with the rooting gods. He can't let vanity get in the way of karma.

The Stardust has two satellite rooms set up in the hotel where the games are being shown on a big screen, buffets are being served, and auxiliary betting tables are taking action. One of them is in the Wayne Newton Theater, and the other is in the conference room that hosted the previous night's shindig. The college kids have tried several times to sneak into the high-roller parties and play with the big boys. Scucci and Lupo know how they feel.

Remarkably, after five months of rooting for the St. Louis Rams to lose every game, Lupo and Scucci find themselves rooting for the Rams to win the Super Bowl. Between the money line and the spread, the book has taken in nearly half-a-million dollars in bets since Friday, with most of that actually coming in Saturday night and Sunday morning. The once-even numbers mushroomed into being $400,000 heavy on the Titans. If the Rams win the game, Lupo will still lose the $500,000 in futures, but counter that with winning the $400,000 on Titans bets. Throw in some winning props and a little luck with half-times and the book could actually break even on the day. Unheard of just twenty-four hours earlier. If only Lupo had worn his blue shirt.

As the game kicks off, Scucci's head suddenly shoots up, as though the ball has been kicked straight from the field through his body. With a possessed look in his eyes he stares at Lupo and says, "Joe, I'm pretty sure this game is gonna land on seven."

"Scooch," Lupo says. "Number one, you're freaking me out with that look. Number two, don't say shit like that unless the cameras are in here. It'll make you look good."

Props pop up throughout the game like land mines, constantly blowing up in Lupo and Scucci's faces. The book needed Rams quarterback Kurt Warner's first pass to fall incomplete. It gets deflected at the line, but is caught. It needed St. Louis to score first, but on an attempted field goal after the first series, the holder drops the ball. Even when the Rams eventually did score first, the Stardust lost $3,000 on a prop that no team would score in the first six-and-a-half minutes of the game.

Nevertheless, as the first half ended, the book was bloodied but unbowed. Despite losing nearly every prop, it had won the first half and St. Louis was winning 9–0 on three field goals. With the Rolling Stones' "Jumpin' Jack Flash" blasting from Lupo's computer, the duo settle on St. Louis minus-3 and a total of 23.5 for the second half.

On the Rams' first drive of the second half, Warner hits wide receiver Torry Holt for a touchdown, the first one of the game. While St. Louis takes a commanding sixteen-point lead, it costs the book $15,000 since the odds on Holt scoring the first touchdown were 12–1. Every small victory has a bitter aftertaste.

Normally calm and collected, Lupo shows his nerves when an ESPN producer asks him how huge this game is. There is a perceptible stutter when he answers. His language and motor skills betray him as he drops the Cleveland Browns' ball and says, "It's, it's, it's very high profile for us. Deep, very deep, deep in the six figures if we lose. Not good." That bite isn't used in the piece.

Scucci, meanwhile, has abandoned Lupo in his office, unable to keep the profanity from flowing out of his mouth and getting picked up by the boom mike hovering above them all like a flying rat. Between the camera lights, the crowd of people, and the tension, the heat in the room could make Satan sweat. If the devil himself were there, Lupo would gladly trade his soul for the score to remain 16–0 Rams.

When the Rams take the field in the fourth quarter, up 16–6 after a Titan touchdown, Scucci has calmed down enough to come back into the office. He remembers back to August, when someone came in wanting to put $400 on the Rams to win the Super Bowl at 200–1. Because the permutation of $400 to win at 200–1 odds calculated to such a big payout, the ticket writer needed approval. "I laughed it off," Scucci says as the Rams are driving down the field. "I said, yeah go ahead and give it to him. Wish I could have seen that one coming."

Watching the fourth quarter feels like the equivalent of Chinese water torture. With a little more than fourteen minutes left in the game, Tennessee fields a Rams punt and begins what would be the longest drive of the game. With nearly $1 million on the line, Lupo and Scucci haven't sat down since halftime. Both of them shake from adrenaline like newborn calves finding their legs. Tennessee quarterback Steve McNair passes for a first down. Then Titans running back

Eddie George runs for a first down. Methodically the Titans march down the field while the bookmakers see the clock dwindling down. With 8:33 left, Tennessee calls a time-out with a first and ten from the Rams twenty-four-yard-line.

When you watch enough games, and when your livelihood depends on the outcome, your body becomes attuned to sports' natural rhythms and patterns. Barring any miracles, you can sense how long certain drives will play out, what plays need to happen for you to keep your lead and what needs to happen if you lose your lead. You don't live in the moment, you live for the next moment to go your way. You're desperate and you know deep down in the pit of your stomach all the telepathic forces in the world will not get you what you want.

But that doesn't mean Lupo and Scucci don't try. When Tennessee takes its time-out, Lupo and Scucci run down the scenarios of what can happen. Normally this is when they encourage each other, bouncing around positive situations the other might not think of.

"Oh my God we are fucked," says Lupo. "If they kick a field goal, we lose the field goal prop. That's fucking $40,000. If the Titans score a touchdown, that makes it 16–13. With not much time left. If the Rams come back and score a field goal, then we still lose the field goal prop and then we still may not cover. That will put us at $1 million. We are fucked. How can we stop this?" Scucci leaves the room again. A minute-and-a-half later, the Titans score a touchdown, making it 16–13, Rams.

On the next possession the Rams look defeated and distraught. Once up 16–0 in the Super Bowl, they are now up by three points and lacking confidence. They go three plays and out, giving Tennessee the ball back on their own forty-yard-line with just over six minutes left in the game. Eight plays later, Tennessee ties the game with a field goal. With a little more than two minutes left and St. Louis starting their post–field goal drive on their own twenty-seven-yard line, the mood in Joe's office is funeral. Covering the spread looks out of the question. Every football fan who has ever bet and needed a touchdown knew the Rams would play for the field goal with no time left. Football coaches don't play to cover, they play to win the game. A slow, methodical drive down the field was the best strategy against the Titans, who had come back too many times in this game and in the playoffs—remember the miracle play to beat the Bills in the first round of the playoffs—to leave them any time at the end of the game.

On the first play from scrimmage, knowing they only needed a field goal, the Rams defied convention and answered the bettor's prayers. Warner threw a seventy-three-yard-TD pass to Isaac Bruce. Suddenly, a hopeless situation in which it looked like the Rams would probably not cover and could lose the game outright had turned into a Rams' win and push. Forget Saint Jude: Rams coach Dick Vermiel, who called the play, would now be considered the patron saint of lost causes. Scucci comes flying back into the room and gives Lupo the possessed look. "I know shit," he says referring back to his instinct that the game would land on seven. "And I'll tell you right now this is going to be the longest minute of our lives."

With 1:48 left and the ball on their own twelve-yard-line, the Titans begin the most spectacular and memorable unsuccessful drive in Super Bowl history. Quarterback Steve McNair, through a daring combination of off-balance throws, scrambling, and sheer will, gets the Titans to the Rams ten-yard-line with five seconds left. On the game's last play, McNair hits wide receiver Kevin Dyson at the five, who then runs four yards before getting tackled one yard short of the goal line and the game-tying touchdown. As Dyson lies face down on the stadium turf and as Rams players jump around him like butterflies on a leaf, Lupo and Scucci slump into their chairs. The game ends as a push, a brilliant stroke of luck for the sports book. Add a couple of college basketball victories to the six-figure win from the Tennessee money-line bets and the potential $1-million loss turns into a decent payday. Not a Super Bowl–caliber payday, but considering the alternative, Lupo and Scucci know they just emptied their karma bank on the last game of the year.

After the game, Lupo and Scucci emerge from the back office and start handing out refunds for those who bet the spread. Rubbing their eyes, they ask aloud when the wave of people is finally going to leave and they can go home. But, already bettors are asking them for sheets listing tomorrow's bets.

Pointing out to the crowd, oblivious to his emotional and physical exhaustion, Lupo says, "It's just another day as far as they're concerned."

Chapter 14

"Without Nevada, This Would Not Have Happened"

There have been more point-shaving scandals in our colleges and universities in the nineties than in every other decade before it combined. These scandals are a direct result of an increase in legal gambling on college sports.

Our legislation may curb illegal gambling by preventing any confusion regarding the legality of gambling on college sports, eliminating the legitimacy for publishing spreads on college games and reducing the number of students who are introduced to gambling.

—LETTER FROM SPONSORS OF SENATE BILL 2021, ANNOUNCING THEIR INTENTION TO ENACT LEGISLATION BANNING GAMBLING ON COLLEGE SPORTS, JANUARY 31, 2000

When he woke up Monday morning after the Super Bowl, more bleary-eyed than a student who just finished final exams, Lupo didn't feel like he just averted disaster. Sitting in his office going over the early predictions for statewide handle on the Super Bowl, scrutinizing them like a studio exec checking weekend box office receipts, he felt more like he had just escaped the minefield only to land on the front lines. The book didn't lose the nearly $1 million dollars as he had feared it might, but handle in the state dropped to $71 million, $6 million less than its peak in 1998. Across the board, those losses were attributed to bettors finding the Internet a more convenient and accessible way to bet on the big game.

With the insidious threat of the Internet challenging his livelihood, Lupo also read the banner headline on the top of the fold of the *Las Vegas Review-Journal*'s business section, which read, "Senators Push Ban on College Sports." The bill that NCAA President Cedric Dempsey had been promising would come to fruition had indeed made its first appearance. The next day, the article's author continued, Senator Sam Brownback, a Kansas Republican, planned to introduce the legislation banning betting on college sports. This wasn't just a puritanical attempt by a Bible Belt senator to curb some illicit games people play—this was a bipartisan effort with heavy hitters on both sides of the aisle lining up to carry the political football into the end zone. Arizona Senator John McCain (R), then a media darling at the height of his popularity while stumping for the presidency, as well as longtime politicos such as Illinois Senator Dick Durbin (D), North Carolina Senator Jesse Helms (R), and Indiana Senator Dick Lugar (R) all backed the bill. Unlike Kevin Dyson of the Titans, they didn't plan on coming up one yard short.

One argument Brownback made was that if sports betting were illegal everywhere, newspapers would no longer print the point spreads. Eventually, he envisioned, the whole notion of sports betting being an acceptable, harmless habit would disappear. "The perception is that young people are desensitized to gambling as something that is illegal," says Bill Saum, the NCAA's gambling-enforcement director. "That is because it is so widespread. If it is illegal in Nevada, that will make it less prominent. Sports betting being legal in Las Vegas validates a young person's reason for betting anywhere else."

Saum, a stout man with a mustache thicker than a steel brush and a disarming Midwestern accent, is the only member of the NCAA's gambling-enforcement office, and he is stuck fighting the good fight on behalf of the NCAA, regardless of appearances or consequences. After all, the NCAA commands billion-dollar ransoms in exchange for broadcasting its games, knowing that without gambling the ratings might not be there to justify such contracts. He spends his time preaching that gambling is bad, an evil poison that will corrupt the inherent beauty of sport. His quest is noble, considering if he succeeds he may have worked himself out of a job. A former high school and college football coach, he took this assignment not because he had a lifelong vendetta against betting, but because he feels that the NCAA stands for something good. And, despite any grotesque displays of hypocrisy by the organization he has committed his life to, Saum still genuinely believes in the purity of sport—which makes his argument for banning betting on college sports that much more compelling, and Saum himself that much more endearing.

To underscore their point that college athletes are easily corrupted by the evils of gambling, the senators trotted out Kevin Pendergast, a former Notre Dame kicker who, for a while, served as the poster boy for gamblers gone wrong. Pendergast is considered the mastermind behind a point-shaving scandal that sent two Northwestern University basketball players, as well as Pendergast, to jail.

In a packed Capitol Hill conference room, with blinding camera lights causing beads of sweat to glisten on the former athlete's forehead, Pendergast described how, by the time he graduated college, he had rung up credit card debts totaling more than $10,000. While working in Chicago as a bartender, Pendergast, always a casual gambler, was introduced to Dion Lee, a Northwestern basketball player, by a mutual acquaintance. Both were deep in gambling debts, too deep to know right from wrong. Lee, in fact, had already been suspended for gambling a month before meeting Pendergast, his habit discovered when Lee approached a booster about securing a loan so he could pay off his bookie. Lee's suspension led federal agents to start investigating the campus bookmaking operation. Yet, all the while, Lee continued unabashedly betting and, eventually, shaving points for Pendergast. At first, the tasks were simple, like making sure Northwestern lost by more than fourteen to Penn State. No one who followed college basketball would question a sorry Northwestern team losing by fifteen or twenty points to a mid-level Big Ten team like Penn State.

Eventually, in 1995, Pendergast took $20,000 in cash from Chicago to Las Vegas to bet at Caesars Palace on the University of Michigan, minus-25, against Northwestern. Lee objected at first, knowing Michigan's tendency to let up at the end of a game against lesser opponents. A twenty-five point spread would be tough to control. But Pendergast persisted, offering to double the player's payment from the normal $4,000 he usually got paid to $8,000. Despite his instincts that told him to do otherwise, Lee relented. And then he watched helplessly as Northwestern only lost by seventeen points. Pendergast lost the money. Within months, the FBI investigation of campus bookies that had started with Lee's gambling troubles had come full circle, with those bookies giving up Lee, Pendergast and their betting mates to avoid prosecution.

"This was something that basically fell out of the sky," Pendergast admitted. "I took it and did the wrong thing. I blame all the mistakes I made on Kevin Pendergast."

Well, he didn't take all the blame. Later in his press conference, he delivered what the bill's backers hoped would be the death knell for gambling on college sports. "Without Nevada," Pendergast said, "this would not have happened."

The last time the sports-betting industry faced such a threat was during the Kefauver hearings in the early 1950s. Kefauver had concluded that sports betting, and the deep ties it held with the mob, was a danger to the integrity of sports and, following his hearings, Nevada leveled a 10 percent tax against all sports books on every bet they took in, win or lose. In the mid 1970s the tax was lowered to 2 percent and then, in the early 1980s when gambling in general and sports betting specifically became more acceptable, the tax was lowered to one-quarter of 1 percent—making it possible to make a profit as a sports book. Only then did Vegas sports betting become a must in the casinos.

Senators like Brownback and McCain were asking many of the same questions Kefauver had posed: What is gained by sports betting being legal? Not much, was their answer, and politically only Nevada would be affected by any legislation. There were also legitimate law-and-order concerns. While the Vegas sports books claim independence from the seedy underworld of illegal bookmaking, they are not immune, and can easily serve as Laundromats for bookmakers looking to clean up some of the cash they took in on the streets. One example was a massive gambling ring uncovered in 1997 by Brooklyn, New York's District Attorney Charles Hynes and his team of investigators. The D.A.'s office alleged that more than fifty bettors in Las Vegas were intricately linked to betting rooms in New York, sharing in proceeds of nearly $400 million. "Local gambling operations in New York are so intertwined with those in Las Vegas that they are part of the same network," Hynes said at the time. "We don't know how far the network extends."

But while even Hynes relishes the Super Bowl eve gambling busts he has made an annual ritual, he thinks legalizing sports betting is the best way to address the problem. "We should make it tax free, like the bookies," says Hynes. "We could make our money the same way they do, from the vig."

Many who share Hynes's opinion point to the pari-mutuel industry. Once horse racing was the most corrupt of all forms of betting. Whether someone from the mob was working an angle, or a trainer was paid off to make sure his prize-winning trotter finished out of the money, the outcome of horse races in the middle part of the 20th century were as fixed as a Chicago mayoral election.

But, ever since New York State legalized off-track betting (OTB) in 1970, the number of incidents involving corrupt races has dramatically declined. It's harder for jockeys or trainers to blatantly fix a race when so many more people have a direct stake in the outcome and are watching their every move. (With simulcasting and interstate betting now available in thirty-eight states, the American Horse Council estimates that 77 percent of the total amount wagered on pari-mutuel races takes place away from the site of the race being bet on. As recently as 1997, $11.8 billion of the $15 billion bet on pari-mutuels occurred the same way.)

And when politicians looked beyond just sports betting, they found that much had changed since the Kefauver era. "Before nearly every state in the Union legalized some form of gambling, politicians were always decrying the evils of gambling because Nevada was the only state that had it," says *Review-Journal* columnist John L. Smith. "Now only two states don't have gambling of some form so they can't say that anymore."

For some senators and representatives a sort of cognitive dissonance set in. On the one hand, an anti-sports-betting bill seemed like a good idea. But then again, what were the larger repercussions of defying the gaming industry? How does one's vote shape one's political future? As the debate raged in the back rooms on Capitol Hill, several Congressmen couldn't remember exactly why they should or shouldn't support any antibetting legislation.

When Jim Korona heard the first shot, loud enough to get the attention of even his bad ear, he thought he was the target. At long last, his penchant for sneering at the lowlifes who incessantly bummed drink tickets after making five-dollar bets had driven someone to homicidal thoughts. It was just twenty-four hours earlier that one of the regulars had argued with Korona about a line movement, berating the bookmaker so badly in front of a throng of customers that Korona had no choice but to kick him out. As the disgruntled bettor walked away, he looked back sinisterly and promised Korona that he "would get even."

When he heard the second shot, ringing through the nearly empty sports book on the second Monday after the Super Bowl, he patted himself down to make sure he hadn't been hit and dove to the floor. He was twenty-four years old, an up-and-coming bookmaker at a respected sports book in Vegas. He was college-educated and wore a tie and expensive eyeglasses. He had just bought a house. His friends, his brother, and his father were all on Wall Street making six- or even seven-figure salaries. He could have played basketball at Rutgers–The State University of New Jersey, he was that good. All these things went through his mind as he lay face down, sucking on the dust bunnies behind the Stardust betting counter. He tried crawling like a caterpillar toward an exit, never raising his body more than a foot in the air. The shooting had stopped, but because the ringing in his ear was louder than ever, he had no clear idea of what was going on. He was blind and deaf to the commotion on the other side of the counter. All he knew was that the day before someone threatened to get even with him and today gunshots were being fired inside the book, ten feet from where he was standing.

RULE NUMBER SEVEN
You bet your life.

Joe Lupo had been sitting in his office when he heard what sounded like a firecracker explode in the sports book. By the time he reached the back entrance to the book from his office, he'd heard another loud pop. He walked in with his arms in the air, screaming, "What the hell is going on in here?" as if to ask who would dare cause such a commotion in his house. Then he realized he was the only one standing in the entire book. He practically tripped over Korona, who was slowly inching his way towards an exit, unharmed but definitely unhinged. He stepped over three more prone bodies, people he didn't recognize, who were breathing but laying motionless on the carpet behind the counter. Then he saw Ray, his wispy, mild-mannered supervisor who had been in the Marines before coming to the Stardust. Ray looked mad, his face contorted in a way Lupo had never seen before. And he held a gun in his hand. Across from Ray stood Anthony Cuccia, Jr., an older, balding man who Lupo recognized as a regular, albeit small-time player, at the book. "I wondered," says Lupo. "Why did Ray look so mean and how come he was holding a gun on the old guy?"

Cuccia, a fifty-nine-year-old homeless man with a criminal record that stretched back to 1960 when he lived in Brooklyn, arrived at the book early that Monday. He sat in the second row of seats on the race side of the book, next to Phillip Greenspan. The two knew each other from a misspent youth growing up in Brooklyn and misspent adulthood in the sports book. For an hour they sat there, Greenspan talking with fellow bettors and Cuccia silently staring straight ahead, as if catatonic.

At 11:45, without saying a word, Cuccia stood up, walked around the row of desks so he could face Greenspan, who had swiveled his chair so his back was to the betting counter, and pulled out a high-caliber pistol. He fired twice at point-blank range, hitting Greenspan square in the chest with the first shot. The bullet passed cleanly through Greenspan, lodging itself in the formica-covered wood in the first row of desks. Blood sprayed the bettors around him with the force of a firehose. Almost immediately, a darkly colored pool formed on the carpet beneath where Greenspan had been sitting. A carpenter from California named Mark had been standing in the handicapping library when he heard the shot. Stepping out of the library, he saw Greenspan heading straight for him with a gaping hole in his chest and terror in his eyes. "He came up to me and put his hands on my shoulders," Mark told the *Review-Journal* that afternoon. "He whispered, 'Help Me! Help Me!' I responded, 'What can I do?'"

Greenspan pulled away from Mark's arms and ran, literally for his life, toward the sports book's main exit, near where Wayne Newton makes his daily entrance and parks his Rolls Royce. Greenspan was unconscious when he finally reached the glass doors, hitting them so hard, like a bird flying unexpectedly into a window, that blood smeared the clear glass in a red coating. He fell to the concrete and was pronounced dead an hour later.

After firing the second shot, Cuccia remained calm, the eye of the storm that swirled around him. As bettors dove to the floor, covering their heads and fearing for their lives, Cuccia stepped forward to the counter, where Ray the Marine had been standing an uneasy sentry once the shots ended, and placed the gun down. "Okay, relax," Cuccia said. "It's over. I had him in my sights."

"One guy who was standing at the counter when the shots went off—Ray said the guy didn't even duck—turned back around after the shooting was done as if nothing had happened," Lupo says. "He wanted to make a bet and had to lean over the counter, shouting at the ticket writers who were still on the floor, 'So that parlay I wanted'... Another guy walks up to me, right in front of the shooter, and asks me for a betting sheet. He says, 'Pretty exciting, huh, Joey?'"

For the next five hours, as the book stopped taking bets so police could secure the crime scene, interview witnesses, and look for the second bullet, the inhabitants at the sports book seemed lost. They'd walk up to the counter out of instinct, then walk back to their desk, then go to the food stand, then sit at their desk. Without bets to make they were directionless and befuddled, like a television anchor whose teleprompter has blacked out.

"People just lingered in the book all day," Lupo says. "Staring at the yellow police tape."

The next morning, still shaken by the shooting, Korona stood behind the counter, staring down every customer as if looking harder might reveal if someone was packing. The book was busier than usual, partly because some of the regulars had money left over from the day before that didn't get bet while the windows were closed. But it was also crowded because, at the advice of Lupo, the Stardust maintenance staff decided not to repair the bullet hole from the front row of desks in the book. "Come on," says Lupo. "It's a tourist attraction. And right now, we need all the help we can get. Between the Super Bowl future payouts we're still mailing out, the betting bill, and the shooting, it hasn't exactly been a banner month." And indeed, the morbid curiosity seekers were coming in droves, rubbing their fingers along the hole and bending to get a glimpse of the bullet that passed through the bettor. Only in Vegas could death become another sideshow attraction.

Korona, however, didn't need the reminder of what had happened. Everyone was a potential threat. After all, someone was still, "going to get him," as the bettor had said the day before the shooting. Late that morning, as he turned his back to move a line on the computer, he heard a loud crack. He muttered aloud, "not again," and dove to the floor. Sucking on the dust bunnies yet again, just twenty-four hours after the shooting, Korona realized he was the only one taking cover. Then he remembered some building repairs had been scheduled weeks before. "There weren't any shots, but the ceiling panels these guys had been working on fell, right onto the spot where I had been standing," Korona said the next day. "My nerves are just shot. I can't handle this lifestyle."

Other than knowing somehow who won beforehand, confidence is every gambler's greatest asset. Losing your confidence makes you want to change the way you handicap, which changes the way your ratings look, and the rating is the one semirational component of betting to which bettors can apply their logic. Changing your rating alters the way you bet, which leads to losing close games. It's a vicious cycle that requires the gambler to fight through tough losses and stick to his game plan the way a coach needs to be steadfast in the belief that his way is the right way. Change the most minute detail in your approach and the ripple effects can be catastrophic.

February is always the toughest month for any college basketball bettor to keep his confidence high and his bankroll up. The excitement generated by the start of the conference schedule has dissipated and the buzz leading up to the postseason conference tournaments and NCAA tournament is still weeks away. College coaches and players themselves hit the doldrums at this time of year, so it's natural to miscalculate how one team will play against another regardless of record, past performances, or incentives. These are the dog days of the college basketball season, and no one is safe from a slump.

Especially Alan, who has been slumping since mid-January and won't likely bet his way out of it during February. "All any bettor can do right now is get through the bad stretch and make it to the conference and NCAA tournaments," he says glumly. A couple weeks in the red won't put him over the edge, but it's easy to forget the slim margins a working wiseguy has to cover in order to make a salary. Winning 50 percent of the time isn't good enough. To really cash in, taking into account the juice bettors pay on every bet and the discrepancies between winning a $10,000 bet and losing a $20,000 wager, bettors must win at least 56 percent of the time. And that's just to come out on the plus side by a couple of bucks. And, because this is a "put up" business, the less Alan wins, the less money he is able to put up for his next bet. With every passing day Alan doesn't win, he's put out thousands of dollars that won't get a return. And he's not exactly living like a monk. "How would you feel if you hadn't gotten a paycheck in three weeks," he says. "It hurts."

"This season has taken a real negative downturn," he continues. "I won't earn a living all summer. I'm such a degenerate that I put back 25 percent of whatever I win during college basketball into poker, Stanley Cup, NBA Finals, and other stupid bets. When you win people think you are playing with the house's money and that it is okay to give it back. But I work everyday and I want to get paid everyday."

He broke even for two straight weeks at the end of January and the first week of February. Then he got his head caved in. The feeling you get when, going seventy mph, you drive by a cop, your heart in your throat and your eyes on the rearview mirror, is how Alan feels all the time. "We were a peanut winner in January, almost nothing," he says. "And this past weekend was the absolute worst weekend of my life. Worst weekend in my history of betting." Even for someone prone to hyperbole, Alan's statement is a bold indictment on how badly the season has gone for him. With the money he bets, and the games he lost, it may well have been one of his biggest losing weekends ever. And when you lose $30,000-$40,000 a weekend, it can add up.

RULE NUMBER SIX
Everything is a game of chance.

Alan and Billy have done everything they can to curtail the drain on their pocketbook. They are betting fewer games and less money and trying to get down earlier on games they like. Betting early goes against the philosophy they've always adhered to, since it tips off other bettors as to where they're putting their money. But at this point they've lost so many games it's unlikely anyone will want to follow them. On Saturday alone, they lost their five biggest bets—between $15,000 and $20,000—by either half, one, or two points. That's a free throw, a layup or a three-pointer difference between $85,000-$100,000.

As Alan speaks, his voice gets more strained. "I'm not trying to be a doomsayer, but I see the season coming apart. I have no other way of earning money, which scares me." He has flashes of San Francisco beating St. Mary's by nine when he had St. Mary's plus-8.5. He sees Long Beach State losing to Utah State by eight when he bet on Long

Beach State plus-7. "It's just the way we're losing. We've been losing 100 percent of these fuckers on last-second, three-point shots. I hate the three-point shot; it is asinine. Some fucking jerk off thought the fans wanted more scoring so they put it in and it is ruining the game. This fucking sport is so stupid.

"For example, the other night we had a huge fucking bet on LaSalle plus-6.5 against St. Josephs. The whole fucking night St. Joe's doesn't cover the spread. Last play of the game they knock down a meaningless shot and win by seven. We lose. We are running bad. I don't cry about bad luck. But even in the small games we're getting beat. We had a peanut on Minnesota plus-8.5 against Illinois the other night. At the end of the game, Illinois hits six straight free throws to end the game and wins by nine. Just the other night, the day after Valentine's Day, which I spent alone by the way, I bet my fucking balls off on West Virginia plus-7.5 against Villanova and they lose by 10. Two-and-a-half fucking points. One shot. Every game is like that for us this year."

If losing the games weren't bad enough, Alan's just lost another piece of the Vegas betting scene that he once romanticized about. Late in January, the Hilton, which, despite its self-proclaimed title of the Superbook is the least-respected book amongst Vegas wiseguys, took over Caesars, which has always taken bigger limits than most. One afternoon shortly after the merger, Alan walked into Caesars to lay two dimes on the total in a game between Wyoming and New Mexico. While two dimes is considered a steep bet on a total anywhere in Vegas, at Caesars Alan was almost always accommodated. Now the ticket writer, who had taken thousands of Alan's bets, looked at him sheepishly and said, "I can only give you a nickel."

"What?" Alan asked.

"It's nationally televised on ESPN," the ticket writer said, still embarrassed. "I can only give you a nickel on the totals for those games."

Rather than leave behind the nickel bet, Alan picked up his money and walked away. "This whole town is making me sad," he said leaving the dark book. "I better pick some winners soon. I don't want to come back here after the summer."

For the first couple of years that Internet sports-betting sites were in operation, the books in Vegas and the books on the islands peacefully coexisted. As long as they worked together in moving the lines, they would get their fair share of juice and make good returns, while the wiseguys would get squeezed out.

But during the beginning of the football season in 1999 and extending into college basketball in 2000, the Internet sites ceased following the bookmakers' leads. As the industry matured offshore, as the once-novice bookmakers grew into seasoned veterans, they became more aggressive with their linemaking. Instead of stringently adhering to every move the Vegas books made, they made their own decisions. Suddenly, the Las Vegas books were feeling the pinch from the Caribbean books' rebellion. When Maryland played Temple on February 13, the Stardust opened with Temple as 8.5-point favorites. Most of the Caribbean books opened a full point lower at Temple minus-7.5. Scucci, knowing the wiseguys would lay the 8.5 as long as it was the only one out there, quickly moved his number from 8.5 to eight to 7.5. Now the Stardust was open to a middle if the game fell eight. Indeed, the final score was Temple 73 and Maryland 65. It cost the book $20,000.

Scucci knew that, at first, the Internet sites were fledgling operations that bettors didn't trust—sometimes with reason. But, now their annual intake had reached the billion-dollar mark; with estimates that within three years, the amount bet offshore would easily eclipse the $2 billion or so bet every year legally in Nevada. And Scucci, Lupo, and the others were realizing that the influence Vegas books have might soon be as irrelevant to wiseguys as the English monarchy is to Her Majesty's citizens. The comparison was apt in more ways than one. It was quite possible to imagine that the sports books themselves could be like Buckingham Palace, tourist attractions for the nostalgic souls that dream of the way things used to be. "As long as there is a desire to gamble, people will still be coming to Las Vegas," sighs Scucci. But he knows something fundamental is changing. "What the Internet has done is drive the bigger amounts of money and wiseguy money out of the books. And that was the fun part of this job."

Still, Scucci had some hope. (Doesn't every gambler, no matter what side of the counter?) And it came from an unexpected source: Janet Reno and her prosecution of the twenty cyber-bookmakers, including Jay Cohen and his cohorts at WSEX.

Reno was basing her case on an interpretation of the 1961 Wire Act. Therefore, the essential questions concerning both the defendant and prosecution in the Cohen case were: Can a law written almost forty years ago with no concept of the Internet be applied to this new technology? And how broad is the United States' jurisdiction in terms of geography and technology?

For ten days in February, the federal prosecutors in Manhattan explained to a jury how WSEX and Cohen targeted American clients. The company advertised in U.S. newspapers and magazines and accepted wire transfers so accounts could be opened and bets made on NFL games, college football games, or any other American sporting event. Prosecutors then described how FBI agents were able to access the site—using a telephone wire and their computer modem—to gather information about teams and players they were thinking of betting on. Finally, they explained how these same agents opened accounts and were able to make bets using both the Internet and an 800 number set up by WSEX.

The defense could not deny the facts, but it raised questions about whether the Internet was what the writers of the 1961 Wire Act had in mind when they restricted the use of telephones for trading bets and information? No, they said emphatically. And could a server processing the bets in Antigua, where betting is legal, fall under U.S. jurisdiction? Not a chance, they argued.

But, Cohen never really had a shot, since this case had become as emotional as it was technical. To prosecutor Joseph Demarco, Cohen wasn't just a neighborhood bookie running a corner shop; he was a bookmaker to the Universe, and, more important to Demarco, Cohen was a bookmaker to the 270 million Americans who could access his site. With the click of a mouse, they could lose the house. Cohen sought them out through advertising, made it easy for them to open accounts and, according to Demarco, finding Cohen not guilty would open a Pandora's box of illicit activity on the Internet that could tear the fabric of the country apart.

The jury agreed. Cohen was convicted and sentenced to one year and nine months in prison and given a $5,000 fine.

Even after his partner was sentenced, Steve Schillinger, still on safe ground back in Antigua, defied the government to stop him or any of the other 650 Web sites offering sports betting and casino games.

"When they shut Western Union down, people still found a way to send the money in," Schillinger said after the trial, in reference to the agreement between the Florida Attorney General and Western Union to not send money to offshore betting sites. "They can still send a cashier's check or a money order. When they started shutting down our 800 numbers, we just put more up so people could get through to us.

"There really is no slowing us down. There's no stopping us."

That's what Korona is afraid of. Eating a steak sandwich at the Pepper Mill restaurant across from the Stardust, Korona is at home in the Las Vegas diner, a relic that has been around since 1972. Despite his slick clothes, slicker hair, and fancy glasses, he's a 1940s traditional guy stuck coming of age in the 1990s. If he had his druthers, he'd follow the horses, make book, and never think about the Internet again. Las Vegas is the place he wanted to become a bookmaker, not Antigua or Costa Rica or some other island he couldn't pinpoint on a map. Like Alan, he had a romantic notion of matching wits against the best wiseguys and having the work he does at the Stardust resonate throughout the entire industry.

But, like any twentysomething who is seeing kids his age earn millions while he struggles for a midlevel manager's salary, he's a little envious. And a little nervous that, if he doesn't jump on the Internet highway soon, he will have missed out on the biggest gold rush this century. In Vegas logic, the real suckers are those who sit on the side.

"Everyone talks about how the computers are changing this industry," he says, emphasizing computers as though he were unfamiliar with the concept. "They say offshore is where it is going. Hell it might be where it is at."

Five years ago, an educated, ambitious bookmaker like Korona would have been marked as a surefire book manager. But, just as many other industries suffered from a brain drain during the Internet craze of 1998 and 1999, Las Vegas bookmaking is on the precipice of losing its most talented people.

"I'm not gonna hide it, I am money hungry," says Korona. "I don't just want to get by. And I give that guy Jay Cohen credit for going down there and getting something started. He is a visionary for doing it, something I don't think I am. But I do wanna be where the action is. Where they are making big moves and taking big bets and making lots of money. How much longer will that be what's happening at the Stardust? I don't know. But things don't look good."

"We're going big on Northwestern today. How the fuck can we not. You think Michigan cares about this game?" Alan asks Billy over the speakerphone.

Northwestern, on pace for one of the worst records in Big Ten basketball history, is the kind of team bettors love to bet on. While it sounds clichéd, they do play hard every night, even when they are getting blown out by more than thirty points, a common occurrence in 1999–2000. Their opponent on February 26, Michigan, has been an inconsistent but talented team whose scouting report reads that they play up to or down to the level of their opponent. On top of that, Michigan's best player and leading scorer, Jamal Crawford, was recently suspended for financial assistance he got from a family friend while he was in high school. The Northwestern game is the first game in which he won't be suiting up. With Michigan as 5.5-point favorites, this game seems like a steal to Alan and Billy. "That's a good bet," Alan reiterates.

When Northwestern is down 25–10 with 3:40 left in the first half, Alan's supposedly good $20,000 bet looks like pure insanity. "More fucking money down the drain," says Alan.

Instantly, both Alan and Billy try to rationalize how the bet could have gone wrong. Simply misjudging how good each team is based on talent isn't the answer. They are both too expert as handicappers to so egregiously miscalculate the outcome. Perhaps it's a question of pop psychology. "I guess Michigan has an NIT shot," Alan says. "That must be what they have in their heads."

The game's second half turns into a microcosm for Billy and Alan's season. Down sixteen points, Northwestern fights back to tie the game with no time left on the clock. Alan and Billy were right; Northwestern would play for forty minutes. Michigan would play down to its opponent. If there is such a thing, it was a good bet. Unfortunately for them, a Northwestern tie at the end of the game is worse than a loss by two points. With the loss, they've won their bet. With the tie, there is overtime, and anything can happen.

Shoveling egg whites into his mouth at Jamms, Alan half listens to his friend Artie talking about the poker games the night before. Alan is incessantly checking his ticker for updates on the Northwestern game. In the overtime the Wildcats score first, taking a brief lead, 53–51. But

Michigan scores the next five points in a row and goes on to outscore Northwestern 12–6 in the extra period. Ultimately, that's a six-point loss, half a point too much for Alan and Billy. Clenching his teeth, tightening his grip on the ticker, Alan drops his fork. As the waitress walks by, he orders a short stack of pancakes, his third breakfast in the span of half-an-hour. This is his brand of punishment, eating until he wants to puke, if the game hasn't made him feel like that already.

"The whole fucking year has been this way," Alan says. "If not for these fucking overtime games we've lost we'd be up $1 million. On top of all that, I got retrograde starting next week just in time for the conference tournaments."

Retrograde, as in Mercury in retrograde, which is the illusion that Mercury is somehow moving backwards while all the other planets move forward. For those who think they are affected when Mercury is in retrograde, straightforward thinking and logical conclusions get interrupted, like TV reception in a lightning storm. As far as Alan is concerned, it's another ingredient in the witch's brew that makes up his ratings. He used to think retrograde was silly and, "then I got retrograded right out of a Kent-Temple game last year.

"There was no other explanation for losing that game. At first I laughed at retrograde when someone told me about it last year. But, I ended up 0–7 that day. And retrograde laughed at me."

The beauty of betting is that every day starts fresh; the day before a distant memory, the day ahead full of opportunity. When the conference and NCAA tournaments start, that feeling is intensified. The slate is wiped clean. Even better, instead of wasting the first month of the season getting to know the teams and himself, the wiseguy has a season's worth of intimate study under his belt. He should know a team's bad habits as well as his own. "Typically," Alan says. "This is the time of year when everyone should get their stroke back. It's not just a new season for the teams but for me."

For the truly wise wiseguys, those who approach betting as an art form and lifelong career, the chance to study the season from a broad perspective is invaluable. This is what Alan is doing on the last Sunday in February, the last weekend before the conference tournaments begin. The atmosphere in his white living room during his season postmortem is a stark contrast to a usual Saturday. With all the action between the phones, televisions, Internet connections, screaming, and virtual bloodletting that takes place on Saturdays, this Sunday morning must be what it's like in the ER when it's been scrubbed down after Halloween.

Piano Jazz, a radio show on National Public Radio, fills the hollow living room with songs like "I'm Old Fashioned" by John Coltrane. Without the usual static that accompanies most radio stations, the momentary silences coming from the radio only magnify how still the house is and amplify the ticking of Alan's wall clock. Laid out on his immaculate desk like scalpels, ready to dissect his last day, last week, last month, and last season of betting, are his different-colored pens. Red for his power rating. Green to compare schedules. Blue to keep track of his opening line, the sports books' closing line, and the final score. The ubiquitous three-ring binder holding the schedule, scores, and bets he made on every team all season is the body that needs examining. Taking a look inside, it is a sick one at that.

What he sees are not just wins and losses, but a steep decline in confidence. He had been doing a good job handicapping. His reasoning behind picking one game over another and one team over another was sound. But in the morass of losing by half-points and on three-point shots and in overtime, it's easy to think you've lost the edge. And, over the last six weeks, having dipped below the break-even point and on the verge of doing serious damage to his original bankroll, Alan is suddenly responsible if everything continues to slide.

As he lost confidence, he's deferred to Billy too much. For example, the day before he saw that the University of North Carolina–Charlotte was a 7.5-point favorite over Tulane University. "Even though they had lost five of their last six games, I like their coach, they play seniors and Tulane features some freshman, and I thought they would play out of it. But Billy didn't think it was a good value. I had a feeling yesterday Charlotte would play well and had a fire in their eyes.

"That is what I mean by being inside a team. I just knew it. But I let myself get talked out of it. Instead of making a medium bet at 7.5 we made a small at minus-6.5."

UNC–Charlotte won by nineteen points.

RULE NUMBER FIVE
Seniors may struggle but freshmen will falter.

But what he sees inside his book, more than a declining confidence, is a season-long disregard for money. As a gambler, he's expected to bet his balls off every once in a while. But as a professional, he is also expected to be disciplined with his money management. That was one of the reasons he went in with his partners: to keep the leash tight. But from the first day of the season, beginning with Stanford vs. Duke, through St. John's vs. Ohio State, and even with Northwestern vs. Michigan, he has overbet. The pattern was the same every time. The game looks good so he gets some money down early. Then it moves his direction and he puts a little more down. By game time he's acting like a full-blown addict, binging on the line in massive doses, unable to hold back from tossing around obscene amounts of money.

"I have to stop fucking off money amateurishly. Most people write down immediately what they think a game is worth and stick to that, but I'm too reckless," Alan admits. "But next week I will write down a reason why I like every game and what I think it is worth. I have no choice. I have to get paid. If the goal is to make enough to get back next year, right now I'm in jeopardy of not making enough to meet that goal."

Chapter 15

Everyone Jump in the Pool

I hear people saying that the $6 billion contract is partially because of the interest of gambling and that ratings are related to gambling. But two things in response to that: One, there has never been a study to back up that claim. Which leads to the second point that, when people say that it's nothing more than innuendo, like two guys sitting in a bar and one of them is saying Peyton Manning is not a good quarterback, it's just opinon.

I think it is just the opposite; as a result of great competition and a great interest in the sport of college basketball, sports wagering has increased. People haven't become more interested in sports because they are betting more.

—BILL SAUM, NCAA GAMBLING ENFORCEMENT DIRECTOR, WINTER 1999

n **May of 2000,** one month after Michigan State beat Florida to become college basketball's national champions, distinguished Yale Professor Edward Kaplan stood before the spring conventioneers of the Institute for Operations Research and the Management Sciences and delivered a lecture on this paper: "March Madness & the Office Pool." Kaplan is no lightweight researcher. His particular field of expertise is applying scientific methods toward better decision making in the battle against AIDS, a discipline for which he has won several awards of high distinction from his colleagues.

But, the NCAA pool had always vexed him and his colleague, Stanley J. Garstka, the deputy dean of Yale's School of Management. "We decided we'd like to win once in a while," Kaplan said of himself and Garstka, who coauthored the paper with him. "We have unsuccessfully participated in such pools for more than a decade."

In the NCAA tournament, there are 9.22 billion possible outcomes, Kaplan explains. When he tested his model—which considered the probability for predicting game winners based on regular season performance, professional sports rankings, and Las Vegas odds—against actual past results of the NCAA and NIT tournaments, the model accurately predicted winners at a 58-percent clip.

Other than winning, what compels a couple of high-minded academics to research the best way to win the NCAA tournament pool? Well, despite Bill Saum's pleas otherwise, it's the same reason CBS paid $6 billion for the media rights to the tournament. The Gaming Control Board does not discern between money bet on college or pro basketball. But of the $172.4 million bet on basketball in Nevada in March of 2000, most bookmakers agree that nearly $80 million of that, more than is wagered on the Super Bowl, belonged to the NCAA tournament.

And the Vegas numbers are just a reflection of just how commonplace betting on the tournament has become nationwide. It's impossible to calculate total figures gambled during the three weeks of March Madness, but combining pools, illegal bets, and Internet gambling, the FBI estimates, an admitted underestimate at that, the figure is about $2.5 *billion*. That's more than the state of Nevada takes in legally during an entire year of sports. Other gaming experts put the number has high as $7 billion.

Last year before the tournament, the *Pittsburgh-Post Gazette* calculated that, if it takes the average person fourteen minutes to fill out a pool at the office, and 15 percent of the nation's workforce participates—around 10.2 million people—then Americans would spend 2.38 million hours focusing on their pool brackets in the days leading up to the tournament. The paper took it a step further, determining that based on the average American hourly salary of $13.53, the total amount people were paid to fill out their brackets was $32.2 million. When the Society for Human Resource Management conducted a poll in April of 1999, it found that 30 percent of the respondents participated in an NCAA office pool.

A more inexact science for determining the tournament's betting popularity—certainly less precise than Kaplan and Garstky's study—is tracking the variations on the pool that have developed over the years and how the wagers have escalated. The common pool, where a group of friends throw $5 in a pot, fill out the brackets, and the winner takes all, has generally been replaced by more complicated schematics. Now every game is prescribed a point total. The lower the seed that wins, the more points the bettor gets. The pool winner has the highest number of points at the end.

More specifically, the landscape is littered with anecdotes of betting pools being tolerated by those who are supposed to stop them. While giving a speech one year at the Los Angeles Dodgers spring-training facility about the evils of gambling, two FBI agents were asked to wait fifteen minutes while the Dodgers finished filling out their NCAA brackets. Even President Clinton and his secret service staff have faxed in their pool picks while traveling through Central America.

Another form of the NCAA pool allows groups of people to buy a particular team they think will do well. The further their team goes, the more the initial investment is worth. At one high-stakes pool in New York in 1999, the total pot swelled to $11.9 million, with one team paying $2.1 million to own the Duke Blue Devils. In the finals, Duke lost to Connecticut—which paid its investor group $2.6 million.

But where pools have garnered the most spectacular coverage is in the country's exchanges. Home to the most pure market-driven economy in the world, places like Wall Street, the Pacific Exchange that Jay Cohen and Steve Schillinger used to call home, and the Chicago Board of Options Exchange are petri dishes for risky behavior. One popular approach is for traders to assign dollar amounts to every team in the tournament and allow the players to buy, sell, or short those teams as the tournament progresses. (This is the style of betting that Cohen and Schillinger thought would revolutionize gambling when they opened WSEX in the late 1990s.) Partially because the notion of buying futures and shorting stocks is so complicated, the NCAA tournament as stock market has mostly been confined to those who play with money for a living. That might be just as well. In 1991, a clerical assistant at Paine Webber lost $330,000 selling short in Duke, hoping the Dukies would eventually flounder, while the Blue Devils instead won the whole thing. Another clerk once lost $200,000 doing the same thing with Kentucky when it won the title in 1996. One pool that started in Chicago and extended to New York in the early 1990s became worth more than $1 million. It had become so distracting to the traders that the chairman of Lehman Brothers delivered a memo declaring that participating in pools was a fireable offense.

Appropriately, the phenomenon of high-stakes betting on Wall Street and small-time NCAA pools coincided with ESPN helping the tournament evolve from a weekend championship into a three-week serial drama. The same people betting on the games, predominantly college-educated, professional men, were the same guys who watched ESPN twenty-four hours a day. And, even more than the Super Bowl, March Madness lends itself to social betting, because it's likely that someone you know went to a college that is playing in the tournament.

With the advance of the Internet over the last four years, the pool of bettors has increased, as have the social aspects of betting. The majority of sports-related sites, including CNNSI.com, ESPN.com, and Sportingnews.com, have pools for which the winner is awarded prizes equal to thousands of dollars. At all of these sites, bettors can create smaller communities linking them with friends all across the country in the same pool. "I think these are the office pools now," said Mark Mariani, president of sales and marketing for CBS Sportsline. "Now the Internet plays a role in every pool."

In 1999, Sandbox.com's pool attracted 300,000 entrants total. In 2000, combining with sports site Rivals.com, they offered a $1-million bonus prize to anyone who could correctly pick all sixty-three games. They also spread out $500,000 in prizes to three thousand other top finishers.

The tourney fever is most obvious on selection Sunday, the day the matchups for the tournament are announced. Selection Sunday is treated almost as a holy day by every sports fan. And the network analysts are the pontiffs. At 6 P.M., CBS broadcasters begin running down the brackets for each of the four regionals—East, Southeast, Midwest, and West. Unlike the Super Bowl, the depth and breadth of teams involved lends itself to being more inclusive for the fans. And while most Super Bowls produce an endless stream of buildup that leads to a lackluster game, the tournament always delivers high drama and stunning upsets. The tournament's pageantry isn't produced by Disney and doesn't star Christina Aguilera or Enrique Iglesias. It comes from college bands, cheerleaders in short skirts, and fans with their faces painted. But, most of it all, it comes from the do-or-die nature of the event and the fact that, for most college players, their lives will never be as great as it is right then. Everyone watching knows it. And so do the players.

That's why they play with such desperation. And that is why the tournament produces sentimental favorites that are virtually impossible to reproduce at any pro level. If a pro player loses a big game, it's hard to sympathize when chances are good they're making $1 million a year and will have another shot next year. But when a college player loses his last game, the pain on his face isn't just for losing the game, it's for the end of his playing days. More often than not, what lies ahead isn't the privileged life of a college athlete, complete with training tables, free warm-ups, and all the BMOC adulation he can stomach. It's an everyday life spent looking for one moment that matches even a scintilla of the rush he got playing in front of 20,000 people. It's easier for fans to get caught up in the emotion of the moment when they know the college kid has a lifetime of work ahead of him, not a career in the NBA.

The anticipation for the tournament selection is so great that ESPN, knowing how to milk the cash cow that put it on the map, runs a countdown leading up until 6 P.M., when the selections will be announced. It is the day before Dan Marino, the greatest quarterback in NFL history, is announcing his retirement, but on Sportscenter, ESPN's signature show, the talk is about "bubble teams" who may or may not make the tournament and "upset specials" people should consider when filling out their brackets. In honor of the Final Four being in Indianapolis, ESPN even ran a treacly video featuring Indiana rock 'n' roll legend John Cougar Mellencamp waxing poetic about what basketball means in the heartland. The piece included a basketball montage set to the Mellencamp's tune "Your Life Is Now." When it ended, Mellencamp stood in an empty gym holding a ball and, looking earnestly into the camera, said, "Alright college hoops, your life is now." Over the top, sure. But the video's "anyone can win on any day" theme captured the essence of the tournament and why people love it.

It certainly struck a chord with Rodney Bosnich, who showed up at the Stardust at 9 A.M. on selection Sunday to get a good seat for the conference championship games. He needed a pick-me-up and, for an Indiana native and former high school basketball star, a cocktail of Mellencamp and hoops feels like a shot of B–12 directly into the heart. Back in the middle of February, watching games at the Stardust, Rodney overheard another bettor describing his system for betting. Rodney copied it down on a Stardust parlay card and took it home to test it out. "It's pretty basic," says Rodney. "You take the RPI rating [a team's strength of schedule and how well they did against that schedule] for each team and then, for the home team, add four points. Any spread that is within two points of the RPIs plus the home court advantage number is a good value." That Friday night Rodney spent six hours in front of the computer, adding home-court advantages to RPI numbers on every college game. That weekend he won twelve straight college basketball bets, totaling $2,400. "It was better than anything you could imagine."

But only a few weeks later he was struggling for the first time in his fledgling career. Instead of trusting the instincts and innate basketball knowledge that carried him all season, he relied on the system to feed him the answers. The week before the tournament, trying to wean himself off the system, Bosnich suffered his first losing week of the season. He also suffered the indignity of getting rejected after yet another job interview.

This time it was at Harrah's sports book, and Bosnich thought he had a real chance. He went against all his "I could care less what you think" instincts and dressed nicely, arrived on time, and answered questions the way he thought the interviewer would want them answered. When she asked him about his job as a security guard, how he liked working with people, and why he left, he didn't say, "'I hate it, I'm shitty with people and my boss was a dick.' Even though I wanted to. I just said it was great, I was great with people and I left to move out here." He even took a math test of thirty questions that had to be answered in five minutes, the sports book equivalent of the NFL's Wonderlic test that measures the intelligence of prospective draft picks. He answered twenty-eight of the thirty questions and got every one of them right. Still, no call back. Not even to say thanks but no thanks, we're not interested. "I don't really care," he says. "I'm not interested in that anyways. I don't know why I bother. I bet, that is what I do."

But with three weeks left in college basketball and the prospect of only betting on baseball and pro baskets from April until next September, two sports he got killed on when he first arrived in Vegas, a steady income would be nice. Playing the conference tournaments leading up to the NCAA tournaments, he lost $600 for the week. "I don't really know how it happened, actually," he says with astonishment from the front row of the Stardust seats. "I just sort of lost the feeling."

RULE NUMBER FOUR

If you forget your bet on the way to the window,
forget your bet.

Seeing the analysts break down which teams are definitely in, which are definitely out, and which teams could be upset contenders helps him refocus. It's like he's playing the game himself and trying to shoot himself out of a slump. Getting back to basics is the key. What's your first instinct about a game? Why did you have that instinct? Does the research you do support the instinct, refute the instinct, or is it irrelevant?

Those are the same questions Lupo and Scucci and their staff are debating right now on the other side of the counter. For example, Cincinnati, which was the best team in the country all season long, lost its best player for the rest of the year during its conference tournament. How will that affect their seeding? How will that affect their play? The bookmakers don't have an accurate measure of what kind of rating to give the team, compromising their ability to post a spread against whomever Cincinnati plays.

The first four days of the tournament, that Thursday through Sunday, are the most important for both sports book and sports bettor. That's when there are the most games, full of teams no one except the bookmakers and the wiseguys have heard of. Once the tournament enters the second week, the field has been winnowed down to teams that the public at least can make educated guesses on, eliminating the knowledge advantage the professionals maintain. For everyone who makes their living betting, the first four days are when the tournament matters. The rest is just backwash.

At the Stardust, a strategy for attacking the opening two rounds actually developed the night before when Lupo, Scucci, and Korona had dinner at the California Pizza Kitchen in the Mirage Hotel. There's a lot on the line in this year's tournament, more so than in years past, because of financial pressures and, more important, pressure from the Caribbean books. The islands' aggressive line-making is starting to impede on the Stardust's status as the first line posted. Lupo does not want to get beat to that opening line, and he's demanding Scucci and Korona be sharp. Unlike the regular season, Lupo will not wait for the consultants' numbers to come in on the tournament games. They don't have the luxury of wasting even a second if they want to get their numbers first. All three of them must have a solid rating for every tournament team in their head so, as the matchups are announced, they only need to fine-tune before posting a number.

Lupo tells Korona that, as the selection show airs, he will be in charge of clearing the big board above the counter. Gone will be spring training games, the Atlanta 500 Nascar Race and the Masters Futures. It will be black, filled with nothing but the brackets, the teams and the numbers, a cornucopia of money-making opportunities, either for the book or the bettor. Each time a team is announced on the show, Korona will type it into the computer so all the games are ready to be posted as soon as the selection show ends. "I get all the grunt stuff," Korona says.

"Don't worry," Lupo tells his anxious protégé. "You'll get plenty of action. These are the greatest four days of the year. Better than the Super Bowl."

At 3 P.M. Vegas time, CBS comes on the air. After a day of pomp and ceremony signifying the start of a three-week dream, the pretense is dropped. As soon as Greg Gumbel, the host of the show, announces the first matchup, the board at the Stardust is cleared, creating a gaping hole in the betting universe. From now until the first lines are posted, the betting world stands still. There is literally nowhere to make a bet. Not a corner bookie, island site, or betting window will take any action. All the wiseguys, bookmakers, sharps, squares, students, lawyers, doctors, moms, and dads are filling in their empty brackets, making notes about certain teams and planning a betting strategy for the coming weeks. And, emphasizing how the tourney has captivated the sports world, for the first time in its broadcast history, the selection show gets a higher rating than the NBA game being played on rival NBC.

If Lupo has his way, and his team is ready, all of that money, billions of dollars worth of bets, will hinge on the line that he posts. "That is just the way I like it," he says. At 4 P.M. he saunters into the book like a gunfighter ready for a duel, carrying boxes of Girl Scout cookies and casually munching on a chocolate-dipped shortbread. Around him the bettors sit in rapt attention, staring at the big board like expectant fathers, waiting for the first sign of life. He runs through the matchups Korona handed him, talking to himself about every team, leaving clues about how he thinks they will fare and what their number should be.

"Louisville got in? St. John's is out west? That LSU is a dangerous team. The west region is wide open. Arizona is the worst number-one seed I've seen. UNLV is going down hard, which is good so we don't have to worry about not putting up their games. Tennessee is going nowhere. UCONN could surprise people."

Korona walks in and grabs a thin mint cookie. "Man, there is nothing better than these in ice cream." But Lupo ignores him, continuing on with his Jack Kerouac style of line-making, a stream of consciousness dissertation of first impressions that will weigh heavily when he makes the numbers minutes later. "Notre Dame didn't get in. Rutgers didn't get in. Xavier didn't get in. They never got a dinner."

"Huh?" Korona asks.

"Red Buttons, whenever he'd emcee a celebrity roast would go down a list of people who had gotten roasted. He'd be like, 'Dean

Martin got a dinner. Frank Sinatra got a dinner. Sammy got a dinner.' Then he'd say, 'Me? Never got a dinner.'"

Korona looks at him like a confused puppy but Lupo doesn't bother explaining any further. He just moves on.

"Cincy is a number-two seed, huh? They're going down. West is the easiest region. Ohio State has the toughest journey. Hofstra is playing in Buffalo. How far is Buffalo from Hofstra?"

Location, location, location. Nothing matters more in the early rounds of the tournament when it comes to posting totals. The bookmakers and wiseguys have the home and away scoring averages for every team in the tournament at their fingertips. While none of the teams actually play at home, some teams play close enough that it will feel like a home game. Knowing the proximity of a school to the region it's been assigned to is vital to posting a good number. Since Buffalo is only an hour flight from Hofstra's Long Island, New York, campus, chances are good a lot of Hofstra fans will make the trip upstate. That pushes Lupo to use Hofstra's home scoring average, which is a couple of points higher than its away average, in the school's matchup against Oklahoma State. These little details could mean the difference of just a couple thousand dollars, but they are precisely the details Lupo has been stressing that his staff pay attention to since his unpleasant sit-down with them in early January. The islands are taking away too much business to slack off. They cannot afford to assume that what they lose on one game they will make up on another game. The margin for error is slim.

That's obvious two hours later, at 6:15, when the lines are up and Lupo is standing behind the counter, calling on bettors who want to partake in the lottery. There's not a single book that has lines up other than the Stardust. They are the clear winner in the first-to-post sweepstakes. Their prize? A grand total of four people want to bet. In less than a season, the power of the island books has become so enchanting that the lottery, the wiseguy's chance to pound a book's weak number and make some easy cash, is rendered almost irrelevant. As he shuffles the cards, Lupo shakes his head in disbelief, wondering why he rushed, why he risked posting some faulty numbers, in the first place. "The wiseguys are pathetic. Last year there would have been twenty guys lining up for a crack. None of them want to bet now unless the Caribbean is up. That's killing me."

For a bookmaker addicted to action, the silence is deafening. The only commotion is caused when Lupo takes off his shoe and reveals his blue-painted toes, courtesy of his daughter. "Nice huh, there's plenty to say about my toes. How about making some bets?" he says.

At 6:30 the lines at the Mirage go up, giving bettors a chance to see which way the books are leaning on key games. But still, the runners in the front row of the Stardust don't look up from their nachos. They've all got pagers attached to their hips, and when the first Caribbean lines goes up, their boss will page them with some plays. Until then, it's sit tight.

Seven minutes later, at 6:37, Costa Rica International Sports (CRIS) finally posts its line. But by then, Lupo is on his way out the door, disgusted.

At 6:30 on Selection Sunday, Alan Boston had staked out a seat at the MGM, where bookmaker Richie Baccellieri's limits were $10,000. It was another bold move by a young bookmaker trying to turn around a book for the corporate suits while still maintaining his rep with the wiseguys. If he pulls it off, everybody loves him. If he doesn't, he'll be the most beloved exbookmaker in town.

Alan made a stop at the Stardust before going to the MGM, but the limit was just $3,000, surprisingly low for the tournament. With the MGM at $10,000 and several other books at $5,000, the Stardust's reluctance to take a higher limit has as much to do with the lack of action during the lottery as the presence of the island books. "If I'm gonna take half an hour to drive here, I want more for my time than a lousy three dimes," says Alan. Instead he puts down the limit at the

MGM on Wisconsin minus-2.5 against Fresno State, Oregon minus-1 against Seton Hall, South Carolina State plus-34 against Stanford, Cincinnati minus-15.5 over UNC–Wilmington, St. Bonaventure plus-8 against Kentucky, Butler plus-9 against Florida, and Samford plus-14.5 against Syracuse. Almost $77,000 in bets and vigorish are placed in a matter of minutes. That doesn't include the five dimes each he put on Butler, Cincinnati, and St. Bonaventure at the Bellagio. Any issues of money management he had been weighing the week before the tournament have been overcome. "You gotta be fearless right now," he says later that night. "You can't watch every dime in a week like this. If you do then it's too hard to gamble with it. Everyone will bet this tourney; if you see a game you like you have to hit it early and hit it hard. As game days approach, because there is so much time between when the lines go up and when the games happen, you never know what will happen to the lines."

The next three days—Monday, Tuesday, and Wednesday—will be the hardest for any DG (degenerate bettor). Normally, during the season a bettor has maybe 12 to 24 hours to contemplate a line and get down his bets. But, with more than seventy-two hours between the posting and the tip-off, and with every square in the country making a play, the numbers can move like EKGs. And a bettor's eyes spin like pinwheels. With so much time and so many games, suddenly numbers you didn't like get closer to numbers you do like. The line between value and sucker bet, between fiscal responsibility and feeding your fix, gets wiped out with greenbacks.

Every Tuesday before the NCAA tournament begins, a group of old-guard, hardcore bettors and bookmakers, past and present, get together for one final toast to the season. For 364 days of the year they are strangers. But once a year they gather, like a family meeting for Christmas. They are a band of bettors and bookmakers considered the last of a dying breed in Las Vegas—Jimmy Vaccaro, Alan Boston, Dave Malinsky, Richie Bacciellieri, Arnie Lang, and Billy—even though none of them is any older than his mid-fifties. They are transplants, betting vagabonds, who settled in Las Vegas because this is where they could do what they loved. What they gave up in terms of family, friends, and human connections they felt—and some still feel—could be replaced with a good number, a winning bet, and some cash in their pockets. They developed their craft before the corporations turned hotels into theme parks and before computers made the sports books almost obsolete. A wiseguy lifestyle, devoid of any attachments that could make them feel like betting on sports for a living was irresponsible, was what they craved. In return their support group isn't a wife and family, but each other. And these dinners served as an anchor that tethered them, however loosely, to other people floating in the same ocean.

But, this year, all that has changed. The life they wanted when they were thirty is not the one they need when they are in their forties. The industry has changed. Their needs have changed. They all know that this is the last year they'll all be around to toast each other, share stories, and reminisce about the way it used to be. Vaccaro, once the man who ruled the books, is moving back to his native Pittsburgh. Lang, who hosted the Stardust Line, was fired by Lupo in favor of a younger, more energetic host. Baccellieri, tiring of the corporate structure, is contemplating offers in the islands. Malinsky has already spent most of his time during the college basketball season helping some investors set up a book in Panama. He's only in town to pack up his things. Billy, Alan's partner, is moving to Los Angeles and may only make it to Las Vegas to bet on the weekends. One by one, by sheer coincidence, they all decided this was the year they would move on. All of them that is, except for Alan. And so this year, it is out of respect and sympathy for him that they gather. "He was the one who organized it," says Malinsky. "Partially because he knows the people he has always relied on in the past, even if he never spoke to them, will be gone next year. The odds of all of us being at this table again are not very good."

Alan chose Hugo's for dinner, where he knew he would get his usual star treatment. As his friends gathered, he ordered bottles of wine, spoke loudly, and acted like the gregarious host. For all his talk about wanting to be alone forever, he truly loved being with these people. They had seen him when he was broke, when he was high, when he was fat, when he was rich, when he was sober, and when he was sculpted. They knew him as well as anyone in the world. And he appreciated that.

When everyone was seated, Alan stood up to toast his fellow wiseguys.

"I know this is probably the last year that we will all get together like this. And it's sad, because everyone is quitting for the same reasons college basketball disgusts me so much. Television turned this tournament that I love into something worth so much money everyone has gotten greedy. Meanwhile, the corporations have made it impossible to get down in this town, taking all the joy out of betting. They don't want to take bets; they just want to make money and that has changed everything. It makes me sick." Alan paused, taking a big gulp of his wine.

RULE NUMBER THREE
Vegas doesn't root for Vegas.

He continued: "But the guys here, like Jimmy and Richie, did it right. And guys like Malinsky played it right. That wasn't as eloquent as I had practiced in my head, but you all know what I mean. Amen."

"Cheers," Vaccaro says, raising his glass. "I have something I'd like to say also. You three guys across the table [Alan, Lang, and Malinsky] made all the years I've been here great. When I leave for Pennsylvania, it will be the bets you guys made and times we shared across the counter that I miss most. I'm sorry it all had to end. I can't stand this fucking place anymore. Next year we'll all meet at my house in Pennsylvania. But it is the end of an era."

For the next few hours they talked about the tournament, about the hot teams, about what a football hotbed Pennsylvania was and how the islands were taking over Las Vegas. Vaccaro tells a story about a bettor named Bruce Jarrett who got beat up at the Mirage one day by someone he owed money to. When the paramedics came, he sat in the middle of the book with a towel wrapped around his bloody nose, refusing to leave until he found out whether or not Barry Bonds was in the lineup so he could make his bet. Then Vaccaro spoke proudly how his college-aged son was traveling through Europe and picking up some culture at the museums. Baccellieri complained that the island books are killing him on the Louisville vs. Gonzaga game, forcing him to move off the number he wants. Alan talked about getting high on cocaine while working as a substitute teacher. He even suggested he wouldn't mind getting high right there and pretended to call a dealer he once knew. He was only kidding, but in an instant Vaccaro goes from teasing Alan about some of his worst bets to genuine concern that Alan is serious. "Come on, Alan, you know that stuff is no good." It's a sweet gesture, the kind that reminds Alan why he needs these dinners.

"An old bettor named Willie," Alan announces, "who I really respected told me once to never go against the direction the money is going in. Because the people betting all that money have it for a reason. He also told me don't ever try to guess why someone would bet one team over another. Everyone can find a reason for liking a bet."

"Everything is happening early this year and no one is making a bad bet," Malinsky says.

"I'm just going to bet golf from now on," says Alan.

"It may be easier than college basketball," says Malinsky.

At dessert there was the complimentary Hugo's tray of chocolate-covered fruits and pastries followed up by bananas Foster, cherries jubilee, and chocolate cake. They ate in honor of the end of an era, toasted the end of an era, and reminisced about the end of an era. But until it was time to leave, no one anticipated the actual end of the era.

It happened fast, like the games they bet on. As it neared midnight, Vaccaro slammed his palms on the table and matter of factly said, "Okay, that's it."

As if warding off the final goodbyes, Alan ignored him, singing Kenny Loggins's song, "This Is it." Vaccaro said it again and started to stand up. Everyone at the table followed suit. Then Alan looked at Vaccaro and asked, "This is it?"

"The end," Vaccaro said.

Alan paid for dinner, refusing to accept a dime from anyone. As he walked to his car with Malinsky and Baccellieri, he was obviously full of adrenaline, ready to keep the night going. Malinsky and Baccellieri meanwhile were ready to call it a night. As they walked away, Alan turned toward them and said, "It wasn't enough. It can't be over."

He was talking about more than dinner.

Chapter 16

The Final Four

By Sunday I'm saying to myself, "What the fuck am I doing with my life?" I haven't left the house in four days. I'm not kidding myself. I was pretty close to empty by the time I got here after last summer, and it will be the same once this summer is over. Probably worse since we did so bad this year.

I have some money set aside in a retirement fund. Some equity in the house and a few lame horses. But that's it. Everything else goes into action. My goal is simple. Make as much as I can now, pay the bills, go through the summer, and get back next year. That is all I want to do.

—ALAN BOSTON, MID-MARCH, 2000

As far as the teams are concerned, and as far as the fans of those teams are concerned, the most important weekend in college basketball is the Final Four. But, for fans happy just to see their team play an extra weekend in March, the opening rounds are as special as any championship weekend. For the NCAA, which sees greater aggregate television ratings from the first- and second-round games—games like St. Bonaventure vs. Kentucky or Utah State vs. University of Connecticut—than the actual Final Four ratings, it's the first four days that have become worth billions.

For the wiseguys and the bookmakers, the first four days of the tournament are like working retail during the holiday season. Every game, like every customer, is a money-making opportunity. The Final Four is irrelevant. By then even the squares have figured out which way to bet. The lines are solid and there's no advantage to be had. But those first few days, when the traders and the lawyers and the bankers start acting like they know the difference between Samford and Stanford, that's when there is money to be made. Some bettors and bookmakers can turn a losing season into a winning one with some well-placed bets or smartly crafted lines during the first two rounds of the tournament.

As far as the guys looking for action are concerned, it's the tournament's first four days that signal the end of the college basketball season. They are the four days to pad their season's total winnings. They are the four days to redeem a season's worth of losses. To the pros who lay it on the line all season long, those days are the real Final Four.

DAY 1

Thursday, March 16, 2000

The Stardust sports book will be open for ninety-one of the first ninety-six hours that constitute the beginning of March Madness. It will be a living and breathing entity taking bets, rocking to sleep lonesome losers long after the games have ended, and serenading self-satisfied winners just before tip-off. Joe Lupo won't be there every minute, but since he'll be up for most of those ninety-one hours trying to calculate where his book stands, he might as well be.

For the first day of the tournament, Lupo shows up to work in a pressed black suit, crisp white dress shirt, and red power tie. His seven-year-old daughter, Kelsey, gave him the tie and while driving to work this morning, even she sensed today was bigger than usual in the book. There had been clues: Normally the drive to school is a good time for Lupo to catch up with his son and daughter, hear how their day will be and what they are working on. But today, when they were strapped into their seats, he needed to get pumped up. As he pulled onto the road he looked at his daughter and said, "Today, we are going to listen to some rock 'n' roll."

"Are we listening to some guy named 'The Boss' again?" asked Lupo's son, Julian.

"That's not his name," said Kelsey

"The Boss," repeated Julian, defying his sister.

"His real name is Bruce," said Kelsey. "The Boss is just his nickname."

"I have a nickname," said Julian. "People call me 'Jules.'"

While Lupo laughed and his daughter looked at her little brother with a mix of bewilderment and disdain, she said to her father, "Good luck, Daddy. I hope you win your basketball games."

There is one battle Lupo and his Vegas colleagues won before the tournament even started. The congressional hearings concerning the betting ban that had been scheduled to begin during the last week of the tournament were canceled. While neither the NCAA nor spokesmen from the office of bill cosponsor Kansas Senator Sam Brownback (R) gave reasons why the hearings were postponed, sources close to the hearings intimated that they were having trouble getting relevant witnesses to commit during the NCAA tournament.

On a high of well wishes from his daughter and a reprieve from Congress, a tanned Lupo, rested from a day of skiing (a rare day off), walks into the book looking like his hero, Michael Corleone, ready to conquer the world. It's 7:30 A.M. and a special edition of the Stardust Line radio show, broadcast daily from the book during the tournament, has the standing-room-only crowd waiting on every tip like traders listening to Alan Greenspan. Lupo has thirteen ticket writers on staff for the day and night shifts and every window is open, yet the lines still stretch from the counter to the wall. Juice, a Stardust ticket writer from Chicago, was walking down the Strip toward the book wearing his Stardust shirt, and two fans yelled at him because the book was so crowded they couldn't even get into a line.

"It's all small stuff, a lot of small stuff," says Lupo, watching the writers punch out an endless stream of tickets. "We are just going to let them bet. Keep it coming. It's all about the money. Lots of action."

Not only is the pressure to win greater during the tournament because of the perceived advantages a seasoned bookmaker should have over "squares," but this is also due to the new challenges the book is facing. The damage from both the Caribbean books and not winning the Super Bowl has put Lupo behind the eight ball to meet his budget for the quarter. If he fails to do so, he's playing catch-up for the rest of the year. And because the Stardust has held around 7 to 8 percent of its tournament handle over the last two years, as opposed to the standard 3 to 5 percent, the suits upstairs have unrealistic expectations of what the bookmakers can achieve.

As do the bettors. They're like children who need immediate attention when they have a question, no matter what the circumstances. Such was the case when Lupo arrived at the book and saw Scucci locked in a heated discussion with one of the regulars.

When the conversation ended, Scucci walked over to Lupo to say good morning and to tell him what a snappy dresser he was. Lupo's tan face blushed, and then he asked what the regular wanted.

"I can't even tell you," Scucci said. "It's too unbelievable."

"What?" Lupo asked.

"He had some papers he needed to file for small claims court and asked if I would help him fill them out and tell him how to get the case into the system," Scucci said, exasperated. "Like I fucking know? And like today is the day for me to deal with something like that?"

The Stardust is about $10,000 heavy on every favorite tipping off on the first day. And if the first few games are any indication, it's going to be a weekend filled with moments of near apoplexy for Scucci and Lupo. The Stardust had nearly $14,000 in straight bets and parlays riding on St. Bonaventure, 7.5-point underdogs against Kentucky, the same amount on Creighton to cover the 3-point spread against Auburn, and $38,000 on the line if Indiana State covers the 11-point spread against Texas. With 2:23 left the Kentucky vs. St. Bonaventure game is shaping up to be a classic David vs. Goliath matchup that makes the tournament so endearing. The twelfth-seeded Bonnies were leading the fifth-seeded Wildcats, a perennial Final Four team, by two points. While the rest of the country is marveling at St. Bonaventure's spirit, the sports books are praying the lead would inch higher, eliminating the risk of overtime. Bettors, on the other hand, are praying for as many overtimes as it takes for Kentucky to cover the 7.5-point spread. The crowd of nearly 300 people at the Stardust is silent. "That's always good," says Lupo. "A quiet crowd means good things for us."

When UK freshman Tayshaun Prince hits a three-pointer with seven seconds left, tying the game, the silence is broken. Instead of counting the thousands they would have won, not to mention thousands more that would have been knocked out in parlays, Lupo and Scucci scramble to put up an overtime line. "Gimme two, gimme two," Lupo screams. "Two-and-a-half, two-and-a-half," Scucci responds. They settle on Kentucky minus-2.5 for the OT with a few hundred dollars coming in. (Incidentally, the fact they are the only book in Vegas or the islands to post an OT line is worth more to them than the potential OT windfall.) Meanwhile, Creighton misses a last-second, 3-point shot against Auburn, losing the game 72–69, right on the original number. It costs the Stardust $14,000. Also, with ten minutes left, Indiana State is easily covering the 11-point spread against Texas, down just seven points.

Back and forth through the five-minute OT, Kentucky goes up, St. Bonnie's ties it. With four seconds left, up by three points and victory seemingly at hand, a UK player foolishly fouls a St. Bonnie player behind the three-point line as he is about to shoot. That's three free throws for St. Bonnie, a chance to tie and set it to double-OT.

"We should not lose this fucking game," says Scucci, the first words he has spoken in nearly ten minutes.

"I can't believe we have to sweat this game," says Lupo, wiping some Ruffles potato chips grease on his tie. Scucci catches him fingering the tie and can't help but say, "Real lucky fucking tie you got there Joe."

The St. Bonnie player makes the first two free throws and, after a UK time-out to ice him, calmly sinks the third. Double OT. Another OT line from the Stardust.

In the second OT, St. Bonaventure runs out of Cinderella dust, losing by a final of 85–80. Not good enough to advance, but good enough to cover, giving the Stardust a $14,000 win and knocking out several thousand in parlay bets that included Kentucky. After two games and several fits of adjeda, the Stardust is even, prompting Lupo to say, "I don't know if I can go on."

In contrast to the smoke-filled, beer-stained atmosphere at the Stardust, Alan Boston's pristine white living room was perfumed with the smell of Tennessee barbeque. Ribs, pork shoulder, and baked beans, flown overnight from Corky's barbeque restaurant in Memphis, filled the air as Alan tended to the food and his guests like a gracious Southern host. Kind of.

"Come and get these ribs if you want them," he said. "I'm not gonna fucking serve them to you."

There are forty-eight games played over the first four days of the tournament, enough wall-to-wall basketball for the average hoops fan to skip a couple of days of work and take up residence at a local bar. But for a wiseguy like Alan, those forty-eight games over four days are two-thirds the number of games he would need to pay attention to on a regular season Saturday. His bets for the first two days—excepting the occasional halftime wager—are all made. His work is done, and now all he can do is wait for the results. Like he did back at Penn, Alan has ordered enough food for four days, this being the one day a year he will eat red meat. He has invited friends to drop by whenever they feel like it. He has been magnanimous and gracious, exulting in his hosting responsibilities and appreciating, actually craving, the human relationships. Along the way, people who normally would be afraid to call him during the season get a rare glimpse at how he works the phones, makes his halftime bets, manipulates lines, and reacts to wins and losses. With steaming plates of barbequed meat piled high on their laps and Alan handicapping in front of them, it's as if the invited guests—including Artie, Billy, and one of his harness horse drivers visiting from the East Coast—are catching the Vegas version of dinner theater.

Alan, with friends sitting in his living room and pulled pork heating in his oven, remains calm when he loses nearly $20,000 after number two–seeded Iowa State fails to cover the sixteen-point spread against fifteenth-seeded Central Connecticut State. At some point, you have to let it go; if you don't you'll be too scared to ever bet again. "Nothing I can do," he says matter of factly. "Damn Mercury is in retrograde." But instead of pulling back and cutting his losses, Alan picks up the phone and starts pouring more money onto games he's already made heavy bets on. While he may be more calm and collected than the bookmakers after a loss, they are guaranteed paychecks next week no matter what happens in close game. Alan can't afford more tough losses like Iowa State. He needs to make up ground.

After a series of calls, he's down for twenty more dimes on Utah as 3-point favorites over St. Louis (he'd push), twenty more on Northern Arizona as 14-point underdogs against St. John's (he'd win), fourteen more dimes on 27.5-point favorite Arizona against Jackson State (he'd lose), and ten more dimes on Wisconsin to cover the 4-point spread against Fresno State (he'd win). The action—his frenzied phone calls, quick calculations, fearlessness at putting down nearly $65,000 combined on four basketball games—leaves his guests stunned and speechless.

RULE NUMBER TWO
Winning is a work ethic.

All eyes are on a smiling and slightly buzzed-looking Alan instead of the game being played in life-size form on the big-screen television. Then the phone rings again, breaking the tension. It's Alan's accountant, calling about his client's quarterly tax payments that are due.

"Alan, I have some tax information for you," says the accountant.

"Oh fuck," Alan says, sitting down.

"Are you sitting down?"

"Oh dude, oh dude, oh dude," Rodney Bosnich says breathlessly as he surveys the day's damage. "God I just did not do good today. I lost one game by a point and another game by half a point. I never do that."

In his first tournament as a professional, Rodney exercised more discipline than most during the tantalizing first day. He bet five games at $200 a game. However, even after a season spent learning how to read line movement, he still didn't have a good feeling for which way spreads would move and whether or not there was value to be had. He bet Utah minus-4 against St. Louis as soon as the line was posted. Alan bet the same game at Utah minus-3, ignoring the opening line of four because he knew it would go down. St. Louis had had a mediocre regular season, but during the Conference USA tournament, it made a spirited run to the finals, earning a bid to the tournament and a bevy of national press, thus attracting the public's attention. As soon as the line was posted at minus-4, Alan knew the public would bet St. Louis because of their emerging status as an underdog. Rodney however, still learning how lines can be manipulated and how to factor public sentiment into his betting, bet early. Utah beat St. Louis 48–45. That one point was the difference between Rodney losing his bet and Alan pushing his. That loss bookended his first defeat of the day, when he bet Samford plus-13.5 against Syracuse. During garbage time, a Syracuse player hit a meaningless layup to give the Orangemen a 14-point lead, covering the 13.5-point spread by half-a-point. Half-a-point too much for Rodney. His tally for the day: Five bets, four losses, down $800. He had hoped his losing streak would end once March Madness began. It certainly hadn't.

Angry and desperate later that night, the once-confident Rodney who magically turned three- and four-team parlays into $1,200 wins stared wondrously at his computer as Missy slept. He searched for a clue that could help him break his slump, a pattern that could help him predict a winner the next day. Just a game was all he asked for. Just one game to get himself turned around. The electronic blue screen reflected off of his glasses in the dark room and his feet, the true barometers of his anxiety, sweated in his Birkenstock sandals. Looking for a game to bet while under duress, a feeling he was unaccustomed to, is probably the worst time to wager. It's like going grocery shopping on an empty stomach: Everything looks good no matter how much it costs.

One contest he had been tracking since the selections were made the previous Sunday was Utah State vs. the University of Connecticut. His reasoning was sound. UCONN was struggling and earned its number-five seed as much on reputation and the fact they were defending champions as they did on their prowess. Utah State meanwhile had won nineteen straight games and the Big West conference title, only to sink to the number-twelve seed because of its lack of tournament experience. The game opened at UCONN minus-9 and the wiseguys were taking Utah State for hit after hit. Because of UCONN's high profile, however, the public money coming in on the side of the Huskies outweighed the big wiseguy bets on Utah State. So, the line had actually gone up from minus-9 to minus-9.5, and, at the most bettor-friendly book in town, the MGM, the game was at minus-10. Instead of cowtowing to the wiseguys, bookmakers were moving the line in favor of the public money and UCONN.

Rodney hadn't yet discovered the phone accounts, and he still didn't trust the Internet. The only way he knew how to make a bet was by walking up to a window. At 12:30, down $800 for the tournament and a few thousand more than that for the month of March, he grabbed $400 in cash from his stash in his shoebox. He begged Missy to go with him, waking her from a sound sleep. Racing to the book in the middle of the night to make a bet conveyed he had more of a problem than he was willing to admit. But if Missy and he just happen to be heading to the Strip and he happens to stop at the MGM for a bet, well that's a different story. She waved him off, unwilling to participate in the charade.

As he peeled out of his complex onto Tropicana Road, the street was quiet and empty, which suited his needs perfectly. The minus-10 wouldn't last long at the MGM. A wiseguy watching the lines would surely recognize the value and call in a bet. But, Rodney couldn't afford to speed and get a ticket, since he still hadn't gotten auto insurance. It was a long, slow ride. The adrenaline pumping through his veins, the cash burning a hole in his pocket, the race to snag the best number in town on a game he thinks is a lock, is all part of the bettor's rush. It would be strange to say Rodney was enjoying himself, but it wouldn't be wrong either.

Like a drunk staggering for the bar, Rodney walked through the immense MGM hotel toward the sports book in a single-minded haze. He dodged tourists who ignored him as he asked them to move. A couple from Wisconsin, strolling leisurely toward the blackjack table, stopped in the middle of the aisle and blocked his way. A change cart came out of nowhere and almost hit Rodney in the knee.

Finally he made it to the counter. Out of breath he mumbled, "$440 on Utah State plus-10." The number was still there, no one had taken it from him. He counted out his money. The ticket writer counted out his money. Then she handed him his receipt. He held it in his hands, stared at it, and folded it in two before putting it in his wallet.

This could be his ticket, literally, back into the win column.

DAY 2

Friday, March 17, 2000

"You know what today is don't you," Joe Lupo asked as the second day of games tipped off.

"St. Patrick's Day?" said Scucci.

"Today's the day we go in for the kill," Lupo answered. "And it tastes good."

On the first day of the tournament, the momentum from that Kentucky vs. St. Bonaventure win helped the Stardust sweep nearly every game on the board. Their final tally for the day: $150,000 won. Listening to Stevie Wonder on the way in to the book, the sun rising in front of him as he drives ninety mph, Lupo can't wait to get in to work. To win $150,000 during any tournament is an accomplishment. To do it when your business is being pecked at from all sides like a carcass in the desert is a credit to your bookmaking and prognostication skills. If two of the next three days are even half as good as the first, Lupo will make his budget for the quarter, which back in January seemed imposssibile. More than that, it will vindicate his skills as a bookmaker and a manager at a time when many in the industry are wondering how much a Las Vegas sports book manager really matters.

"It's gotten so bad these last couple of months, with such a change in the industry's dynamic over where the money is going," Lupo says. "Now saving money because of smart moves is as good as winning money.

"I don't really know how it happened, but it is really depressing me and stressing me out. I don't know if the Carib has gotten good or...I just don't know the answer. We just couldn't find a rhythm for two reasons: One, when we got early money this year it was sharper than in years past, wiseguys betting earlier than normal. This hurt us because we put up the first number, which means we've got sharp bettors hitting us. Two, if the sharp guys didn't bet us early, the really big money was going to the Carib before it came to us. We didn't know how to adjust our lines and we were always chasing instead of setting the agenda. We would ask ourselves if someone made a big bet what their thinking was? Are they setting us up just to move the line in the islands? Are we not doing good enough handicapping?"

That's certainly what he was asking himself later in the day, when he'd lost four straight games because of what, in retrospect, seemed like tentative line-making. In the DePaul against Kansas game, the line moved in half-point increments from Kansas minus-1, to minus-1.5, to minus-2, to minus-2.5. In the Missouri vs. North Carolina game, the line moved in half-point increments again from UNC minus-2 to minus-3. And, with two big underdogs, Appalachain State vs. Ohio State and Hofstra vs. Oklahoma State, the managers and Lupo made the same mistakes twice. From the beginning of the year, as if he could sense last year's record-setting season was more a mirage than a harbinger of things to come, Lupo had been preaching to be aggressive with line movements, not to be afraid of moving a full point if the bettor was a wiseguy or if the money coming in was big. The slightest hesitancy could cost them serious dollars. With those four games, the young bookmakers under Lupo's watch repeated their mistakes four times.

And those were the last four games of the night. At the time, the Stardust was up $50,000. By the time the DePaul game ended on four points with Kansas winning 81–77 in overtime, the fifty grand was gone and the book was even.

"I'm here for fifteen fucking hours and we don't make any money. Spend fifteen hours working in a department store on the busiest shopping day of the year and I guarantee you make money. At least that is how my general manager is going to see it," Lupo says. "Man, I was in such a good mood today when the day started. I went wrong with the Stevie Wonder.

"I should have listened to Aerosmith."

When you're betting upward of $20,000 a game and you're counting on the tournament—the first four days of the tournament—to double your bankroll, winning $10,000 in one day isn't winning. It's losing. Betting is a cash-intensive business and upping your stash by ten grand won't give you the freedom to increase your bets the next day, nor will it feel like a very satisfying return on your previous day's investment. This is essentially what happened to Alan Boston on Thursday, which means he's desperate to make up ground on Day Two.

Unlike the day before, when friends were over and a collegial atmosphere filled his living room, Friday is more like a regular-season Saturday. There's too much work to entertain.

"What's the Cincy-UNC–Wilmington total?" he barks into the phone. "One-hundred-twenty, huh? They're not gonna score 100 points in that game. We gotta get down on that. Gimme the under 120 for the limit. Thank you."

"Hi," he tells a new operator. "Game 535 Cincy total? 119? Okay, thank you." He hangs up.

"Hello," he says after dialing another book. "What's the Cincy total? 119.5. Thank you, goodbye." He hangs up.

"What the fuck?" he says aloud. "One-hundred-twenty is what we wanted and it is fucking gone everywhere. Make one freaking move and every bettor and book jumps on the fucking bandwagon moving the game. What a fucking joke. We can't do a fucking thing. We only got twelve dimes down on the Cincy total. Normally you feel more comfortable betting during the tournament. This is the time of year when you will get down your biggest bet easily. But this is a fucking joke. We can't get anything down before the lines start moving away from us."

He dials Billy.

"What the fuck, we got nothing on the Cincy total. We got 100 dollars [$10,000] on App. State plus-13.5 and 140 [$14,000] on Tennessee over Louisiana–Lafayette. I'm conflicted on that Tennessee game. My first thought is that they would kill them. My second thought is that they are a rat team that plays down to the level of their competition. My third thought was that they got blown out last year in the first round and may have some pride. You know what this all means?"

"What?" Billy asks, playing along.

"I've got no reason to bet, and I am a degenerate who shouldn't have even bet on the game."

"That's great, Alan," Billy responds, glossing over what might be the most introspective comment his partner has made all season. He has no choice. What Alan says about himself is also true for Billy, and it's not something he wants to admit. "Listen, we are fucking balls out on Penn vs. Illinois plus-nine," Billy responds.

"I'll tell you right now I am going to get violent when Penn gets the whistle shoved up their ass," Alan says, his introspection having passed like a case of bad heartburn. Like losing a close game, the more time he spends dwelling on his shortcomings, the less he'll be able to pull the trigger on a big bet.

"I'm not even gonna watch it," Billy says.

"I will," says Alan.

"I know," answers Billy. "Don't call me."

"Thanks for your support," Alan says, somewhat bitterly.

"You see Butler on your screen just went up to plus-9.5 against Florida," Billy interrupts. "We want more of that?"

"Yes, not a chance Butler loses that game by ten points. They may even win it," Alan counters.

Alan's right. Butler not only easily covers the spread against Florida, but it has the lead most of the second half and in overtime, before losing on a last-second miracle shot by Florida's All-American

Mike Miller. Unfortunately, Alan was right about the Penn-Illinois game also. Penn opened up an early lead on Illinois before its starting point guard was called for his second and third fouls of the game within a span of two seconds on the clock. With more than eleven minutes left in the first half, the refs had put the Quakers best player, and best chances of staying close, on the bench. Illinois opened up a fifteen-point lead before Penn's star came back on the floor for the closing minutes of the half and scored six straight points, helping his team cut the lead to five going into the second half.

As usual, while the outcome of the game was never in doubt, the outcome of the bet was nip and tuck. With seventeen seconds left and his team up by ten points, Illinois junior forward Marcus Griffin hit the second of two free throws, pushing the lead up to eleven points in the game and two points more than the spread. At this point in the game, Alan has finished a jar of peanut butter he started eating as the second half began. With seven seconds left, Illinois sophomore forward Lucas Johnson hits two more free throws, pushing the Illinois lead to thirteen and essentially putting the game out of reach. But, to add insult to the tens of thousands of dollars Alan lost on the game, Penn's bench-warming sophomore Dan Solomito hits a twenty-three-foot, three-pointer with no time left to make the final score 68–58 Illinois, one point from a push and one basket out of the money.

Later that day, Alan is calculating the wins and losses, which, for the second day in a row, are disappointingly even. But he doesn't lament one game or one bet or one fluke play that costs him a win. Instead he laments the loss of a season.

"It's hard on me when the season is over," he says. "When you work constantly at something you are good at, good feelings come from it. Then that's all gone. That's hard. Then I am just another jerk who has got plenty of time on his hands."

DAY 3

Saturday, March 18

Las Vegas is known as Convention City. And what is the NCAA tournament if not the world's biggest convention of sports fans? Hotels are booked at capacity months in advance, with packs of rabid hoops fans stuffing four and five people in a room. The lines for betting on Saturday and Sunday morning start forming at 6 A.M. and don't let up until the last game has tipped. The truly committed don't bother going back to the room for sleep. They lounge around the blackjack tables all night or jockey with the wheelchair-bound for space around the slots. More than the wiseguys and even the bookmakers, these are the people who need the tournament. It is their break from reality, their chance to live like a wiseguy for 48 hours, talking about point spreads, betting lines, three dime bets, underdogs, favorites, lucky bounces, and bad breaks. Come Sunday night they all go back home to school or their wives or jobs. But until then they are bettors, making action happen.

"I can see how people could do this for a living," says Geoff Holley, a thirty-three-year-old high school basketball coach watching Saturday's games at the Las Vegas Hilton. "The rush is undeniable, and, if you look at this schedule, there are so many games, everything looks good. Like it's an easy bet."

For five years, Holley has been coming out to Las Vegas with his parents and his wife for the first weekend of the tournament. It's the only time of year that he bets and he never puts down more than $20 a game. His wife, Chris, won't let him. "And even then he better win," she says. "Otherwise I cut him off."

Chris is a tough lady who gives as good as she gets with the wannabe wiseguy frat boy crowd at the Hilton. With a friend's baby shower coming up the next weekend, she had started sewing a Winnie the Pooh blanket to take to the party. Rather than waste the time staring at the TV screen, she put a sawbuck down on the number two horse to win the fourth race at Gulfstream, cleared space for herself on a counter at the back of the book and settled in with a beer, her pattern and a needle.

"Hey lady," a college-aged kid in a Hawaiian shirt yelled at her. "There's no sewing in the sports book."

"Back off punk," she snaps. "I know what's up with these games. I'll sew in here if I need to."

"I've got to get my jeans hemmed," he answers back. "Can you do that for me?"

"Gimme UCLA plus-4 and I'll think about," she says. It's a shrewd comeback, considering the game is not even listed on the board, and, if it were, UCLA's opponent, Maryland, would be favored by only three points. The college kid's tone changes from Bart Simpson to Boy Scout.

"Say," he says meekly. "Are you using a cross-stitch on that?"

"I am," she says, stunned.

"Well, you should get a loop for that fabric," he says. "Otherwise your tension will be screwed up."

"Thanks honey," she says sweetly now. "And don't worry about me taking advantage of you on that UCLA game. I'll let it go. This time."

Geoff catches the tail end of the conversation and laughs off his wife's insouciance. The Michigan State vs. Utah game is deep in the second half and Chris wants to know which team she's rooting for.

"We're rooting for Utah, plus-14.5," Geoff answers, dutifully.

"Win this one honey," she says. "You know what I mean?"

With Utah leading the entire first half and trailing by only one for the first five minutes of the second half, Geoff looks safe. Then Utah goes cold from the floor, even missing an alley-oop dunk. Suddenly, Michigan State balloons a one-point lead early in the half into a ten-point lead with plenty of time remaining. It's not out of the question that Michigan State will cover the 14.5-point spread. When the Spartans' All-American senior guard Mateen Cleaves drains a three-pointer with just over seven minutes left to give his team a fourteen-point lead, it looks as though Geoff's betting day may come to an early end.

"It's not losing the money that annoys me," Geoff says. "It's the fact that I could lose at all. That's what makes me want to bet again, just to prove I am not an idiot."

"That's alright honey," Chris says comfortingly. "I feel a comeback coming on."

She's right. Utah holds strong, making enough shots to keep the point spread at bay yet not really threatening in the game. They never trail by more than thirteen again. However, the last twenty-seven seconds are among the most compelling in college basketball history for a game that is so obviously over. The Spartans are up by twelve as Cleaves casually brings the ball up the floor. There is still the slim chance the minus-14.5 contingent in the book can win their bet if the Spartans somehow score three more points in the next twenty-seven seconds. A small chant starts in the back of the room, "Shoot the ball, shoot the ball." Another chant counters it, "Hold the ball, hold the ball."

By the time there are ten seconds left, and it's obvious Cleaves has no intention of shooting a random three-pointer to cover the spread, the chants in the book are deafening. Chris sucks down the last of her beer and, screaming above the din, says, "That's what I love about coming here every year. No one here cares who wins, they only care about how much."

Then she looks at her victorious husband and adds, "Okay honey, who are we betting on next?"

DAY 4

Sunday, March 19

On Thursday he lost $800. On Friday he lost $600 and on Saturday he lost $400. Over the last three weeks of the college basketball season, Rodney Bosnich had watched his bankroll dwindle faster than an old man's dignity at a Britney Spears concert. By Sunday, the normally calm, cool, and collected demeanor Rodney had exhibited during his brief tenure as a professional gambler had degenerated into that of a square in town for a weekend and looking to get even on one roll of the dice. Deep in debt for the tournament, he wanted to make up his losses and he needed to do it fast.

Taking $2,200 in cash from his apartment, Rodney arrived at the Stardust on Sunday morning, determined to let it ride on one bet. He wasn't a wiseguy anymore, at least not on this day. Waiting in line, fidgeting as he stared up at the board, he was a bettor, an addict and, worse yet, he was acting like a square. For the first time his desperation got the best of him. This bet wasn't being made because his instincts told him it made sense, it was being made out of spite. The game owed him, dammit. For the first time in his fledgling career he didn't just want to win—he needed to win. And those were the most dangerous bets to make.

If Rodney intended to make this his livelihood, he had reached a rite of passage. The hole he dug himself forced him to reevaluate the prophecies he had been preaching all season. "I don't get upset when I lose because I am so far ahead; I'm actually playing with the house's money," he had said many times during the season. "I'm too attached to my money to make stupid bets. I need to have a certain lifestyle and when I lose I'll just stop until I feel better," he'd say about his bankroll. Problem was, he had never been down this much at one time. His will had never been tested. And now that it was, Rodney was failing.

When he finally got to the window, he counted out his cash deliberately, as if he had to ask himself if he really wanted to make this bet with every dollar that passed through his fingers. "Seton Hall plus-11 for $2,200," he said. Even Lupo and Scucci, standing behind the counter, were surprised at how much Rodney had bet. He had never been more than a nickel player at most, and now he was throwing down two dimes.

The game started at Temple minus-11 and, as Rodney watched Seton Hall trailing early by six points, he wondered aloud how he was going to make up his lost income from the last couple of weeks. It wasn't just a matter of working to fill his time anymore; if he lost the Seton Hall bet, he'd be working to fill his coffers. His job prospects were dim and almost farcical. Beginning in the summer, a friend of his who dredged golf-course ponds retrieving balls for a used-golf-ball salesman, was going to be doing a tour of duty in Las Vegas. If Rodney was interested, his friend was willing to pay him three cents for every ball he salvaged from the water. Rodney figured the gig would be worth at least a couple of grand for the summer—as much as he bet on the game he was watching.

"I don't know," Rodney reflected, his eyes glued to the game. "It's something."

As the second half unfolded, it looked as though Rodney might be able to put away his wet suit. Seton Hall, seeded tenth, led second-seeded Temple almost the entire half, before eventually winning in overtime. After an anxiety-filled morning in which the merits of working in scum-filled ponds had been weighed, Rodney had won his bet. He had pulled even in the tournament, and, although he didn't act like the professional he claimed to be, the lesson he learned would serve him well.

"I've got gray hair, no fingernails, and I am about twenty pounds heavier," he said walking into the bright sun of the Stardust parking lot. "And this whole thing has taught me I would be a lot better off if I took more underdogs next year."

For Rodney Bosnich, the light again was green.

In the twilight of the first weekend's final day, Alan is moving forward at a furious pace. As the Duke vs. Kansas game comes to an end, next weekend's UCLA vs. Iowa State game hangs on the board like a juicy apple ready to be plucked. "Alright, let's go, let's go," he says to Billy. "That game is moving. Billy we gotta get it. Whatever we can: ten dimes, five dimes, three dimes, five dimes, anywhere, anyhow."

They don't just need the game for the rush, they need the game for the win. Like they do every Sunday night, Billy and Alan tallied their winnings for the week. Neatly stacking his winning tickets in one pile and his losing tickets in the other, Alan rattled off the figures he had calculated. Last year the duo won as much in these four days as they did during their best week of the season. But this past weekend was just a symbol of their entire season. "We lost $8,250 on the first day. Fuck, we lost $10,000 on the second day, we won a peanut on the third day, and we dropped $23,500 today. Jesus fucking Christ, I thought we had a good week and we got clobbered. I've got us up five dimes total for the week.

"Fuck it. What a waste of a life. I quit."

He's bluffing. For all his self-loathing, Alan is a wiseguy. He'd no sooner abandon betting than a mother would abandon her baby. As he claims he's quitting, he's grabbing the uncashed pile of winning tickets from his desk and a wad of cash from a desk drawer and heading for his car. Even though the last game of the second round just ended, the spreads for next week's games are being posted in rapid fire, and the MGM lines are plump with opportunity. The earlier Alan gets down the better, considering every square in the country has a line on the games and will be backing up their opinions with hard-earned cash. This is the bettor's biggest challenge during the tournament: Finding values in the spread before an ignorant public throws everything out of whack. And who knows: This could be the day that Mercury's retrograde works in Alan's favor, the day he turns out to be right, not just about one line or one game but about everything. It could happen. Isn't that why you gamble?

RULE NUMBER ONE

The only sure thing is that there is no sure thing.

Alan's viscosity doesn't dissipate once he's reached the MGM. Only one thing can soothe his soul, break him out of his funk, and take the edge off. The cocaine never did it, the vegan cookies never did it, and even the working out has never been full-proof. Until he gets to the counter he won't see straight or think straight. Only the numbers— lines, spreads, plusses, minuses—swirling in his head like a malfunctioning stock ticker can ease the pain. Once he sees them he'll feel right. Or at least as right as he can feel. Every other second of the day is misery.

The supervisor at the MGM spots Alan coming through the sports book entrance with his fist clenched around his tickets and his eyes swirling like pinwheels. The board is lit up like a Fourth of July night. And Alan is drawn to the lights.

"How ya doing tonight, Mr. Boston?" the supervisor asks.

"I hate myself," Alan says, taking a deep breath and handing over his winning tickets. "Now gimme game 621 plus-1.5 for $11,000."

Epilogue

November, 2000

Rodney Bosnich finished the NCAA tournament the same way he started: losing. The desperate $2,000 bet that brought him back to even during the tourney's first weekend was a false positive. He lost nearly every game he bet down the home stretch, accumulating $3,500 in losses, which equaled about 10% of his bankroll. The bad luck continued into the start of baseball season when, although he promised himself he'd never bet on his beloved Chicago Cubs again, he did just that, costing him even more money.

However, as was always the case, what basketball takes from Rodney he always gets back. And during the NBA playoffs, he was money. "I took the underdogs," he says, repeating the lesson he learned during his college hoops losing streak. "Every time." As the playoffs ended and his bankroll became bloated again, Rodney celebrated his one-year anniversary as a professional bettor. And then, in August, life got even sweeter. The ticket writer's job that had eluded him for so long finally found him. The sports book manager at the Las Vegas Hilton—a native Chicagoan and Cubs fan—noticed Rodney's e-mail address on the job application included Sammy Sosa's name. He called Rodney in for a meet-and-greet, but the interview was a mere formality. By virtue of his fandom, Rodney finally had a job. At last, he had made some money off the Cubs.

Rodney's parents, once so unforgiving of their son's lifestyle they kicked him out of the house, have not only embraced his gambling, but Las Vegas as well. Looking ahead to their eventual retirement, they bought a swanky new townhouse in the toney Vegas suburbs. Missy and Rodney are still together and happily living there, nearly rent-free, until his parents move in for good. Between his low-cost life and newfound job, Rodney's tolerance for betting has increased and his bets per game have grown from $200 to $400. But in Vegas, that's not called addiction, it's called progression. Ultimately, Rodney got what he wanted when he was back home in Indiana; he resides under his parents' roof but lives by his rules.

He just had to go to Vegas to get it.

Jim Korona left the Stardust on June 1, about five weeks after the hammer came down on sports betting. But, it wasn't the passage of the college betting ban bill by the Senate Commerce Committee in mid April that sealed the sports books' fate. About a week after the bill passed, Korona, standing at his usual post behind the counter, spied an officious looking man walking toward him. The man reached slowly into his bulging breast pocket and pulled out…a list. He was an FBI agent, presenting Korona with a list of client phone accounts and safety deposit boxes to which they wanted access. A joint sting between the FBI and the Gaming Control Board uncovered what they alleged was a multistate illegal gambling operation involving several local gamblers. Both groups raided accounts at several casinos looking for what they believed to be money laundered through the sports books. For the next three days, FBI agents scoured through the safety deposit boxes seizing hundreds of thousands of dollars. On top of that, they shook down all the runners normally congregated around the first row of seats, taking thick wads of cash, tickets, ear pieces, and even the quarters runners used to call their players.

Korona, once Joe Lupo's golden child, had been thinking about leaving the book for a while. He saw Lupo, divorced and alone. His heart broke when Lupo told him about the time his four-year-old son Julian, sensing how hard the divorce was on his father, grabbed Lupo's leg and, for no reason at all, said to him, "I love you Daddy." Korona saw Scucci, never married and also alone. The young bookmaker realized that everyone he knew in the business was divorced, in a bad relationship, or unmarried, and he wondered if that would be him in twenty years. When an offer to work in marketing came along, even Lupo and Scucci told him to get out. They were dinosaurs in a dying field, they said. But he still had a chance.

The Stardust—and Lupo and Scucci—has struggled in the aftermath of the raid. With the runners and bettors alike scared off by the FBI, business has been slower and more difficult. The famed Stardust lottery, which was already losing its luster, became irrelevant without the runners' action. Now it was just a bunch of squares and small-time players betting no more than a nickel a game. And while the betting ban bill hasn't been sent to the full Senate as of this writing, even Nevada Senator Richard Bryan (D) expects it to pass by an overwhelming majority in 2001. Lupo and Scucci both joke with their boss that it may be time to go to dealer school. They all signed up to make numbers, challenge wiseguys, and win big bets. "But, the day of the raid," says Lupo, "that could have been the last day of true wiseguy action. Ever."

If Alan Boston's goal every college basketball season is to win enough money so he can do it again next year, he came perilously close to failing in 1999-00. It's a testament to how much he won early that he still made his yearly summer retreat to Maine, bought a new Corvette, and picked up an expensive habit, golf, before returning to Las Vegas in October. He did so reluctantly however, because, the fact is, he was broke. He hadn't had a winning week since early January, and he desperately wanted to stay back east. For the first time in twenty years, the thought of making a bet repulsed him. He seriously considered something that had once been thought of as the ultimate cop out: consulting for bigger players.

Then he realized, like Willy Loman looking to close one big deal, this is the life to which he's consigned himself. He's a bettor. Not rich enough to quit, not qualified to do anything else. Alan didn't get "horny" for college basketball anymore, as he used to say. The relationship between him and the betting actually felt something like the middle of a dull marriage; the comfort of knowing what to expect outweighed the discomfort of starting over. Come October, while still in Maine, he dutifully bought the preseason college basketball preview rags. He combed the pages for insight into Drexel and Hofstra and every team in the Big Sky conference. Then he boarded a plane bound for Las Vegas, sat in his first class seat and talked himself into doing it one more time.

This year, he'd close the deal.

Index